2016

THE LAST
INDEPENDENCE DAY

Other Books by A. H. Krieg

The Satori and the New Mandarins

Marketing Your Product Through Distribution Channels

Plate Forming Machines

The Problems with Welding Fume and How to Slove Them

Distributor Marketing

July 4th

2016

THE LAST
INDEPENDENCE DAY

BY

ADRIAN H. KRIEG

HALLBERG PUBLISHING CORPORATION

Nonfiction Book Publishers – ISBN 0-83719

Tampa, Florida 33623

This book is a companion to:

The Satori and the New Mandarins

ISBN Number 0-87319-044-0

ISBN Number 0-87319-047-5

Library of Congress Catalog Card Number 99-094567

Cover design and typography by Michael X Marecek

Printed in the USA. First printing February 2000.

For information concerning Rights & Permissions or other questions
contact:

HALLBERG PUBLISHING CORPORATION
P.O. Box 23985 • Tampa, Florida 33623
Phone 1-800-633-7627 • Fax 1-800-253-READ

To my Wife

Audrey

and my sons

Ivan & Alistair

CONTENTS

Illegitemus Non Tatum Carborundem!

"Mankind's problems can no longer be solved by national governments. What is needed is a **World Government.** *This can best be achieved by* **strengthening the United Nations system.** *In some cases this would mean changing the role of the UN agencies from advice giving to* **implementation.** *"*

— United Nations Human
Development Document
page 88, 1994

FOREWORD

The Last Independence Day... So What?

The argument for Global, One World Government goes much like this:

Anyone with any brains knows that the US economy is global. US citizens and businesses own stock in companies all over the world and people from all over the world own stock in companies in the United States.

This is the 21st century, not the 18th. It is easier today to travel from Chicago to England or Japan than it used to be to go from Chicago to St. Louis.

We need a global government to control the global economy. Just think what a mess the United States would be in if every State was an independent country with its own money, army, import and export taxes, etc. Independent, sovereign nations are a thing of the past. Global government is the system for today's global economies.

Sounds good and much of it is true, with one big exception — *we have always had a Global Economy.* Where do you suppose the money came from to develop business in the United States? It came from all over the world because the United States was the "land of opportunity."

The right of private property was guaranteed only in the United States. The freedom to invest your private property and engage in business without government permits and restrictions was available only in the United States. The money was backed by GOLD in the United States. Taxes were almost zero in the United States.

The government got its rights from the people in the United States and as a result money and people flowed into the United States from all over the globe. It was "the land of the free and the home of the brave." And, there was no other country like it because in every other country the people got their rights from government.

In fact, as we begin the 21st Century, there still is no other country like the United States because in all other countries, the people still obtain their rights from government.

The Globalists and One World Government people like to say that all nations, with a few exceptions, are alike because we are all "Democracies." "We are all free people who freely elect our government officials." Well, I remember many an election in Communist countries in which the people "freely" voted, but I doubt anyone would say that the people in those countries were free. Whether or not people vote means nothing. The power controlled by the government means everything.

Here is a small example:

When radio was invented, businessmen in the United States rushed to establish broadcasting stations. This did not happen in Canada, or England, or Mexico, or any other country because their governments had not given the citizens the right to own broadcasting stations.

When TV was invented, the same thing occurred. Ditto with the invention of the steam engine and railroads — and everything else you can think of.

In fact, the English and Canadians only recently won the right to own and operate radio and TV broadcasting stations. I have no doubt that Canadians were finally given the right by their government to own TV broadcasting stations because 90% of their citizens listened to US broadcasting stations instead of their government stations. Our FREEDOM embarrassed them.

Thinking of inventions, can you imagine the look on the commissar's face should an inventor like Cyrus McCormack stop by the Farm Production Bureau and say he had invented a reaper for harvesting crops which would allow them to lay-off 80% of the work force? Do you think he'd be given permits to build such a machine?

There is no question in my mind that without individual freedom and the right of private property, 7 out of 10 people would still be working on the farm.

The word "govern" means to limit. When a governor is put on a car it limits the car's speed by limiting the amount of gas. People who wish to control use government to limit the rights of their fellow citizens and limit their business activities.

All current "free trade" agreements have nothing to do with free trade. Under the various proposals and treaties such as NAFTA and the World Trade Organization, trade is more controlled than ever before by international government bureaus. The word "free" has only to do with import/export taxes. Thus the words "free trade" are being used to take away rights that once belonged to citizens of the United States (i.e.) to produce, buy and sell in a free marketplace to whomever they wished. You must remember that only the citizens of the United States obtain their Rights from their Creator, (God) and not from government. In every other nation on earth, citizens rights come from government, Canada and England included. The shot heard 'round the world was not the sound of guns, but the words of the Declaration of Independence on July 4th, 1776.

It seems odd that any free person would want to be a serf. It seems impossible that we can have our freedom taken away and we do not even resist. In fact, we vote to have it taken away. In reading this book you will learn how modern methods of brainwashing will soon accomplish what Hitler and Stalin could not. That is, to establish a one world socialist government in which the citizens are but serfs.

If liberty and personal freedom, the freedom of enterprise, the freedom to try and to fail or to succeed, is to live on and continue to serve as a light to the oppressed people of the world who get their rights from government, we must not join their system. We must bring into being a world in which all people receive their rights from God, as do we in the United States. Ours is the global model for the future of mankind. The things that made the United States great — individual freedom, and right of private property, the right to buy and sell and trade where, when and how we wish, with whom we wish — this is free trade. It is the change that needs to be reinstituted in the United and States and brought to all the nations of the earth. And it is the change that the new global economy and global citizenship require. We must re-light the lamp of Liberty as it was lit for us on July 4th, 1776.

CHARLES HALLBERG
PUBLISHER

PREFACE

In writing and researching my previous book, *The Satori and the New Mandarins*, my object was to inform the reader about that topic using the term "Satori," to identify the "hidden masters," and "Mandarins" to identify those who put into effect and administer the wishes of the Satori. I also included membership lists of the master Mandarin organizations such as: the Council on Foreign Relations (CFR), the Trilateral Commission (TC) and the Bilderbergers. This in itself was a worthwhile effort that helped citizens become aware of, and thereby resist the *New World Order.* Since then, I have come to the conclusion that in order for citizens to more effectively resist the Satori plans they must be made aware what those plans are, and how they are implemented. This work is an outline of the modus operandi of the Satori in their efforts at world conquest. It demonstrates the odious plans that these people have — not only for America — but for the entire civilized world.

Every bit of information in this book is the result of dedicated research. All information was derived from books, web-sites, pamphlets, white papers, reports, and Satori surrogate organizations, as well as personal interviews. This is not an author fantasizing about secretive conspiracies. It is information about the conspiracy which comes from members of the conspiracy, as well as governmental sources.

The plan for implementation of the Satori's desired outcome is manifest in a complex plan designed to make you malleable to their effort. The incrementalism of political and social change in the direction of that plan is the modus operandi. As you read this book the plan is well on its way toward maturity. The acceleration of political and social change in the last 50 years has been exponential. Never before in the history of the world has change been so organized or so rapid.

The time of fruition for the Satori plan has been changed often. The latest target date was publically announced by America's then Secretary of State Warren Christopher in speeches during the last year he was in office. Although consistency was not Christopher's hallmark, he announced in speeches in Buenos Aires, Asuncion, and Rio that the hoped for date was 2006. Although not officially announced, this date, due to Clinton's loss of fast track authority to include all of the Americas in the expansion of NAFTA, has been changed to 2016. The exact time for the plan to be finalized is impossible to predict. Hopefully we can delay it indefinitely. (The original time was to be the turn of the millennium, 2000 A.D.)

My previous book dealt with the "who" of the conspiracy, this book deals with the "how." The several and varied tenants of implementation toward Novus Ordo Secalorum are discussed in detail. Together we will examine the various methods used to direct you into a route of thought and action which is contradictory to your self interest, and the ways utilized to hide the real consequences from your notice.

Unlike my previous book which was international, this book deals primarily with America. For obvious reasons reference to the international aspect of the conspiracy forces us to consider implications of a foreign nature. The conspiracy is worldwide. Developed sources for this book came from America, Canada, Germany, Switzerland, and Great Britain. One of the major reasons for this is the fact that numerous Satori-sponsored think-tanks function in an international scope, and that there is not one government, or multi-national institution that is not affected by them. The conspiracy is trans-national and centered in numerous international organizations such as the Club of Rome, Bilderbergers, Trilateralists, CFR, Bones, and multi-national corporations.

One may term it the "Messianic Goal" of some of the richest family dynasties on earth, to re-establish — on a world-wide basis — a State comparable to the Roman Empire, through which they will establish their New World Order — with the assistance of our mainstream churches.

Flash-Back

Dateline: 1934

Issuance: **Congregation Christian Churches Council for Social Action Resolution**

Source: **Social Action Bulletin**

That same year, the Congregational-Christian churches established a Council for Social Action after passing a resolution to work toward:

"The abolition of the system responsible for these destructive elements in our common life, by eliminating the system's incentives and habits, the legal forms which sustain it, and the moral ideals which justify it. The inauguration of a genuinely cooperative social economy democratically planned to adjust production to consumption requirements, to modify or eliminate private ownership of the means of production or distribution wherever such ownership interferes with the social good."

Flash-Back

Dateline: 1942

Source: **John Foster Dulles' Commision, Delaware Ohio Conference**

Issuance: **Federal Council of Churches**

Resolved: ". . . a world of irresponsible, competing and unrestrained national sovereignties, whether acting alone or in alliance or in coalition, is a world of international anarchy. It must make place for a higher and more inclusive authority."

The above Flash-Backs are quoted from a new book by the Reverend Edmund A. Opitz, The Libertarian Theology of Freedom.

INTRODUCTION

At The Outset

It is important to understand just exactly how the Satori have been so eminently successful in the 20th century implementing their plans. First, the Satori are wealthy. We are not talking about a few million dollars, we speak of billions. As such they have learned an important lesson from the capital markets, namely that you can easily control a corporation with less than 10% ownership of the stock. Please bear with me while I explain that the Rockefeller family has controlled Chase Manhattan Bank for years while owning less then 10% of the outstanding voting stock. Such control is also helped by numerous tax exempt foundations which control millions in stock and vote in accordance with the wishes of their board of directors, which often have overlapping directorships with the principal. The same holds true for a very large portion of the world stock markets. Through a process of controlling the board of directors and the procedure of proxy voting, a business can stay under the control of minority stock holders indefinitely. You, as a stockholder, are given the privilege of selecting things like who the auditors are to be. You may be sent a package of 50-plus pages outlining some arcane change in the by-laws, or be asked to vote for a new slate of directors selected by the Board of Directors, self-succession being the rule of thumb.

This lesson, with some important twists, has been put to use by the Satori in controlling society. The first and foremost premise is that 90% of the individuals involved are totally unaware of the plan. They do not even know that there is a plan. This offers the masters ample opportunity to ridicule any accuser. Why are so many people in government, as well as the private sector, supportive of the plan? The answer is simple, but the explanation is not. The use of peer pressure, financial benefit, and pension benefits are the wheels which make it work. The process of peer pressure, in which, if you do not conform to required norms of behavior you do not ascend in the power structure, is also employed in controlling the output of the scientific and research communities. Consider yourself an employee of a supremely hierarchical governmental department, or a large corporation. Let's choose, for arguments sake, the State Department. Now, as an employee of the State Department you are told quite clearly by your department head exactly what is expected of you, what policy is, and that your job is to follow directives to the letter. You are also informed that if you carry out your job in a manner as outlined by your superiors, you have no place to go but up in the hierarchy. Lets face it, this is not a job which requires or demands inventive thought, or problem solving ability. It rather obligates dogged slavish obedience to command. Such a person need not be aware of the ulterior motive of the Satori, or even that they exist. He does not need to know of any master plan. Indeed, for him to do so would be detrimental to the entire cabal and his career. Once a level of upper management has been attained the individual is in his 50's. He now relies on his pension. He is, as they say, locked in. Disagreement may well be a personal opinion, but it is never openly admitted. The mold, as they say, is set at an early age, and once cast is only rarely broken.

You were probably a graduate of some college, lets say Dartmouth, in political science. When I was doing research for the predecessor of this book "The Satori and the New Mandarins" I required a research assistant. Living within driving distance of Dartmouth, I placed ads stating that I required a research assistant from the political science department, either a senior or a graduate student. I interviewed 12 seniors and one graduate student. Not one of the seniors knew who the Bilderbergers, the

Trilateral Commission, or the Council on Foreign Relations were. Not wanting to embarrass them further I did not mention the Club of Rome. The Graduate student had heard of the CFR and TC but not the Bilderbergers. It is my contention that if the political science department at Dartmouth does not teach students of these organizations which control society, they should give up education for something else.

The heavy, ever present hand of the Satori is pulling every imaginable string in an effort to negate disclosure of their brotherhood, from the publication of such books as *"Conspiracy"* actually written by a CFR member who referred to the CFR and Trilateral Commission as a club, to *Salmon Day* by Douglas Lamont who argues that the Europeans should embrace the EMU and accept *ex-officio* voting status for a European central bank.

Then, of course, there have been dozens of movies and newscasts all ridiculing in one way or another the fact that there is a conspiracy in progress. With such films, as the latest James Bond film in which we have a Ted Turner gone megalomaniac, the entire conspiracy is made to seem like a delusionary dream. Last, but certainly not least, there exists a concerted effort to prevent the publication and distribution of books exposing the entire matter. This I know firsthand as my first book on the subject was refused by every major publisher I approached. Excuses were more than just ridiculous: "Conservative books don't sell;" "No one is interested in the topic,"etc.

The largest problem facing America in the twenty-first century is the fact that our people have been taught not to think. Only a scant three percent of our population regularly visits libraries. Our population reacts on an emotional level, according to "batch conditioning" as put forth by the elites. The media spews forth distorted propaganda, and the populace accepts it as fact. The "long range penetration" of the Satori has, to-date, had a devastating effect on our society. The processes of "FUTURE SHOCK," "SOCIAL DRUGS," "CRISIS ADAPTION," and "PEOPLE CONTROL" is what this book is about.

The Satori establishment permeates the social and political fiber of our nation. You will see that the environmental movement, the socialists, even the major religions are infiltrated and related in the master plan, which is all drawn together in the ending chapter. Historical improvisation, the communist process of rewriting history to suit future goals of the establishment, is a prominent act of the Satori. Everyone including the federal government and educators are involved in this process. A new history book for secondary education was written by a staff at UCLA. The book mentioned the KKK seventeen times. It left out Edison, Samuel Adams, the Wright Brothers and Andrew Jackson among others. It glorified the Mayan civilization (human sacrifice), and the claim is even made that America's form of government was copied from the Iroquois Indian culture.

I state clearly, that of the people involved in the conspiracy, 90 percent are unaware of its existence, and will deny it exists. They will deny this, if for no other reason than the prospect that their entire lives have been spent in the service of a conspiracy makes them look very foolish.

Flash-Back

Dateline: **1922**

Source: **Council on Foreign Relations**

Issuance: *Foreign Affairs Magazine* (CFR's house organ)

In one of the first *Foreign Affairs* quarterly published, Mr. Philip Kerr (CFR) states:

> "Obviously there is going to be no peace or prosperity for mankind as long as the earth remains divided into 50 or 60 independent states . . . until some kind of international system is created."

CHAPTER ONE

CONSPIRATORIAL HISTORY

As there are so many people who claim the conspiracy is but a poor theory, some history may well prove useful. I delve into the last century, only to touch on some important matters which impact us today. There is ample evidence as we shall see.

The two most incriminating books published on the topic in the twentieth century are those by Professor Caroll Quigley: *Tragedy and Hope,* and *The Anglo-American Establishment.* Quigley makes no bones about the conspiracy when he states: "I know of the operations of this network of (influence) . . . and was permitted for two years in the early 60's, to examine its papers and secret records. I have no aversion to it."

Not to be forgotten are two decidedly different, but nevertheless cogent books by Zbigniew Brzezinski (National Security Advisor under President Carter): *Between Two Ages* and *The Technotronic Era.* These volumes give us a more vivid view of our planned future, and not a very nice one. Spoken of is an era in which an elite moneyed class rules a socialist feudalistic world. Personal freedom and individual rights are but remnants of the past, and where a drugged, stupefied population functions as serfs to the ruling class. Envisioned are four classes of people: Serfs, which represent the vast majority; a military police class used for control; a mandarin class used for administration; and the ruling elite which I call the Satori. This pyramidal structure is envisioned as worldwide. The upper 15% of the pyramid representing the Satori, military police and Mandarins, the rest (or 85%) are serfs, whose only function is to ensure the opulent well being of their masters.

It is impossible to address the issue of a conspiratorial 20th century without serious consideration of the British Fabian Society and Cecil Rhodes. The Fabian Society — which for the greatest part was funded by Rhodes — represents the inner circle of organization which extended the conspiracy into the 20th century. Rhodes considered the British as the normal inheritors of the world in conjunction with their controlled or allied commonwealth, and America. To put it in a nutshell, Rhodes envisioned a world government under British and American control. To these ends he created several complicated and secret wills, some of which were later published in 1902. One of these was for the creation of the Rhodes scholarship fund, the purpose of which was the creation of a school at Oxford designed to teach one world socialist dogma to a very specially selected group of college graduates. The requirements of acceptance were partially academic, a high IQ being mandatory. Some unsavory personal traits were also part of the requisite.

The Fabians first ulterior motive was the control of certain special aspects of society. These are: banking, journalism, politics, economics, education and mainstream churches. Their success in that endeavor is a matter of current world history.

In the fall of 1890 Rhodes sent a letter to his good friend W. T. Stead. The letter outlines most of his plan, and, as excerpts will demonstrate, the astounding to-date success of that plan. *"The key of my idea discussed with you is a society* (the Fabian Society) *copied from the Jesuits* (It is important to understand that the Society of Jesus [Jesuits] established in 1540, has a unique, centralized, military-type of organizational structure. The title given their leader, who is elected for life, is that of general, whose authority over the centuries has at times challenged even that of the Pope) *as to organization . . . an idea which will ultimately lead to cessation of all wars and one single language . . .* (English is now the common language in Scotland, Ireland, England, America, Canada, New Zealand, Australia, India 2nd required, Pakistan 2nd required, Russia 2nd required, China 2nd required, and over twenty less important nations.) *. . . the only feasible way to carry out this idea is a secret society . . . gradually absorbing the wealth of the world* (a process we now call mergers, acquisitions and global business) *to charm young Americans* (into membership) . . . *to share in a scheme to take the government of the whole world."*

As it turns out, the plan was to come to fruition 100 years later. It was at that time that then president George Bush reiterated the words of "The New World Order" in a speech. In Quigley's books (1967) we learn that there were between two and three thousand graduates of the Rhodes scholarship programs active politically around the world. The unsavory characteristics of the participants specified by Rhodes were: *"smugness, brutality, unctuous rectitude, and tact."* A veritable description of Bill Clinton as well as his fellow Rhodes scholar advisors.

In 1890 or so, the Milner group, named after Lord Milner, was formed, and shortly after that the Round Table and the Society of the Elect. Members included Rhodes, Stead, Milner, Brett, Esher, Webb, H. G. Wells, and G. B. Shaw among others. Those not members of the Elect were called helpers. In 1890 they also formed the London School of Economics, which came to dominate an entire school of socialist economics. H. G. Wells later published numerous books dealing with plans hatched by the group, most notably, *The Open Conspiracy, The New World Order,* and *Blue Print for World Revolution.*

Between 1902 and 1911 numerous auxiliary organizations appeared on the scene. These included: The Carnegie Trust, The Carnegie Foundations, and The Carnegie Endowment for International Peace. It is a well publicized fact the J. P. Morgan was enamored of the Rhodes plan, and was instrumental in the funding of the aforementioned organizations, along with Andrew Carnegie. The first president of the Carnegie Foundation (1902) turns out to be none other than Daniel Gillman (The Order). This represents the beginning of the assertion of the Order, the senior society from Yale University whose secret hidden hand is so very prominent in America's political stage. David Boren (The Order) became president of Johns Hopkins University where he introduced to American education the destructive new German educational philosophies. He went so far as to invite the Webbs — at whose home the Fabians had their regular meetings — to address the faculty in closed session. He hired Stanley Hall as a professor, who subsequently schooled John Dewey, the father of modern education. In 1904 Gillman funded, through the foundation, radical experiments in eugenics (the process of selected breeding of humans).

Beginning in 1912 New York bankers began their push for the FRS (Federal Reserve System.) Then President Wilson published an article in *The New Freedom*. In it he made the following statement: *"Since I entered politics, I have chiefly had men's views come to me privately. Some of the biggest men in the U.S. in the field of commerce and manufacturing, are afraid of something. They know that there is a power somewhere so organized, so subtle, so watchful, so interlocking, so complete, so pervasive that they had better not speak above their breath when they speak in condemnation of it."*

In 1914 the First World War was set up. We have it straight from Col. House, who was Wilson's "alter ego." On May 29th about four weeks before the assassination of Arch Duke Ferdinand (June 28) in what is now Bosnia, House sent a letter to Wilson from Berlin. *"Whenever England consents, Russia will close in on Germany and Austria."* Toward the end of July the British Secretary of State Sir Edward Grey (Milner Group member) misled the German Ambassador to Earls Court, Prince Karl Marx Lichnowsky, into believing that England would not enter a conflict between those powers. Had he done otherwise and told the truth there would have been no First World War.

In 1918 *The Declaration of the Federation of the World* was published. It was subsequently endorsed by a number of state legislatures. The key phrase of that document is: *"that all people of the earth should now be united in a commonwealth of nation."* The Document was authored by Robert Lee Humber, a Rhodes scholar. In 1919 the Wilson administration went all-out in an attempt to establish the League of Nations at Geneva Switzerland. This was the first attempt at the establishment of a World Government.

In 1921 the CFR (Council on Foreign Relations) was formed in New York City. Among its founding members is one Col. House. The CFR was set up along the lines of the RIIA (Royal Institute of International Affairs) London, and was unofficially affiliated to it. The CFR went on to virtually control the entire American State Department as well as almost every presidential cabinet position from FDR onward, and the majority of the Joint Chiefs of Staff of the military. In 1922 Frank Aydelotte (Rhodes Scholar) (CFR) became director of the Institute for Advanced Studies at Princeton, New Jersey, which appears to be affiliated to the University. Quigley, in his book, claims that the operational structure of Milner's Round Table and the ASP are identical in configuration.

In 1928 Shaw published *The Intelligent Woman's Guide to Socialism and Capitalism.* This work makes some of the most idiotic statements of the century: *"under socialism you would not be allowed to be poor. You would be forcibly fed, clothed, lodged, taught, and employed whether you like it or not. If it were discovered that you had not the character and industry enough to be worth all this trouble, you might possibly be executed in a kindly manner."* This is the crux of Fabian socialism, it is a quote which should be read often, it reminds us exactly what happened in Russia, and what is in store for us if the Satori are successful in their endeavor.

1930 was a big year. The plan for war reparations was made and enforced upon Germany thus a second World War was guaranteed. The Bank of International Settlements (BIS) was founded in Basel, Switzerland. The largest influences in the foundation of this mega bank were the great financiers of the 30's: Rothschild, Morgan, et al. BIS is a bank that loans money to nations and banks in financial straights. It is a private bank whose shares have traded between $5500 and $8400 each in the past ten years. Most shares are held by private banks due to their high cost. This in effect is the forerunner of a world bank, with a world currency.

In 1931 Mr. Arnold Toynbee (The Group) addressed the Institute for the Study of International Affairs. He stated *"We are at present working discreetly with all our might to wrest this mysterious force called sovereignty out of the clutches of the local nations of the world."* Just a few months later, in 1932, the Rockefeller Foundation granted the RIIA 8000 pounds sterling per year. The amount was subsequently increased in 1937 (8000 pounds in 1932 would be equivalent to about $500,000 today). On November 23, 1931, FDR wrote to Col. House and in that confidential letter stated: *"The real truth of the matter is, as you and I both know, that a financial element in the larger centers has owned the government since the days of Andrew Jackson."*

In 1936 Joseph P. Kennedy, who was ambassador at Earls Court and the father of JFK, made the following statement in July of that year: *"Fifty men run America, and that's a high figure."* This is also the year in which the Ford Foundation was started. It was eventually taken over by non-Ford family members and financed so many "anti-American" activities that the last Ford family member quit in disgust.

Just a little while later, in 1939, The Group took over the London Times, making it a clean sweep. Between the CFR and The Group, they now controlled all important mainline newspapers and wire services in the US and England. Takeover of American radio and TV production followed, until all networks are under control. New works published include *The New World Order* by H. G. Wells (Group) and *World Order* (Civitas Dei) by Lionel Curtis (Group) a work of almost 900 pages. This then brings us to 1941 and the publication of *The City of Man* authored by a number of Rhodes scholars, including Aydelotte, Yandell, and Eliot.

In 1942 Corbett (The Group) published *Post War Worlds.* He states: *"It must be recognized that the law of nations takes precedence over national law."* Thus we find ourselves ever more affiliated and entangled with the UN, and in myriad's of international trade treaties of UN origin.

I am sure you have heard of the statements made by numerous media commentators in spring and early summer of 1998 about the new plans for an *international jurist court* under UN sponsorship which would have autonomy over American citizens. This is one of the hottest projects of the Satori at the present time. The seeds for NAFTA, EC, GATT, WTO, all are already sown. The rest you will learn in the text of this book.

PREREQUISITE

Before anyone can gain an understanding of the Satori and how they control societies, they must have an understanding of the world's monitory systems. It is not by accident all such information is either omitted in our educational systems, or befuddled to the extent it becomes unintelligible.

The ultimate success of any system of oppression depends on, at least the premise, that the subject of manipulation not be aware of the true cause or planned outcome of the manipulation. This is the reality of all the world's fiat money systems. As Machiavelli so clearly stated: "should the people become aware of the manipulation, then hostilities would ensue."

Barter

Mans first effort at trade was barter. Barter is still used today, more so in rural communities. The process is simple: If I have a skill or commodity which you need or want, and you have one that I need or want, we trade at an agreed upon level. Money is not used, and records are not kept.

Real Money

As societies developed barter became ineffective. Transactions began to include groups rather than individuals and thus an alternative means of trade had to develop. Furthermore the payment of, for example, a military group hired for protection, is difficult through barter. In early history a commodity which shared special features had to be found. The first of these was copper, then bronze, then iron, then silver then gold. As man developed from prehistory a medium of exchange was required. The easiest and simplest commodity due to size, weight, and value were metals. These metals, then as now, were shaped into coins, and represented the actual value of that quantity of metal. The difference between fiat money and real money is that real money has an intrinsic value, while fiat money has none.

Fiat Money

Fiat money is funny money. Its value is based on the say so of government. In fact, it has no intrinsic value at all. We are informed by government that we have inflation and that this has in the last 50 years varied from between 3% to 12%. If we take the lowest figure of 3% and multiply it by 50 we have 150%, and that's not compounded. Inflation is caused by the continuous increase in "printing press" money and credit. Thus the money supply becomes larger than the available supply of goods and services. This decreases the value of the money, and the decrease in the value of money is called inflation. Value in the market is based upon goods or services which are wanted and/or needed by the consumer versus its supply (how much of it is available). The values system of any nation therefore is not based in the value of the currency, but in the sum total of what it produces, and is able to sell at home and abroad. The variation in buy and sell between nations produces a "balance of payment," which is a record of the desirability of its products versus those of other nations. America's balance of payments has been negative for half of the 20th century.

America's funny money policies go way back to the Continental Congress. To finance the War of Independence the congress issued Continentals. These were a fiat currency that came into common use, particularly because the Continental Army was paid in Continentals. I do not know if you have heard the expression "Not Worth A Continental," but that was a very common expression for most of the 18th and 19th century. It stems from the fact that Congress, which had promised to make good on the Conti-

EXAMPLES OF REAL MONEY

St. Gauden's $20 Gold Piece

U.S. Silver Dollar

$20 Gold Certificate

$5 Silver Certificate

*Photographs courtesy of Worldwide Treasure Bureau,
P.O. Box 5012, Visalia, CA 93278-5012.*

EXAMPLE OF FIAT MONEY

THIS NOTE IS LEGAL TENDER FOR ALL DEBTS, PUBLIC AND PRIVATE, AND IS REDEEEMABLE IN LAWFUL MONEY AT THE UNITED STATES TREASURY, OR AT ANY FEDERAL RESERVE BANK.

This statment "Redeemable in Lawful Money" [meaning Silver or Gold] was printed on every Federal Reserve Note issued from 1914 to 1963.

THIS NOTE IS LEGAL TENDER
FOR ALL DEBTS, PUBLIC AND PRIVATE.

Federal Reserve Notes became Fiat Money after 1963 when the promise disappeared.

nentals at the close of the War of Independence, backed out of the deal, and devalued Continentals to the point of one cent to the dollar. They also backed out of a land deal promised the veterans, but that's another story.

With this background information we can now enter into a discussion of currency manipulation and how the Satori utilize money as the means of financing their operations against the people.

First Attempt

If you are going to understand the nature of, workings, and organization of the Satori, then you must of necessity have a clear and concise understanding of the history and operation of the management of currency. The old axiom about following the money is as true today as it was when America was founded.

To understand United States history, it is important to know that England's Currency Act of 1764 replaced the currency of the colonies with English pounds. The Bank of England, who issued those English pound notes, was a privately-owned bank established in 1694. (In 1999, one of the first things the newly elected Prime Minister did was to remove Parliament's oversight of the Bank of England.)

To raise money for Washington's Continental Army, Arthur Lee and Benjamin Franklin went to England and France. Lee wrangled financial support from business interests, i.e. the Bank of England, and even members of the British Parliament. While Franklin, in a treaty with France, dated February 6, 1778, obtained 3 million livre additional grants and loans, a defense alliance, and a trading partner for America's goods.

In return, for the financial support given Lee and Franklin, a commitment was made to the banks. Should the colonists win the war, their "financial interests" would continue as under English rule. (For more information on this subject, read *Whatever Happened to America?* by John Christian Ryder.) Therefore, one of the first actions taken by the newly-formed United States Congress in 1792, at the behest of President George Washington and Secretary of the Treasury Alexander Hamilton, was the establishment of the Bank of the United States. This was a privately-owned bank in which the United States government was given a 20% interest. However, due to Thomas Jefferson's staunch opposition, the bank's charter was limited to 20 years.

Flash-Back

Dateline: February 15, 1791

Source: The Writings of Thomas Jefferson
             ed. by H. E. Bergh, Vol. III, p. 145 ff.

Issuance: Thomas Jefferson

I consider the foundation of the Constitution as laid on this ground — that *all powers not delegated to the United States, by the Constitution, nor prohibited by it to the states, are reserved to the states, or to the people.* To take a single step beyond the boundaries thus specially drawn around the powers of Congress, is to take possession of a boundless field of power, no longer susceptible of any definition.

The incorporation of a bank, and the powers assumed by this bill, have not, in my opinion, been delegated to the United States by the Constitution.

Second Attempt

When in 1812 the charter for the Bank of the United States was not renewed, England attacked and burned down Washington D.C. (the War of 1812). In response to England's action, the Bank of the United States was reinstituted as the United States Bank in 1816, and its capitalization was $35 million. Bear in mind that although such an amount seems paltry in today's trillion dollar economy, it was very substantial in 1816. The charter given by Congress delegated to the United States Bank the monopoly of issuing currency and notes receivable by the United States for taxes and demands due the government. The United States Bank acted like the Federal Reserve System does today. This was a private banking consortium exactly the same as the Federal Reserve is today. So you can see that in almost two centuries almost nothing has changed. To understand exactly where the Satori plans to take us, let's look at the exact wording of the original charter as passed by Congress in 1816:

That no other bank shall be established by any future law of the United States, during the continuance of the corporation (United States Bank) hereby created, for which the faith of the United States is hereby pledged. Provided, Congress may renew existing charters for the banks within the District of Columbia, not increasing the capital thereof, and may establish any other bank or banks in said district, with capitals not exceeding, in the whole six million dollars, if they shall deem it expedient.

Note that the American government gave a pledge to a group of private bankers, giving them not only a monopoly, but guaranteeing them financial solvency at the expense of the republic. Also note that the currency to be issued was not acceptable for the payment of import duties, which was the only income our federal government had. At that point in our history hard currency, i.e. gold or silver, were the only acceptable way to pay federal import duties.

Through this charter our government surrendered its constitutional authority over control of the currency, and to collect revenue. Therefore, revenue was collected though Washington DC and the bank became the sole collection agent for the federal government. This charter was enacted for a term of 20 years, whereupon it was assumed by the Satori that it would be extended forever.

For the privilege granted these bankers, they were to pay the United States an annual bonus of $200,000 per year. Consider the enormous profits that could be made by having the exclusive monopoly on: 1) issuing of currency; 2) collecting of general debt; 3) collecting duties and fees in gold; 4) setting all interest rates; and 5) collecting all interest on outstanding debt. That, however, was just the beginning. Within months of the charter's activation the bank was busy making loans at low interest rates to anyone elected to anything, as well as journalists and news editors. In addition, financial arrangements allowed the bank monopoly rights of issuing and producing the medium of exchange of the country, and to obtain interest payments on that medium of 35 million dollars. They were also provided an additional 5 million dollars which was constituted as primary loan funds, on which all interest came due to the bank. By discounting collected duties revenue they also made profit on the collection of taxes. Within three years of its charter the bank had virtual control of the nation's business, and as a monopoly had the government act as their enforcement department. The financial power vested in the bank became not only corrupting, but it shook the very foundations of the republic.

From 1816 to 1832 the United States Bank (a privately owned corporation) was the sole and only arbiter of the financial affairs of the republic, in both private as well as public matters. Things were about to change. In 1828 Andrew Jackson, the hero of New Orleans, was elected president by a landslide. In his first address to Congress on December 8, 1829, President Jackson announced his resolute opposition to the Bank and that he would not renew their charter.

In 1830, due to the collection of import duties, there developed a substantial surplus of funds in national accounting. In accordance with the charter, those funds were deposited with the Bank, which allowed additional loans and profits to be made. In that same year Jackson proposed that these surplus funds instead be distributed among the states, and in the same address, again opposed the renewal of the Bank's charter. On the 4th of July 1832 a bill to re-charter the Bank was passed by Congress and sent to President Jackson for his signature. The pressure on Jackson was unimaginable. The Bank pressed every outstanding loan holder, especially elected officials and the media, but also business, farms, etc. They forced these borrowers to sign petitions. They threatened to destroy the Republic. They threatened to call all outstanding loans.

In his next address to Congress Jackson eloquently informed the assembly that he would stand fast, and would, to his last day, oppose the Bank. He said; *"In this point of the case the question is distinctly presented, whether the people of the United States are to govern through representatives chosen by their unbiased suffrages (elections), or whether the power and money of great corporations are to be secretly exerted to influence their judgment and control their decisions."* Here we have President Jackson in 1832 recognizing a secret conspiracy to control the government, that conspiracy being benched within the financial community.

Opposition to Satori plans always have dire consequences. The then president of the Bank, Biddle, ensued on a policy to destroy the president and insure Satori supremacy. First he called every loan that was outstanding, then he drastically reduced the volume of currency on the market — depriving business of capital. Expansion and production became impossible, hundreds of thousands were unemployed, businesses went bankrupt, outstanding loan holders in the media and elected officials were forced to support Biddle or they would be ruined.

Andrew Jackson, a true American patriot, stood his ground — he vetoed the bill. He uttered Jefferson's great quote: *"Banks of issue are more dangerous than standing armies."* Jackson showed that with a fixed capital stock of $28,000,000 the bank in actuality had valued its stock $17,000,000 higher, and then through loans on those funds provided over $500 million in loans and was paying the US government a paltry $200,000 per anum. He went on to propose that the bank be liquidated to the highest bidders and that the assets of the sale be used to lower the tax burden of Americans. Then he showed that of the outstanding stock of the bank, a full quarter or $8 million was held by the bank of England (a privately owned bank). This astounding revelation more than any other brought support to President Jackson's position. This brings us full circle. How much of our current national debt is held by foreign interests? We can surmise that it is substantially more than we can repay.

Jackson made a statement that still rings true today: *All its operations within would be in aid of hostile fleets and armies. Controlling our currency, receiving our public moneys, and holding thousands of our citizens in dependence, it would be more formidable and dangerous than the naval and military power of the enemy."*

Jackson proved to be more than just right, the bank after its closure was proven to be corrupt to the core. Loans to the media and members of congress totaled over $30 million. After the bank lost its charter and government funds were removed from its grasp, it continued its policy to attempt to destroy the republic. The bank instituted a policy of currency contraction, and calling loans, its reason given was: "the government is harassing us." The bank refused to be audited by the government. Again we go full circle. Since its inception, the Federal Reserve has never been audited.

The history of the United States Bank is a clear and present warning to Americans of the corrupting power wielded by the Satori in their continuing attempt to control society for their own benefit. In 1803 Jefferson made the following commentary on the privately owned Bank of the United States:

> "This institution is one of the most deadly hostile existing, against the principle and form of our constitution . . . I deem no government safe which is under the vassalage of any self-constituted (private) or any other authority than that of the nation, or its regular functionaries."

Banks wielded great power in the 19th century, just as they do today. People, however, were not well educated in banking and thus America's bankers were able to institute the panics of 1811, 1833, and 1837 to 40. Through these acts, banks consolidated power and began the recently accelerated process of reducing the number of banks. In the United States over 800 banks have disappeared in the last decade. Worse, in over 600 of these consolidations, bankruptcies, and mergers, you the taxpayer, through the assistance of a willing Congress, have made up all the losses in such transactions. This process, which is now more evident than ever, is designed to bring us back to a scenario of similar financial construction as the United States Bank, but on an international scale. There are at present several international banks whose asset base is substantially larger than that of 90% of the world's nations. And, just as in the game of marbles, he who has all the marbles calls the shots.

Even with the economic anchor posed by the banking industry our nation grew economically from 1800 to the Civil War at an astounding pace. The Civil War — which may be directly attributed to financial causes — came about due to the differentiation of industry in the northeast and agriculture in the south. The southern states obtained most of their industrial goods from England because of four factors: England was their best customer; England was their principal supplier of industrial goods; England supplied a major portion of their capital needs; and England's goods were of better quality then those of the north. These facts did not escape England's great adversaries in industrial production and finance in the United States northeast. With a plurality of population the northern states instituted high tariffs on British industrial goods, essentially blockading the southern states. This cut the south off from capital, their major markets, and less expensive and better made industrial goods. The south seceded from the union, as was their constitutional right, because they really had no other choice. The fairy tale that the civil war was fought over slavery is just that. Slavery was on its way out, and had already been brought to a peaceful end in most of the world. The fact is that new methods of farming and producing, plus the exorbitant cost of caring for slaves, simply made the practice obsolete. The facts of the war are clearly demonstrated by the reality that as the two camps, North and South, were marshaling their forces, the British firmly sided with the southern states and in due course financed the southern states' war effort.

August Belmont & Co. were the agents for the Rothschild banking interests in New York, the financial capital of the United States. Then as now the Rothschild banking interests were immensely powerful, with operations in Paris, Frankfurt, Berlin, London and Vienna. They advised August Belmont not to purchase any American financial paper, thus cutting the North off from the largest supply of cash in the world at that time. A very interesting letter was circulated in the United States to banking interests. Its origin may be directly traced to the Rothschilds' through their agents.

> *Slavery is likely to be abolished as it has been elsewhere, and thus chattel slavery destroyed. This we and our European friends are in favor of, for slavery is but owning of labor, and thereby carries with it the care and sustenance of the laborer. In our new European plan, led by England, the capital control of labor is through wages, and the control of currency."*

Just read that one more time! We see here in the 1850's, the clear and distinct premise that labor costs in our present time, as well as in our future, are controlled not by unions, labor or management, but by banking interests.

Financing of the war by the North thus had to be done internally, through the issuance of treasury notes. The exact amount was $150,000,000 an astronomical sum for the 1850's. Principally New York bankers (the same class who now own the Federal Reserve) were able to force Congress to institute the structuring of those Bonds in such a way as to allow them to reap unheard of profit. The Notes were discounted to the bankers at a full twenty percent. Thus Satori interests made an immediate profit of $30 million before the first shot was fired.

The Gradual Approach – National Banks

In the 1860's there were several types of banks. Roughly these could be separated into State Banks and National Banks. Both had the right to issue currency, and were loosely regulated. The National Banks had a plan, which they had instituted into law by the Congress. That plan was to eliminate their competition, the State Banks. This was accomplished through the introduction of the National Banking Act, as brought to legislation by Senator Sherman, February 13, 1862. This odious law placed National Banks in a legally strong position, by empowering them to bring suits at law in the United States courts of original jurisdiction (now called Federal courts) and virtually forced State Banks to become National. It made National Banks impervious to State courts and State jurisdiction. Further, the law doubled the actual net worth (capital) of any National Bank.

1.) Bonds deposited by the National Bank to secure circulation of money they printed drew interest, payable in gold.

2.) The circulating notes issued to the National Bank by the government were promissory notes, payable on demand, and were thus used as collateral for additional loans at higher interest rates.

3.) The government gave the National Banks the right to loan up to 90% of their asset worth, and guaranteed the principal.

4.) Loans (borrowing) by the government from the National Banks allowed the prepayment of interest, i.e. loans were heavily discounted, up to 20%.

All this made the currencies (notes) issued by national banks competitive to the federally issued "Green Backs," and through it, placed our federal financial interests in private hands. The owners of the National Banks were thus able to influence and often control tax rates, money supply, and the entire economic life of the nation, but they did not have monopoly power. This was to come later.

The Final Product

The Federal Reserve System (FRS) was established by the Federal Reserve Act of 1913. Like most banks in the majority of the developed world it is not a governmental institution. The FRS is a private banking monopoly comprising 12 district banks with a total of 37 branches. The inherent power of the bank rests in New York, whose 12 participating banks control just under two thirds of all assets in the system. At the head of this consortium we find the board of governors, which are located in Washington, DC. There are seven board members, each of which enjoy a tenure of 14 years. They are recommended for office by the Satori, appointed by the president, and approved by the Senate. Not once in the entire history of the FRS has any applicant been rejected. Not even an economist like Rivilin whose ideas, to say the least, are unconstitutional. Thus we can understand that the appointment and approval are mere window dressing.

Flash-Back

Dateline: 1993

Source: *The Secrets of the Federal Reserve*

Issuance: **Eustace Mullins, Author**
                 P.O. Box 1105, Staunton, VA 24401

A facsimile of an article which appeared in the *New York times* dated September 23, 1914 appears on the opposite page. Listed are major stockholders of the five New York City banks which purchased 40% of the 203,053 share of the Federal Reserve Bank of New York when the System was organized in 1914. they thus obtained control of that Federal Reserve Bank and have held it ever since. As of Tuesday, July 26, 1983, the top five surviving New York City banks have increased their ownership of the Federal Reserve Bank of New York to 53% of the shares.

THE NEW YORK TIMES.
WEDNESDAY, SEPTEMBER 23, 1914.

BANKS' STOCK LIST FULL OF SURPRISES

Many Names Associated by Public with Big Stockholdings Not Found.

HETTY GREEN'S 30 SHARES

Frank Vanderlip Missing from Among Large Interests in National City.

Publication yesterday of lists of stockholders in some of New York City's largest banks aroused considerable interest in the financial district, as much because of the absences of expected names as of the amounts of the principal holdings. The date at which the lists were compiled was not made known, and important changes may have taken place since, although as a rule there is little activity in bank shares and the controlling interests in most institutions have been in the same hands for many years.

Among the surprises in the lists, as published by Dow, Jones & Co., was the discovery that Hetty Green, often spoken of as a very important factor in the conduct of the Chemical National, owns only 31 of the 30,000 shares of that institution. Frank Vanderlip, President of the National City Bank, is not down among the principal shareholders, while James Stillman, Chairman of the Board of Directors, holds 47,498 shares of the total of 250,000. Mr. Stillman is also a large holder in the Hanover and the Citizens' Central. J. P. Morgan & Co. have the biggest holdings of any firm.

The shareholders, capitalization, number of shares, dividends, and book value, follow:

National City Bank—Capital, $25,000; total stockholders, 1,013; book value, $230; par value, $100; annual dividend, 10 per cent. Stock also includes $10,000,000 capital of National City Company, which pays annual dividend of 6 per cent.

James Stillman..	47,498	W. A. Rockefeller	10
J. P. Morgan & Co.	14,000	A. T. Russell....	8,267
		*H. A. C. Taylor	7,999
W. Rockefeller..	10,000	J. W. Sterling..	6,087
M. T. Pyne....	8,267	U. S. Trust Co.,	
Percy Pyne	8,267	New York.....	4,500
J. D. Rockefeller	1,750	J. P. Morgan,	
J. S. Rockefeller	100	Jr.	1,000
*Trustee.			

National Bank of Commerce—Capital, $25,000,000; total stockholders, 3,013; book value, $166; par value, $100; annual dividend, 8 per cent.

Equitable Life..	24,700	A. D. Juilliard.	2,000
Mutual Life....	17,294	J. J. Gerdan...	1,606
G. F. Baker....	10,000	J. P. Goodhart &	
North. Finance		Co.	1,287
Corporation ..	9,300	J. N. Jarvine..	1,285
J. P. Morgan & Co.	7,800	F. A. V. Twombly	1,250
Mary W. Harriman	5,650	Kidder, Peabody & Co.	1,125
E. J. Berwind..	5,650	J. P. Morgan,Jr.	1,100
T. F. Ryan.....	5,100	L. P. Morton...	1,500
R. W. Winthrop Co., agents..	4,900	H. B. Davison..	1,100
		W. W. Astor....	1,000
S. J. Saltus.....	4,757	J. H. Schiff....	1,000
T. A. Reynolds.	3,175	V. P. Snyder...	1,000
*P. M. Warburg.	3,000	G. Whittell	1,000
A. J. Hemphill.	2,000	E. T. Nichols...	1,000
*Since sold his holdings.			

First National—Capital, $10,000,000; total stockholders, 626; book value, $329; par value, $100; annual dividend, 40 per cent. Of this 28 per cent. is paid on bank's stock and 12 per cent. on stock of First Security Company.

G. F. Baker....	20,000	G. F. Baker, Jr.	5,000
J. P. Morgan & Co.	13,900	J. J. Hill......	4,000
		North'n Fin. Co.	1,700
H. C. Fahnestock	10,000	F. L Hine......	1,400
Garland, Dodson & Emmer, Tr. of est. of J. A. Garland	9,900	H. B. Davison..	1,010
		Mary C. Thompson	9,000

Chase National—Capital, $5,000,000; total shareholders, 309; book value, $299; par value, $100; annual dividend, 20 per cent.

G. F. Baker....	13,408	H. W. Cannon..	1,400
A. H. Wiggin..	6,492	G. B. Schley....	500
C. A. Edwards..	3,500	S. Miller	500
A. B. Hepburn..	2,873	J. J. Mitchell...	500
J. J. Hill......	1,500	Faith Moore ...	500
L. G. Thompson.	1,500	W. H. Porter...	500
E. Tuck.......	1,500	F. S. Thompson,	
Trustees Princeton Univ.....	1,000	U. S. T. Co.,Tr.	1,000

Hanover National—Capital, $3,000,000; total stockholders, 404; book value, $579; par value, $100; annual dividend, 16 per cent.

Wm. Woodward.	6,600	Bessemer Invest.	
James Stillman.	4,000	Co.	325
Wm. Rockefeller	1,540	Wm. J. Clark...	423
Wm. Barbour..	1,200	Wm. J. Halls...	410
Jas. M. Donald.	1,025	C. Wodsworth...	750
		Robt. M. Goelet.	400

A clear understanding as to who runs the FRS is indicated by the fact that the Chairman, Alan Greenspan, and the Vice Chairman, Alice Rivlin, are both CFR members. Both are also members of the powerful Federal Open Market Committee (FOMC). The first Vice President of that committee, Ernest T. Patrikis, is also a CFR member. The Chairman and Vice Chairman of the FRS are appointed from the membership of the Board of Governors by the President (he gets to choose one of seven insiders). Even if we elected a pro-American patriot as president, he could only, in four years, appoint two members of the board of governors, and would have to choose the chairman from the seven current Governors in February of his first term. The possibilities of making any meaningful changes within four years are therefore non-existent.

The powers of this private bank are extraordinary — they:
- Conduct the nation's monetary policy.
- Regulate interest rates.
- Approve credit (banks).
- Supervise all banking.
- Regulate credit, (FRR) Federal Reserve Regulations.
- Regulate markets.
- Regulate American & foreign banks operating on American soil.
- Loan money to the Federal Government, the public, and banks.
- Operate the nation's payment system.

It is important to note that the Federal Reserve System has never been audited by any branch of the government.

The FRS operates the following:
- FDIC Federal Deposit Insurance Corporation
- NCUA National Credit Union Administration
- OCC Office of the Comptroller of Currency
- OTS Office of Thrift Supervision.

In this manner they, in effect, control all functions of State Banks, bank holding companies, non-bank subsidiaries of bank holding companies, branches and agencies of foreign banks operating in America, and all officers and employees working for any of the aforementioned organizations.

I believe it should now be abundantly clear who controls American finance, along with the fact that those who do so are neither audited, nor are they elected. The entire financial system of America is controlled, run by and for the express purpose of the Satori. Consider the national debt. About half of our taxes go toward the interest payment on that debt. Some of it is held by the FRS members, much of it is sold. Regardless if it is sold or held, members of the FRS make financial gains on every single transaction relating to the national debt.

The real money, however, is not made through these acts, but through the guarantee of profits by a government warrantee. For example, the FRS will make a loan, to say, Mexico, as requested and guaranteed by our government. If the Mexicans default on it or devalue their currency (both of which have taken place) you the taxpayer are drafted to make good the outstanding Mexican debt to the banks. Members of the FRS simply can't lose. No matter what they do or how they do it Uncle Sam guarantees their every financial risk. In effect and action, we the people underwrite any and all risks of the Satori. We will look even deeper into this subject in Chapter 6, Finance.

Money

Under constitutional law the only "currency" which may be issued by the government is gold and silver coin. All specie (i.e.) paper money is issued by private banks. I know this is very confusing so bear with me. The confusion in all this is purposeful — why do you think they call it the Federal Reserve System? It is not federal but a privately held corporation, it is not a system but a business, and most importantly there is no reserve whatsoever.

What is written on every American bank note, *"Federal Reserve Note,"* then signed by the secretary of the Treasury, causes the confusion. How can the secretary of the Treasury — who is not a member of the FRS — place his signature on the FRS note? What backs this note? Nothing. The Federal Reserve System has no assets except for the assets of member banks, which could not begin to cover the notes issued. To make things worse, the federal government underwrites any potential loss by the Federal Reserve System. A corporation is a separate entity by law, and thus stockholders are not liable for losses of a corporation. How would you like to own a business, have the government guarantee a profit, and have the government absolve you from any possible loss?

Now you have surely heard that our U.S. currency is backed by the *"good faith and trust of America"* — more poppycock. How can a government who is in debt to the tune of over $24 trillion represent any good faith? Our national debt is greater then our federal assets. The United States collects about one trillion in taxes per anum, and usually spends several hundred billion more. Why is all this debt accumulated? The answer is simple. But it lies buried in the 19th century. When the government issues notes through which it borrows money, it does so through the private banking system — the Federal Reserve System. Thus the same people who issue, distribute, and control the currency also issue loans, notes, bills, and collect the interest, earning a handsome percentage on both ends of the transaction. The reason that the national debt is so high is because the central banks of the Federal Reserve System make compound interest profits on every single cent of the debt. Who pays for this disgusting Ponzi Scheme — you do! Through taxes assessed, you pay the interest due the FRS which has been issued a monopoly money machine.

Debt is the way that the ruling elite prosper. Why do so many Mandarins oppose the reduction of our national debt, which in 1998 reached over $24 trillion? The reason is obvious. The larger the debt, the more money is required to pay the interest charges thereon and as a consequence the more money the lenders make. Consider now the interest rates on personal credit cards alone, at a variance from 6.5% to 18% interest compounded. The total

American private credit card debt is at present over 2 trillion dollars. If we compound that, at say a 10% average, the income is astronomical. The present national debt is financed through the sale of government bonds. During the last years — at least since the advent of the Clinton administration — these papers have all been issued short term, usually 5 years. This was not previously the case — most government paper was issued as 30 year notes. In any event, consider the interest on $24 trillion, much of which is held by foreign governments and institutions. Do not suffer under the delusion that the United States government is in charge of these transactions, it is the Federal Reserve System, which is a private banking group. Furthermore you must clearly understand that these outstanding loans — and that is exactly what they are — have considerable impact on our national trade policy.

Currently outstanding debt (loans) held by foreign interests may be assumed to exceed 5 trillion. Now let's equate that to the most favored nation trade status given China. China has in the last ten years accumulated about $270 billion in American notes. Japan has four times that amount. Other bankers of Satori-run institutions have at least 4 trillion. Can anyone seriously argue that this does not have enormous effect on America's foreign and trade policy? Does it not clearly show that we are no longer able to form foreign policy unilaterally, and that current American foreign policy is heavily influenced by our international financial policies? This is the reason for the Satori-pushed "Free Trade" policy which, categorically stated, is government controlled trade, free of taxes.

The United States Constitution

Without a good understanding of our Constitution any citizen will be hard pressed to oppose the Satori, and therefore we review it at the conclusion of this book. It is unfortunate that the document which is the guarantor of our liberty is only glossed over in our schools. It is not difficult to understand the motive for this. The management of the academic establishment is basically opposed to the Constitution, so we can readily understand the reason it is omitted from the curriculum.

The very first thing to understand about the Declaration of Independence, the Constitution and the Bill of Rights, is that they neither promise nor give away anything which might cost another anything. All rights granted in the Constitution are what are considered God given rights: the right to worship, or not to, as you please; the right to freedom of speech; the very important right to bear arms — which gives to the people the ability to oppose government by force of arms, upon infringement of their constitutionally granted rights. The Constitution is not a document giving entitlements to the populace. It is instead a document that affirms our basic human rights — life, liberty and property.

The basic principles of the Constitution were devised in such a way that it would require no basic change. The document guaranteed the right of self-determination without undue government interference. What would the framers say if they saw what our legislators have done? How the judiciary, law enforcement, and the executive, in a continuous cycle, violate the tenants and principles of the Constitution. Above all, the Constitution limits government. It restricts, in the tenth amendment, exactly what the federal government is allowed to do. The Constitution does not make provision for the entire alphabet soup of federal agencies that enforce a myriad of social programs. These programs — every one of them — are unconstitutional.

What in fact has taken place over the last ninety years is that thousands of politicians and bureaucrats have created a dependency-class of citizens (i.e. voter fodder) for their next turn at bat in election. No one was more skillful than FDR in capitalizing on the changes made by President Wilson in 1913. He created more government dependency programs then anyone before or since. All of these social programs were frauds, as were those subsequently enacted. Take the Ponzi scheme of Social Security. There is no way (NONE) by which such a system could remain solvent over time. FDR knew it. The House and Senate knew it. Medicare and Medicaid are just two more Ponzi scheme lies.

We must as a people escape this terrible "government-will-provide mentality." Government can not provide a damn thing. Nothing. Everything you get from government must first be taken away from the people in the form of taxes, fees, and licenses. Government does not produce, manufacture, or create anything. Government only redistributes wealth in accordance with various schemes to produce dependency voters. All of these socialist (and that is exactly what they are) programs are unconstitutional. They are destructive in that they provide incentive to be lazy. They rob citizens of their self-esteem. They turn productive society into unproductive lay-abouts. They induce producers not to hire, or expand their businesses. This is exactly what the Satori want. The greatest pleasure that the Satori could possibly achieve is to learn that everyone worked for one of their mammoth corporations, and half the population existed in some poverty level social service program.

In an immense effort, the media has expended more time than can be calculated in an effort to destroy Christian beliefs. Consider, it is almost impossible to pick up a newspaper or turn on a broadcast without the usual diatribe about gay priests, ordained homosexuals, or child molesting ministers. In any event, one would come to the conclusion by listening to these reports that the entire Christian ministries were consumed with charlatans and perverts. To this we must now ask a question — what has Christian ideology to do with the Constitution? The answer to that is everything. In a Republic the government reflects the basic values of the society. The very concepts of God, and Christian moral beliefs are inculcated in our Constitution. Not a single one of the founders was an atheist. Most were Freemasons and committed to a belief in God. They showed us who they were in the words of the Constitution and by their courageous deeds of declaring independence. They originated the concept of a government for the people, by the people and of the people who obtain their rights from God, not government. This concept is rooted in Masonic origin, for the master of the lodge is elevated to that stature not by social position but by personal ability and common vote. All Masons meet on the level — meaning in equality among companions.

We are all preoccupied with the effort to stay financially solvent in a society which has been economically perverted. I came to America in 1952. Not one of my friend's mothers worked a full-time job — some had part-time positions. With one earner in the family we all survived, and most had a considerably higher standard of living than we have today. There can be no question but that we all had a better social life. Today almost all families must have two workers to keep themselves in a similar degree of well-being. Many people work two jobs. Home life is non existent. Divorce rates are at an all-time high. Children are brought up in state socialist incubators, there to be brainwashed with government mush. The American dream is rapidly disappearing. As an example, when I was born in 1938 America's population was 129,969,000. An average three bedroom house cost $3,900.00 and average annual income was $1,996.00. This indicates that a house cost about two times annual income. Today a similar house costs $139,000.00 and average income is about $28,000.00, an increase in cost of housing of 100%. An automobile cost $650.00 in 1938 and today the average cost of a car is $15,400.00. Therefore, in 1938 you could purchase 3.07 cars with one year's salary whereas today you can purchase 1.81 cars with your annual income. This is touted by our elected officials as an improvement in standard of living. All this relates to the effort of the Satori to destroy the Constitution, and to reduce our standard of living to that of other nations.

Much of this is caused by a horrendous increase of taxes on every level. The cost of taxation in America has risen on an exponentially accelerated level for decades. An American worker now spends more than $6^1/_2$ months a year just to pay for the cost of government, and pays 49.20% of his total income to government in the form of various taxes. This amount is greater than what is spent on a family basis for shelter and food. This is related to the Constitution, in that all of these increases are based on a spoilage system of government, by which a huge social dependency class, as well as an entitled over-bloated and overpaid bureaucracy, has been established.

Just by example, about 84% of your property or sales taxes are attributable to education. These are local taxes. Added to this are billions of dollars doled out to schools by the federal government, which then mandates a variety of programs as a requirement to become eligible for those funds. The government has no business in education. The elimination of government-sponsored education run and subsidized by taxes should be our goal. By calculating the reduction of taxes paid by individuals and spent by government on education, you can rapidly see that no one is getting their money's worth, and would be far better in an arrangement of private schooling. A quick look at how our high school graduates compare with those of other nations verify that point. We are, as of 1998, number 19 in mathematics, 16th in science, and 35th in literacy. Legislation like the Americans with Disabilities act, and (SE) Special Education, a program that has seen a cost increase on the national level of 4% per year every year since enactment, and is now up to an average of over 30% of cost for less than 14% of the student body, represents nothing more than another entitlement which society can not afford. All of this is in violation of the Constitution.

The Social Security Administration, for example, spends 70% of every dollar collected in administrative burden. Think about that — every dollar you pay in Social Security tax is doubled by your employer and 70 cents of every dollar collected is spent in a bureaucratic morass. If we as a nation hope to survive then we must return to a system of local taxation and strict constitutional interpretation.

What You Can Do

The solution to this problem is very simple. Disneyland on the Potomac must be placed on a strict diet. We must change the way taxes are collected, and the way they are distributed

The New Tax system

1.) Elimination of all federal taxes not specified in the Constitution or ratified by the states (IRS).
2.) No federal, individual, or corporate taxes collected by the Federal government, as per the Constitution.
3.) All States pay a federal tax based on a per capita population apportionment as per the Constitution.
4.) States can collect taxes any way they like.
5.) Privatize Social Security, Medicare and Medicaid.
6.) Support a Constitutional Amendment declaring all Executive Orders and Treaties not in keeping with the original intent of the United States Constitution null and void.

CHAPTER TWO

INFORMATION OVERLOAD

The first and most important concept in the plan for total world control lies in the requirement of the governing authority to command citizens in support of their goals. This is not a simple accomplishment given our unique laws and heritage of freedom. What the planners must do, in this instance, is to convince the populous in supporting, and in sustaining, a plan which essentially is contrary to their own personal self interest. Furthermore they must do this in a manner not suspect by the populace of the actual objective.

During and since the Korean war, methods of mind manipulation have dramatically improved. Early experiments into "brainwashing" have evolved into complex theorems of mass population manipulation and control through the tampering of information so as to make it conform to a pattern which will ensure the desired outcome. This is not to say that simpler processes were not previously utilized. Dr. Goebbles, Hitler's propaganda minister, was considered the father of this process in modern times. In these early efforts, information alteration, information omission, and information creation, were common. The process of tying good information to unrelated information for a specific outcome is also not new. These tools are commonly used by our media in order to achieve a desired outcome of public opinion. The Satori, in addition, utilize a process which is not only a great deal more shrewd but that is very difficult to detect by the novice. This process is called **information overload (IO).**

The human mind is a processor of information. Information Overload deals with the procedure of altering the imput of information in such a way as to attain a predetermined outcome. It also deals with the method by which your mind processes the provided information, and how to control that course of events. One way by which our minds process information is through the creation of verbal images. This procedure is very rapid and is reached subconsciously. If, for instance, I say "BABY" you will have in your mind a picture of what you think a baby looks like, perhaps one of your children or yourself. One of the functions of Information Overload (IO) is to create such images in your mind through the use of indoctrination. Usually such created images are tied to an emotional cause, which strengthens them. Often word patterns or phrases are used the same way. Let's look at some: *"Cop killer bullet"* and *"Assault rifle."* Neither one of those exist in reality. "Cop killer bullet" refers to a metal clad cartridge, as used by every military in the world. As of 1998 one police officer had been killed by such a bullet, none since. Likewise "assault rifle" is a nonexistent entity. There is simply no such device. Both phrases, however, carry an emotional feeling. No rational person wants to see police officers killed, and neither does anyone wish to be or see someone else assaulted. Thus images have been created in your mind that lead you to the desired conclusion.

Another method by which Information Overload works is through the massive amount of information on a specific topic. In almost all cases this is carried out in a negative manner. The reason is that your tolerance for negative information is substantially lower than for positive. This is done beyond the edge of boredom. Information on a specific topic is made available in such enormous quantity, that after a few days of being inundated by it you simply tune it out. An example of this would be the Clinton scandals, and his continued presumed popularity. Once you have attained Information Overload, you begin to ignore new information and to tune out from further developments.

Information Overload is a devised process specifically engineered to direct you to a predefined outcome. IO was developed by think-tanks on both the Allied and Axis sides during the Second World War. The process was used on enemies and indigenous population. To create IO at that time, two specific processes were utilized: Information was collected from newspapers and radio programs, and pollsters were used to collect public opinion on specific issues. The collected information was then processed and re-issued with a predetermined, planned, desired outcome.

The most pronounced remainder of this process today are Public Opinion Polls (POP). POP as used today, is a concerted Information Overload process. Frankly polls are just plain bull. The manipulation of polling information is carried out in several different ways. The most common is through the phrasing of the question, and the topic introduced in that question. It was found that public opinion could be gradually altered through these procedures. Both the Allies and Axis used IO from 1941 onward. A by-product of this is the extreme difficulty of WWII historic research, due to the inability of the researcher to separate fact from fiction. Literally hundreds of these procedures operate at any one time. They are issues like "Church Burnings" of 1997 and 98, a complete hoax, fueled by Satori surrogates and expanded upon by state-captive information disseminators like the Southern Poverty Law Center (reported to be partially funded by the Justice Dept.).

Society, it seems, works much like the human brain. We seem to have a sort of collective conscience. And like individuals, societal conscience is also subject to Information Overload. Thus if a certain specific outcome is desired by the manipulator, information is simply adjusted in such a way as to attain that outcome. What we wind up with instead of NEWS, is manipulated CREATED NEWS.

Let's have an example for the sake of clarity. The entire basis for the Gulf War conflict was false. First: Kuwait is a dictatorship by an Emir who would not allow a citizens' assembly. Second: International oil companies in Kuwait were drilling oil wells on an angle into Iraqi oil fields. Third: Iraq repeatedly asked Kuwait to stop this practice, and only after they refused were they invaded. Fourth: Kuwait is about the size of a postage stamp. To create a viable reason for Allied action and to whip up the public, the daughter of Kuwait's ambassador, who was a college student in America, testified before Congress about Iraq's soldiers murdering children, stealing child incubators from hospitals, and shipping them to Iraq. She was coached for her testimony by a Satori think-tank. The public and our legislature were treated to hours of phony information by the media, who is always part and parcel of such an operation. The vilification of Sadam Hussein continues to this day. By the end of the IO process for the invasion of Kuwait, 84% of the population of the United States was in full agreement with the war. The end result was the death of 130,000 Iraqi solders, a strip of land taken from Iraq so the international oil companies can now drill straight down into Iraqi oils fields, and the Dictator Emir was reinstalled. The real reason for the war? It was a training exercise for the new UN army, and an object lesson for anyone who would violate Satori controlled property. Kuwait's principal customers are all Satori proprietors. Who's next?

We can now postulate that there are several distinct plans of operation. The first is carried out by the media through the manipulation of information so as to achieve a certain predetermined outcome. The second is the omission of information in order to arrive at an outcome contrary to factual occurrence. The third is the creation of information fabricated out of unrelated facts in order to achieve a specific end. The fourth is to do this so often that the targeted population becomes virtually numb to the process, but retains only a specific and planned attitude about it. This is **Information Overload (IO).**

A fourth process is not controlled by the media, but is fabricated in think-tanks working for the Satori and is fed to the media as news. Quite often sources of such information are not revealed by the media concern that informs us of it. They report such information as if they had in actuality developed the item in their news department or from UPI, Reuters, or some other news wire service. The fact that wire services are Satori surrogates, or so infiltrated by Mandarins as to render them useless as a viable unbiased news source, is significant.

The fabrication of news in the latter half of the 90's has primarily been directed at a special Satori process designed to separate our society into warring factions. It is a fact that a huge effort is directed solely at class envy, racial disharmony, gender conflict, generational discord, and an effort to play all segments of the population off against each other. This is all part of IO (Information Overload). The effort to vilify any patriotic, or constitutionally supportive group, which naturally runs counter to Satori plans, is usually thrown in for good measure. The effectiveness of IO is profound in its resultant impact upon society. It (IO) restructures thought patterns, changes minds, and alters personal as well as public opinion. The impact on society is monumental. If we consider the many various processes called into play by the implementation of IO and what the resultant outcome often is, we can only be amazed. Wars, legislation, society's direction, infanticide, all of them are Satori goals attained through IO.

Let me provide yet another example: "GLASS CEILING" is the ludicrous concept that females are oppressed by males. All facts in this so-called gender war are completely ignored. If we remove gender norming (the process of changing tests to make females attain higher scores) we find that males have higher mathematical skills, higher spatial relation skills, outperform females in SAT, LSAT, and MSAT tests. The male brain functions in a completely different manner, and, *on average*, produces higher scores on cognitive ability tests. No amount of hokus pokus is going to change the aforementioned facts.

Women, as a whole, posess qualities men lack and vise versa. As A.J. Nock once wrote: "women civilize men." There are vocations in which women are superior to men due to their ability to "nuture." And, women climb to top executive positions in many areas, publishing being one of them. But, by nature, men are the ones who build the bridges and skyscrapers while women excell at the interior design. There are exceptions to every rule but one does not pass laws in an attempt to force women to become men. In a free society, people, both male and female, with exceptional talent in any field of endeavor rise to the top of that field.

Germaine Greer, Ph.D., is a noted female scholar. She worked on a book studying the question of male and female bias in the basic skills of art. She produced an entire book on the subject. *The Obstacle Race: The Fortune of Women Painters and Their Work.* At the culmination of all her research she concluded that men, historically, have been better artists than women. She was unable to locate one female Salvador Dali, Rembrant, or Michelangelo. Her conclusion: females egos were damaged through male dominance.

In fact, the entire "GLASS CEILING" issue can be put to rest with one simple example: The Military Academy at West Point. Scholastically, most West Point cadets were directed toward engineering courses. About 65% persued that direction. Females were failing in alarming rates so the curriculum was changed. It is now possible to graduate West Point in Public Affairs, Language, or the Humanities. Great — instead of fighting we can just talk our opponents to death. Changes on the physical end were also made. Male: each semester physical education test – 42 pushups, 52 sit-ups, run 2 miles in 15 minutes. Female: 18 pushups, 50 sit-ups, 2 mile run in 19 minutes. Obstacle course: Males must complete in 3 minutes 20 seconds. Female: in 5 minutes 30 seconds. Are we training combat soldiers or engaging in a social experiment? The result: during Desert Storm, as a group, military females were non-deployable at a 400% higher rate than males, and that does not count pregnancy which was at a 10% level by the beginning of the conflict and increased substantially when deployment was announced.

Israel tried using female combat troops. Result: male casualties increased greatly. Why? Because instinctively the male soldiers tried to protect the females during the battle. As a result, Israel decided not to attempt to change natural instincts and removed women from combat positions.

Gender should not be a barrier to advancement in any occupation. However, to make laws requiring female firemen, combat soldiers, and street police officers, is an out and out stupid idea. Even though there are exceptions to every rule, we cannot make laws based on exceptions or contrary to human nature.

Examples of Distortion

Black Church Burning

For a considerable time all of America was treated to a continual diatribe about the burning of black churches in all the southern states of the union. Stories were aired by all major media sources, all network news and all wire services. In fact the news was so prevalent that even if you did not have a radio or TV, and read no newspaper during that time you could not have escaped the miss-information campaign. The usual victim class promulgated, expounded, and howled without letup. Jessie Jackson and all his friends were immediately elevated to expert status, and promptly spewed forth their venomous attacks on society. Clinton chimed in with several speeches chastising white America for allowing such terrible racist action. The FBI, BATF, Secret Service, and Treasury, along with the US Marshall service, were immediately pressed into service to find what White Supremacists, and vile Militia, were responsible for all this mayhem. The network media, ever in need of more pulp fiction to boost ever declining ratings, clung to the fairy tale like a pit-bull. It was Information Overload. The entire story died. Why?

After thousands of hours of investigation by dozens of federal agencies no link to any organized effort to burn black churches could be established. None, Nada, Zero. Out of over 500 church burnings investigated, two were burned by the same white people. Most burnings, it was determined, had been started by blacks to collect on fire insurance. In fact more blacks were arrested than whites in the investigations which ensued. Not one iota of evidence linking church burnings to any militia, or organized white or other racial organization could be established, and believe me it was not for the lack of effort. Did one single media firm apologize, or even admit to error? Not a single one. In fact the racially motivated victim class, the Al Sharptons, and Morris Dees of America, continue to speak of this matter as if it had been fact. This is an example of NEWS CREATION. The manufacture of news from a nonexistent occurrence, fabricated into a racially motivated act, for the purpose of denigrating white Anglo Saxon males. Is it not peculiar that not one of the news agencies in either of the aforementioned or following matters checked out sources or even checked the facts before reporting them on the national media? They were just provided the information, and then reported same. The goal in this instance was the creation of racial disharmony, which was attained. More IO.

Painting Swastikas in the Military

With the onset of the Clinton administration slandering the military, making officers act as butlers, telling generals not to wear their uniforms in the White House, and in any way possible denigrating military personnel, while cutting the defense budget by over 30%, has been standard modus operandi. So when two swastikas miraculously appeared on a barracks door at the Army's Fort Brag in North Carolina, the literal s_ _ _ hit the fan. All white soldiers were restricted to barracks. The hateful symbols were shown on every network. News was brimming with the racist evil military. Never mind that the Chairman of the Joint Chiefs of Staff, the single highest officer in the entire military was held by a black man (Colin Powell). Never mind that the military is the one place where a black can advance through the ranks without any racial obstruction whatever. Disregard the fact that whites are retiring at unheard of rates from the military, because only blacks and women are being promoted. The diatribe of misinformation contained, among other things, statements by race baiters that the white supremacist militia had infiltrated the ranks of our Army.

How Did This Happen?

Masked gunmen who legally kill American men, women and children (Waco, Ruby Ridge, etc.), and a legal system in which a person is guilty until proven innocent (Rico Laws), is not our America, the "Land of the Free and Home of the Brave." (From The Satori and The New Mandarins*).*

In the end it was determined that two black soldiers had committed the heinous act. The issue, just like the previous, disappeared from the limelight, and no apology for misinformation ever reared it's head. More IO.

In the United States the consolidation and expansion of federal police forces can not be denied. Their expansion continues at a bragged rate of 30,000 per year, according to President Clinton. Presently the United States has 130,000 armed federal police, at current rate of expansion there will be over 200,000 by the time you read this book. Most recruits are laid off military personnel, the Military having been shrunk by 36%, under the Clinton administration.

- It is imperative that the reader understand that military and police functions are not compatible. Presently 86% of all new federal and local police are being recruited from the military. It is the function of military to seek, destroy and kill. It is the function of police to serve and protect. Even the Nazis understood the difference.
- The Posse Comutatus Act, which strictly prohibits any military involvement in civil affairs (which was violated at the Waco massacre by then Attorney General Janet Reno), was written for exactly that reason.

The National Debt

The most bogus information presented by our government is the national debt. We are informed that this number is $4 trillion. When we total all the outstanding debt from all unfunded programs, (Social Security, Government Pensions, Highway Trust Fund, US Patent office, etc.) the real number of $24 trillion appears. The reported balanced budget, which it is not, cuts spending in the projected future by one percent, and this based on the ridiculous assumption that national economic growth will continue unabated over the next seven years. As everyone knows a new budget is put in place every year and is changed every year. Therefore, seven year projections are pure B.S.

Opinion Polls

We appear to live in a society where decisions are not based on facts, morals, ethics, or common sense. In today's America, all political and social, as well as economic decisions, are based on polling. As Seneca so aptly put it, "The proof of a bad cause is the applause of the mob." This creates a state of moral relativism in which society has no anchor from which we can base its direction. This is nothing short of a disaster, and plays directly into the hands of anyone wishing to bring about change. Forget about the Ten Commandments, disregard the norms of society, "If It Feels Good,

Do It." No society can survive with that sort of behavior. Unfortunately this is only the beginning of the problem. The polls, you see, are fixed. Think about it. Who pays to have polls done? Why do they want to conduct a poll in the first place? They come to the pollster with a predetermined outcome plan. Questions are phrased in a way to give the desired answers. This is Information Overload at its best. Through the manipulation of altered information, and the fixing of the questions for desired outcome, an alternative reality is created. That altered reality is the desired goal of the Satori, who through this process alters the outcome to their own ends.

News Fabrication

For years numerous news agencies, programs, and specials have been using a raft of so-called experts in an effort to substantiate their position. This has created an entire industry of soothsayers, whose actual knowledge of the subject is vacuous. The Union of Concerned Scientists is such a group, it does not even require a high school diploma to become a member. The Southern Poverty Law Center instituted Status Quo Sources inside the administration, who usually refrain from being recognized, and pepper us with a continual diatribe of untruths. So, in collusion with the media, these individuals twist and torture reality until it becomes unrecognizable.

This of course represents only a minuscule portion of the news fabrication business. Think about all the thousands of special interest foundations, associations, and clubs, all of which produce a continuous stream of misinformation in an attempt to bolster themselves. Their propaganda is then picked up by one of the news services and reported as fact. By example CCHW (Grass Roots Movement for Environmental Justice, Center for Health, Environment and Justice). They are an organization whose sole purpose is directed at manufacturers, to force them to follow their convoluted ideas as to what is environmentally safe. These people are not scientists, not one of their directors has a Ph.D., not one is a doctor of anything. Neither are their pronouncements subject to peer review. Not one of their board members, to the best of my knowledge, actually qualify to make environmental industrial decisions of any sort. They produce news releases, they publish a magazine *Everyones Backyard* (that's right — it should be everyone's — they can't even spell). They claim 8000 affiliate organizations, but when they had a national convention the total turnout was 300. What we see here is repeated in one organization after another, the false creation of scientific expertise and mammoth size to garner media attention.

News Omission

The amount of scandal associated with the present Clinton administration is a superlative illustration of IO. We have as a nation been subjected to so many misdeeds by members of Clinton's government on a daily basis, that it is unprecedented in American history. Watergate, Filegate, Travelgate, Chinagate, Webster Hubbell, James McDougal, Susan McDougal, David Hale, Gov. Jim Guy Tucker, John Huang, Vincent Foster, Jerry Parks, David Watkins, Ron Brown, Mike Epsy, Henry Cisneros, Hazel O'Leary, Jennifer Flowers, Lani Gunier, Henry Foster, Joycelin Elders, Ira Magaziner, Frederico Pena, Craig Livingstone, Bernard Nussbaum, Lloyd Benson, Susan Thomases, Maggie Williams, William Kennedy — well, I don't want to go on. Not one week has gone by in the last two years without another new revelation. It is sickening to see our presidency dragged down in this manner. In fact so much intelligence on corruption and illegal acts has come to light that people have become numb, and as a consequence most of them completely ignore news reports about the Clintons. Added to this are numerous deaths of high administration officials which must be viewed with considerable trepidation. It can be stated with absolute certainty that Clinton's uncanny good fortune has been the untimely deaths of numerous individuals who, if they were still alive could have incriminated him in more than one illegal act. Jerry Parks, Vince Foster, Ron Brown, James McDougal, Johnny Lawhon, and Pena Gomez immediately come to mind.

The above examples of News Omission are some of thousands which could be listed. To mind come such things as: The Branch Dividians at Waco; first they had an arsenal of guns, then they had a drug factory, then they were child molesters. In the end we found out that they owed $200.00 in back taxes. Over 80 Americans among them many women and children, were murdered in that case over the paltry amount of $200.00, and not one single federal agent was ever prosecuted.

A strong case can be made for the omission of news by the fact that in the Oklahoma bombing there are presently over 300 individual citizens, mostly survivors of the bombing, suing the federal government in regards to the incident. Not one major mainline news source has even mentioned all these suits.

In the Randy Weaver case, in which over one million dollars was spent by federal law enforcement agencies, an unarmed mother was murdered (shot in the head), her teenage son was shot in the back and Randy Weaver was wounded. All this over a shotgun whose stock was $1\frac{5}{8}$ inches below the federally allowed law (unreported) and which had been used as an entrapment device by the BATF. The FBI agent in charge was actually promoted. Murder charges against the FBI sniper were transferred to federal court from the legally jurisdictional state court. The federal government then dismissed the case against the FBI sniper stating that he was carrying out orders from a superior. At the Nuremberg war crimes trial defendants tried the same defense, but the outcome was different — they were executed.

Entrapment is the process by which agents of the government attempt to induce citizens to commit an act in violation of some statute. Such a crime was not contemplated by the person, who in fact, only committed the act at the inducement of an officer of the court. Until the 1970's this was of little consequence since when citizens were able to show entrapment, a violation of the due process clause of the Constitution, cases were dismissed. In 1973, however, the Supreme Court in an opinion given by Judge Rhenquist changed all that, by forcing attention on *"subjective disposition"* of the entrapment of citizens. The Supreme Court said that if you have the disposition to commit a crime, even if you are unaware of the statute, you are guilty of a crime. (I wish someone would show me that in the Constitution).

There is but one cause for such legislation, to create fear of the government, and to give the government false authority to enforce false law. In applying their newly found police powers various agencies, mostly federal, have used sex, drugs, guns, assault, robbery, and extortion, to entrap often innocent citizens who were enticed into a crime. Subsequently laws like the RICO statute then allowed the enforcing agency to confiscate property and convert it to their own use. This violates civil and criminal law, as well as the Constitution. The explosion of the federal office building in Oklahoma City, OK, which started as a BATF sting operation went completely out of control, and cost the lives of many good federal employees, and civilians, who are now suing the federal government. (Although the suit is common knowledge, it went unreported by all major media concerns.)

These above incidents relate to omission of information in order to make the news item appear different from reality and fact, and to cover up governmental misdeeds.

This is conclusive proof of a concerted effort to manipulate public opinion and to overload information in such a manner as to alter public opinion away from the truth to one desired by the Satori.

Z. Brzezinski is without doubt one of the brilliant purveyors of IO. In his many writings we can glean much useful information about Satori plans. Remember that it was Brzezinski who proposed the formation of the TC (Trilateral Commission) to Rockefeller, who subsequently financed the founding of TC.

Flash-Back

Dateline: 1973

Source: **CFR David Rockefeller**

Issuance: **Trilateral Commission**

Several members of the CFR together with David Rockefeller announced the formation of the Trilateral Commission. The commission was the brainchild of One-World Guru, Zbigniew Brzezinski, who proposed the formation of the new organization to D. Rockefeller, who was at that time Chairman of the Council on Foreign Relations. The Trilateralists, as they would later be referred to, have memberships from Europe, Asia as well as America. All founding members of TC were CFR members. The founding meeting was held at the Rockefeller estate in up county Westchester, N.Y. This organization differs from the CFR which only allows US citizens to be members, thus Trilateral. In short order this newest of the semi-secret world government organizations would prove to be a very potent force in the New World Order, challenging even the secret and very powerful Bilderbergers for leadership.

"America in the Technetronic Age" is a paper written by Brzezinski for the Club of Rome. It relates to a new era in which citizens will act like robots programmed by the state through information manipulation and IO. Pointed out in this document is the fact that through IO it will be easy to create a dictatorship, *of the chosen.* This paper was authored in the late 70's, and we can clearly see that we are well on the way toward his prediction. The paper explains that America is now a society in which an information revolution has taken place, and that this revolution is based on advanced IO. The citizens are confronted with only so much relevant factual information and so much fictitious information, which is presented in a media circus of entertainment that average people no longer are able to distinguish between fact and fiction. He goes on to state that this is an opiate for the masses.

Not only are the aforementioned factors relevant to the Information Overload phenomenon, think of these opiates of the people: cable porn the sexual opiate, which recently has been augmented by adult video rentals; rock music and gansta rap whose lyrics appeal to the basest of instincts; drug addiction which is being fostered by government sponsored policies; health problems such as AIDS, which is treated not as a communicable disease, but a political phenomenon. Through the efforts of the homosexual lobby, NY state enacted laws that made it a crime for health officials to inform on an AIDS carrier. This gives AIDS the distinction of being the first communicable decease in history which has legal protection against cure and prevention. It is an actual violation of NY Law for the health department to inform the police that a specific person is infecting others.

These efforts are sustained by governmental regulations such as the expansion of federal law at a pace of over 80,000 pages per year. The expansion of armed federal agents, which are slated to increase by 30,000 in each of the next three years, bringing the total to over 150,000, to enforce those regulations. A tax code which is incomprehensible by anyone, and enforced by an agency which routinely violates all tenants of the Constitution. Federal agencies who, on a daily basis, assault and murder citizens for arcane and non-sensible rules which are unintelligible. These are the foundations of Information Overload.

Compiled together they frustrate the "Masses" (Brzezinski's word, not mine) with Information Overload.

The report which was finally published in 1993 states that information retrieval systems inculcated in the super computer will allow government to retain unparalleled information on all citizens. It then goes on to state it will allow individual control of health, social, political and licensing information to be centrally controlled. Everything, even the most personal preferences will be contained in this system. These files will be subject to instantaneous retrieval by authority, and thus make control of the masses

---

Flash-Back

Dateline: March 2, 1998

Source: **United States Senate**

Issuance: **105 Th. Congress S 1594**

The Digital Signature and Electronic Authentication Law (SEAL), was introduced to the Senate by Senator Bennett. If enacted it will be the force behind the cashless society and the end of personal privacy. If enacted total electronic transfer of all funds, private and public, will be faced by every citizen. The bill gives banks and all financial institutions the authority to transfer funds by relying on "identity authorization." Total electronic transfers will necessitate the use of some form of authorization such as Radio Frequency Identification Device, or Fingerprint, or Retinal Scan. Given the fact that RFID is by far the least expensive, and the new federal law requiring a national system of driver licensing (fingerprint by 2000 at present), what are the chances that United States citizens will soon have to carry a national security ID card?

---

simple — no card, no health service — no card, no job — no card, no pension — no card, no drivers license — no card, no social services — 100% control of your life.

Don't be overly alarmed if the system is not serviceable in the United States — yet — it's only in the planning stages. A national ID requiring finger print verification was scheduled to be instituted in October of 2000 but has since been suspended. It is part of a law passed by Congress which requires finger print ID on all drivers licenses. In Europe the system is operational and awaiting final EC consolidation under direction of the Bilderbergers. The computer complex is ready for operation in Brussels Belgium. It is referred to as "The Beast."

Flash-Back

Dateline: **May 16, 1997**

Source: **US Congress**

Issuance: **HR 1385**

The United States House of Representatives passed HR 138S with an overwhelming majority. The proper name of the legislation is: *The Employment Training and Literacy Enhancement Act of 1997*. This act federalizes schools in America by instituting Goals 2000. Goals 2000 is the chosen vehicle to bring *Outcome Based Education* to our public schools. The bill is designated as the method by which federal authority will be enabled to control the nation's work force. Under this bill local school boards have the choice of either accepting the program, and thus continue to obtain federal funding for their district, or to opt out and lose federal funding. Under this program children's careers will be chosen for them by federally appointed administrators, *(work force development boards)*. Schools will be restructured to teach labor skills, and to focus on changing attitudes and social behavior in accordance with federal guidelines.

Check out America's School to Work program, one of the Clinton administration's strongest incursions into local school control. It is to contain a card to be issued upon high school completion. The diploma will be done away with. The card will contain all information on the student. The program will determine what additional education is to be permitted the bearer. No longer will a student or parent be allowed to decide what trade or which college. The program will determine what industry you work in and in what capacity, will contain your health records, and commentary by your teachers upon completion of their given courses. The card is intended to replace the Social Security card. You will have to present it to any future employer in order to be considered for a job. Written in 1973, published in 1993 it is planned for implementation in 2000. Strongest supporter, NEA (National Education Association) teachers union.

IO has more facets then a gem stone. The concept, however, remains the same. The various differing facets of IO are:

1.) Information manipulation – the process of subtle alteration of factual information to be predetermined by the manipulator's desired outcome.

2.) Information omission – the process of removing certain relevant information from a reported event so that the omission changes the cause-effect relationship.

3.) Information tied to unrelated and derogatory known fact – the process of tying a known unrelated negative to information.

4.) Impossible to follow expansion of law – the process of creating statute that is nonsense: illegal to mail liqueur though post office; outlawing a gun due to its silhouette; draconian tax laws which are impossible to understand; OSHA safety laws which when read make no sense, etc.

5.) The creation of incomprehensible statute – the process of writing laws in such a way as to make them unintelligible.

6.) The creation of fear of government in the population – the process of selectively enforcing statute by force of arms, IRS audits of opponents, FBI files in the White House, BATF raids on legally licensed gun dealers.

It is surely interesting to note that many of these very IO factors were present in Germany at the end of the Weimar Republic. IO concepts were used by the Nazis. Let us therefore consider some historic similarities between Germany of 1930 to 1940 and America 1990 to 2000.

Politicization of Governmental Agencies

Without any apprehension, the most striking similarity of these decades is the expanding politicization of governmental agencies. In our present government who can dispute that the Department of Justice, The Department of Commerce, The Department of the Interior, and all the federal police agencies have now been completely politicized. Janet Reno (Justice) acts more as an apologist for the administration, and any independent thought on her part is purely accidental. Ron Brown (Commerce), who died under more than suspicious circumstances, was under investigation. Commerce even had foreign spies employed in our government with top secret clearance. The Department of the Interior is nothing more than a collection agency for the Democratic National Committee (DNC) as well as the committee to re-elect the president. The FBI, DEA and BATF, as well as the Secret Service, at least superficially appear to be employees of the executive. It is a known fact that the White House, in violation of federal statute, has a list of over 250,000 names of political opponents. This list exists in government computers, and is completely in violation of statute.

The process of political correctness (PC) which I call Cultural Marxism, is used to bully and cajole people into submission. The basic philosophy of Nazi Germany was that of Wundt, Hegler and Nitsche, the gods of altruism, whose basic philosophy is that individuals are unimportant and must be sacrificed to the glory of the state. This is exactly what the Satori have achieved in our public education systems. It is what is being introduced in the classroom, they call it the TEAM concept. It is the binding force behind the association between the greens and the socialists/communists in their ROT/GRUEN (red/Green) alliance which is now fact in Germany. In 1933 a heckler at one of Hitler's many speeches, said "I will never join the party or become a national socialist." To which Hitler responded "Your children already belong to us." Today our schools are at the forefront of the indoctrination process. As of January 1998, America is 39th in the world in literacy,

16th in science and 19th in mathematics. The dumbing down of our population is going well as previously mentioned.

Bogus Numbers

On an almost daily basis we are bombarded by government statistics. These emanate from the Labor department, the Department of Commence and any number of agencies. It is a fascinating exercise to review any of these statistical lies by simply examining how the numbers are arrived at, or in fact, not arrived at. One example: the UNEMPLOYMENT percentage numbers. We are informed that America has the lowest unemployment numbers in our history at under 4%. This is simply not true. Not only is the 4% number bogus, but the entire report is false. To understand this we must first determine how the percentage is arrived at, i.e. what questions are asked in determining the total number of unemployed citizens. In other words who is not counted. Not counted are: the homeless, the disabled, the infirm, those on welfare, or any other social support programs, and those whose unemployment benefits have expired. When we add all these in a very conservative manner, to the reported number we get at least 12%. This does not even consider the "Plug Factor," a number added by the Department of Labor to new job creation figures on a monthly basis. They presume that 35,000 new jobs are created every month in the unreported underground economy, (that's 420,000 jobs per year). This, however, is only the tip of the iceberg. No government published statistic publicly reports information on wages earned by laid-off workers and by newly employed workers. Considering that most lost jobs are in the manufacturing industries, thus the highest paying jobs, and almost all new jobs are in the service sector industries, which pay on average 40% less, we begin to understand just exactly how crooked the reported numbers are. Actual per person net income in America has been declining for decades, if the numbers are correctly adjusted for inflation. This is the plan of the Satori, to reduce the individual wealth of all Americans. Only in doing this will it become possible to integrate the economies of all nations in a one world government. This plan holds fast for all the original G7 nations, and was outlined by the Club of Rome in detail. Only when per capita incomes in trading nations become level can integration of systems take place. All government statistical information must be considered suspect of severe manipulation, just as Hitler's was in the 30's. All of these factors combined create a state of mental confusion, which subsequently leads to the process we call Information Overload.

On the legal front, the Congress has enacted (through the IRS) such arcane rules that when Money Magazine prepares a hypothetical tax scenario and gives it to 10 Certified Public Accountants and 10 IRS officers, no two develop the same tax liability. The Byzantine tax code was bad enough before the last congressional "improvement," supposedly to make the system more citizen friendly, but the Taxpayer Relief Act of August 1997 actually added 285 new sections to the code. It now contains 8 million words. So much for tax-relief. This strengthens the government's ability to intimidate citizens, and to arrest them, or confiscate their property, on feloniously instituted grounds.

The only agencies which outperform the IRS in subversion are BATF and the DEA. The Bureau of Firearms Tobacco and Alcohol has created a bureaucratic nightmare so draconian that no person with any common sense could possibly support it. Why is a shotgun required to have a specific stock and barrel length? Why does an AK47 with a pistol grip violate the law, while one with a hole in the stock is legal? Why is it required to have a special $200 license for a gun noise suppressor? Why outlaw military clad bullets and call them Cop Killer bullets when only one police officer has ever been killed by them? Why outlaw the larger capacity magazines in guns when it is a commonly known fact that magazine exchange takes less than 5 tenths of a second? Why does a black powder in-line muzzle loader, which has been available for

150 years require a license, while a side hammer does not? There is only one reason for such laws, to give armed government agents an excuse to arrest citizens who disagree with, or do not understand them. This all adds up to IO.

The DEA along with the BATF are the two agencies which specialize in violating citizens constitutional rights. They are given considerable support in this by an unconstitutional law (RICO act) which permits such agencies to confiscate property without due process, then convert it to their own use. This restricted statute, we are told, was instituted for the sole purpose of arresting organized crime figures. To the best of my knowledge the currently most common use is against organized religion, and everything else but organized crime. These two agencies specialize in dressing up in black storm trooper outfits with the addition of ski masks, when conducting one of their raids. There is no reason, in a civilized society, for police forces to dress up in black costumes and hide their faces in performance of their legal duties. Such acts may be expected by some Hitler or Stalinist dictator but not in America. The fourth amendment to the Constitution is supposed to protect citizens from unwarranted search and seizure. The Fifth against property seizure without due process. The Tenth amendment limits the authority of the federal government to what is specifically stated in the Constitution. The Posse Committals Act forbids the use of military personnel and equipment in training and assistance of federal and state police forces. I don't know about you, but I am not aware of any police in America who have tanks and helicopter gun ships (Waco). So much for the Constitution; more fear, more confusion, more IO.

The Media

Most assuredly it would be impossible for the Satori to carry out their Information Overload project without the complicity of the upper management of major media concerns. The fact that all news in America is produced by a "controlled" media should not come as a surprise. Consider the reality that regardless of which network you watch, all TV news seem to carry the same news stories. We realize that the amount of news available daily has a finite quantity, but does it not strike you as peculiar that all of these various news organizations who claim to spend billions of dollars on news are all running with the same stories? Furthermore when I watch DW (German TV) or Italian TV on my satellite dish, the international news is completely different. The same is true of the BBC. Although these are also controlled, they are not internationally integrated with ours as yet.

The cinema, the entire entertainment industry, are part of the propaganda scheme directed at you. The easiest way to prove this is through an examination of earnings and ratings in the industry. Movies are continuously rated as to the earnings that they produce, while news programs are rated by numbers of viewers. Entertainment is rated on earnings. If we examine various films we find that all the depraved films which carry an anti-moral bias or which oppose general societal morays have lousy earnings. The news network programs, due to their biased one sided reporting have been losing viewer share for over three decades. Today a scant 40% rely on network TV news for information. All media producers know this. Why then, if you have the option to produce a film with a positive message, or an unbiased news program which will produce good profit, would you make a movie that you know will not be as profitable, or news programs that suffer from mediocre ratings?

The News

Very rarely do I watch network news, but on Friday the 21st of November 1997 I turned on one of the networks. This was the day on which there was more breaking news on the Democratic National Committee and the Teamsters, three of which had already pled guilty to fixing a union election, and accepting and channeling illegal funds to the DNC. But not one word of this was mentioned on the news, instead we were treated to a discussion of the Tapes of President Nixon 25 years ago.

In the November 1997 issue of *Time* magazine was an article entitled "The Secret GOP Campaign." The story goes on to tell us of new evidence that the Republican National Committee actually spent money, and discussed spending such money with supporters. They single out Grover Norquist as one of the evil culprits who actually spent money on behalf of Republican candidates. I am not a Republican, but really — The DNC and Clinton/Gore were recruiting foreign nationals for money (not allowed under federal statute), they were collecting funds in the White House (violation of Federal law), they accepted funds from religious organizations with tax free status and Gore even went to collect the money (violation of federal law), they used telephones in the White House to solicit campaign contributions (violation of federal statute). They gave foreign nationals, who were communist Chinese spies, secret security clearance and briefings, and had the same people work as fund-raisers for the DNC and the president reelection committee while employed by the department of commerce, (so many violations of so many laws I cannot list them all) and *Time* magazine reports on the diabolical Republicans coordinating their campaign with supporters!

The most common methods of new misinformation are omission and a process called "linkage." Omission is simple to understand. It is the process of selectively reporting only those items that one decides are of sufficient importance to report. In this manner any news contrary to the espoused goals is simply omitted from the news broadcast. The second of these, linkage, is quite different. It is the process that is most commonly utilized in villanizing a group, process or individual. The best example that comes to mind is Morris Dees and the Militias. In every instance Dees links the militia movement with the KKK and Skinheads, which is more then just ridiculous. I personally know at least 20 members of different militias, and not a single one is in any way a political extremist, a Nazi, Skinhead, or for that matter connected with the KKK or any other hate group. All are patriots, justifiably worried about our out-of-control federal government.

All of these above mentioned matters relate to creating an atmosphere of total bewilderment. These matters, when taken together, cause a sort of mental paralysis. The mind is overloaded and therefore the citizen tunes out. In support of this I give you the last presidential election, with the lowest per capita voter turnout in over a century. People can only accept so much bad news, corruption, and obvious lies. At some point we just don't want to hear any more of it. This is one of the prime vehicles used to implement the Satori plan of world conquest. The process of overloading you with information that you perceive consciously or subconsciously to be false. The implementation and enforcement of statutes which are so bewildering that you cannot cope with them. The creation of fear of government, through intimidation, murder, and object lessons. In a poll taken in 1997 of a random number of 1000 citizens, 78% indicated that they feared their government. When people fear their government that government is called a tyranny. Waco, Ruby Ridge, and Oklahoma City were all major object lessons, thousands of smaller ones are reported in local papers, and in the general media. The process of IO as we have learned is very clever. It was developed for the sole purpose to influence and control friend and foe alike. Most implementers of the process remain unknowing dupes in that they are not aware of an overall plan nor are they aware of the manipulation. The method of implementation is top down, think-tank to Mandarin and from there to the outlet. The process is present in all known mass entertainment, and news functions. It involves everything from book publishing, distribution, magazines, cinema, theater, and news, electronic as well as printed. IO is everywhere.

The largest think-tank in IO development and implementation is the Tavistock Institute, located in England. Tavistock is a truly amazing organization. In a statement made by them they inform:

"we are a self supporting organization and do not solicit outside funds." As such they are the only think-tank which I have run across which are so wealthy that they do not solicit outside financial aid. Their latest development in human control is called RFID.

RFID

Radio Frequency Identification Device (RFID) is a newly developed process which I am sure will interest you. Complete tests of the system were carried out in Salisbury England in 1998. This new system is far beyond the "Smart Cards" about which I am sure you have heard. Primary tests of Smart Cards were carried out at several American Universities from 1994 to present. These cards are the only item required for the student to have for all on-campus services. Door locks, classroom admission, food service, library use, store purchases, everything required is transmitted by the use of these cards. The problem with Smart Cards is that the process of use is active, i.e. the user must show the card, and it must be passed through a scanner in order for the transaction to be registered. The scanner reads either a magnetic stamp or scans a Bar Code. Such devices are practical from a consumer as well as seller point of view, but have little use to a snooping agency, because cash transactions can omit data to the issuer.

The new RFID system is decidedly different. The RFID is actually a chip, similar to those in your computer. The chip is about the size of a letter on this page. The card is therefore able to store considerable information, and the system becomes passive. The card now holds the information, not the computer. The card is activated by a power signal from a source transmitter. Batteries are not required as the magnetic pulse in the transmission is of sufficient strength to activate a return broadcast signal.

In Salisbury, where the tests were carried out, a totally cashless society existed. Let me explain: You would go to the super market for groceries. You took no cash, all you had was your RFID card in your pocket or purse. As you strolled about the market you would pick up items and place them in your cart, every time you did this a pulse would be issued and your card would provide the sending transmitter sufficient information to debit your bank account. Never once did you take the card out of your pocket. When you finished shopping you just went home. Your employer did not pay you, he pulsed your card and thus deposited your salary to your bank account. Your doctors office upon a visit scanned your card in the waiting room, and all your personal medical history promptly appeared on his terminal. When you used the pay public toilet your card was scanned and your bank account debited. Are you getting the drift? You won't be able to sneeze without the appropriate bureaucrat knowing it. The technology includes sophisticated algorithms to prevent confusion between tags, and readers. Present readers are able to process up to 300 signals per minute. This is sufficient for mass population control in cities. The present cost per tag is a mere $3.00 each, but it is anticipated that costs will go down to .20 cents per unit as quantities rise to meet the requirement of national distribution.

Developed under the guise of "retail sales tool," this product in actuality is a step toward total people control. The tests in Salisbury proved to be successful beyond the wildest dreams of Tavistock. Citizens just loved the system, many actually refused to return the cards at the end of the test. Several US military departments have shown considerable interest, the army in particular.

The Swiss Watch manufacturer, Swatch, the largest in the world which produces in numerous countries, has already produced a watch containing the RFID chip. You will be able to purchase a Swatch with pre-loaded credits. You will have the ability to reload credits when charges are deleted. Numerous establishments in Switzerland and Austria have already signed up with Swatch for this, the second test. The third and final test was held at the World Expo in Portugal in 1998, where all billing was carried out using RFID transmission. Other currently running tests include: road tolls in Sidney and Melbourne, Australia; in California monitoring postal efficiency; in the Pacific NW tracking pacific salmon; gas station tests in Pennsylvania. The most insidious is a project in England where systems are used to monitor TV viewing. This system allows TV cameras to receive radio transmissions of RFID viewers and to then automatically activate a subject carrier camera close to the viewer. Big brother will soon be watching you.

What You Can Do

There are always options open to those who wish to resist the Satori. In the case of IO there are numerous possibilities. Below are 10 simple acts which will take you a long way toward active legal opposition to NOVUS ORDO SECOLORUM. Look it up on the Great Seal. There is one on every dollar bill.

1.) Stop watching network TV and listening to network radio. Not only the news, but all network programming is subject to political correctness, misinformation, and a continuous unrelenting pro-Satori propaganda. There are numerous alternate media such as short wave radio, AM talk radio, as well as printed media: The Resistor, The Idaho Observer, The Spotlight, The Free American, Wake Up Call America, and others.

2.) Carefully edit in your mind all information contained in the national print media. Subscribe to alternate print media publications such as: American Freedom, The New American, The Washington Times, Culture Wars, The Barrens Review of History, and Human Events, among others.

3.) Subscribe to some newsletters which are not tainted: The Triple R Report, The McAlvany Intelligence Advisor, Richard Maybury's Early Warning Report, and Miles Franklin Quarterly are excellent. The publications of "free market" foundations, such as the Foundation of Economic Education and the Independent Institute are but two of many such journals.

4.) Do not support any national political party. Do not make any contributions to any political party. Support only individual candidates with whom you agree.

5.) Become active in local politics, either running for office or supporting someone you feel to be good.

6.) Never believe what any professional politician says. They are only interested in re-election and will say anything to get your vote.

7.) Vote in all elections from school board up to the presidency, even if you have to write-in a candidate.

8.) Actively support America's withdrawal from the United Nations and from other treaties as NAFTA, GATT & WTO.

9.) Insist on the strictest interpretation of the Tenth Amendment of the Constitution.

10.) Demand the reduction of our federal government so that it will comply with the Constitution.

CHAPTER THREE

JUDICIAL ACTIVISM
AND CULTURAL MARXISM

Elostis Humani Americus!

An excellent argument may be made in America of the 90's that We The People are in fact subjects of a judicial tyranny. The separations of powers not withstanding, there can be little doubt that the judiciary has supersceded the legislative branch in making law. This is strictly forbidden in the Constitution. Whatever vagaries the judicial branch misses in their assault seem to become instituted through Executive Orders by the executive branch, also in violation of constitutional precepts.

Let me be very clear in this point: Article I, Section I of the US Constitution states: "All legislative powers granted shall be vested in a Congress of the United States, which shall consist of a Senate and a House of Representatives." I have no problem understanding that, as I am certain you don't either. I would like to know exactly what part of the word "all" our president and judges don't understand. Neither judges nor the president are allowed to make or institute any law whatever.

- *Stone vs. Graham* . . . The court prohibits the display of the Ten Commandments on a school bulletin board. This decision was reached citing the separation of church and state clause, which does not exist anywhere in the Constitution. "Congress shall make no law respecting an establishment of religion . . ." we know very well that the framers, in this article, were referring to the establishment of an official tax-supported state church as existed in most European nations at that time. Furthermore our entire judicial system can be traced back to the Ten Commandments and Judeo-Christian concepts, such as a person must be treated innocent until proven guilty.

- *Roe vs. Wade* . . . The court held that a woman, without consent, had the right to terminate her offspring at will. 30 million American children have been so terminated as of 1997. The ruling judges stated that this right was inculcated in the Constitution, and the Supreme Court concurred with that opinion. In over 200 years no jurist, lawyer, or politician was able to find that "right." Would someone please inform me exactly where in the Constitution termination of an unborn child is legalized?

- *Romer vs. Evans* . . . Judges acting in violation of Constitutional law struck down a people initiative in Colorado, passed by a vast majority of the electorate in referendum. The law passed prohibited the granting of special privileges and rights to homosexuals. Justice Kennedy, without doubt the most activist member of the court, stated: *"Law of this kind now before us raise the inevitable inference that disadvantage imposed is born of animosity toward the class of person affected."* As of this morning homosexuality was a chosen predilection, not an innate factor, such as race or gender.

- The Religious Freedom Restoration Act (RFRA) was passed in the House of Representatives by unanimous voice vote. In the Senate it passed 97 to 3. The president signed it into law. The Supreme Court on June 25, 1997 ruled it unconstitutional.

- In California a state-wide referendum was passed by an enormous margin. It would prohibit the payment of state benefits to illegal foreign immigrants (Proposition 187). This was particularly directed at over one million Mexicans illegally living in that state. (Inciden-

---

Flash-Back

Dateline: 1965

Source: U.S. Senate

Issuance: Congressional Record

Fielded by Senators Kennedy and Katzenbaum, a new immigration act is instituted. This is to be the most destructive initiative ever passed by the Senate, in that over the coming twenty years it will change the racial makeup of the United States. Immigration laws are altered to allow the indiscriminate immigration of non-European races, while European immigration is thwarted.

California is rapidly turning Latino, with 8 million Central and South Americans in residence today, just over one million illegally. The change in immigration quotas and laws has altered the makeup of immigrants from mostly west Europeans to:

Mexicans	27.2%
Asians	26.7%
Caribbeans	10.5%
Latin Americans	11.9%
Canadians	2.7%

---

tally, if you have an accident while you are in Mexico, as an American you had better have cash or they *will not* allow you in the hospital door.) A judge, Thelton Henderson, struck down the peoples initiative stating that it violated the illegal immigrants constitutional rights. How a non-citizen attains the constitutional rights of a citizen he neglected to say.

- Again, in California Proposition 209, a ban on "affirmative action" passed the electorate with an overwhelming margin, only to be struck down by a federal judge. His stupidity was affirmed by a subsequent reversal in higher court.

- In federal statute enacted, the court ruled against the Communications Decency Act stating: *"The act violates the freedom of speech amendment."* In other words it violates children's constitutional right to pornography. How a minor attains constitutional rights, which, by statute, are attained only when legal adulthood is reached, was not explained.
- *Planned Parenthood vs Casey* is a landmark case. It will surely lead us down the slippery slope of depravity. In a 5 to 4 opinion Justices Kennedy, Souter, and O'Conner made the following majority statement: *"At the heart of liberty is the right to define one's own concept of existence, of meaning of the universe, and the mysteries of human life."* What in essence they stated is that the prime concept of American jurisprudence which is a basic cornerstone of not only the Constitution but our legal concepts, was no longer valid. **All men are endowed by their Creator with certain unalienable rights … was no more.** In *fact* what these people did was to produce out of thin air a concept that it is not the Creator God who gives us our laws, we can give these to ourselves. So whatever suits you, go ahead and do it, it's OK, the judges say so. The passage of their ruling is referred to by lawyers as the Mystery Passage. It will, in short term, be used to legalize same sex marriage, polygamy, inter-species marriage, and yes, any other depravity you can think of.
- Judge Russell G. Clark ruled that the citizens of Kansas City were incompetent to manage the schooling of their children. He took over the school system and mismanaged it for 20 years, finally to bankruptcy.

  A few gems:
  - A 25 acre farm with air conditioned meeting room for 100
  - A 25 acre park for wilderness study
  - New construction codes to require all new construction to conform to neighborhood compatibility, drove construction costs up 300%

- 2000 sq. ft. planetarium
- A large greenhouse
- Broadcast studios for TV and radio
- A 3500 sq. ft. dust free diesel mechanics room
  Property taxes were doubled. A $150 million dollar bond issue had to be made. A state wide 1.5% surcharge on state income tax had to be instituted. Total cost for the district: $1.8 billion. Kansas City now has the dubious distinction of having the highest education cost per student in the world.

- Judge Stephen Reinhardt found the right for your doctor to kill you in the Constitution.

- Judge Diane Wood, a Clinton appointee, ruled that an Illinois prison inmate had the right to sue the federal government under the Eighth Amendment (cruel and unusual punishment) because he was not imprisoned in a smoke free environment.

- In what was the most bizarre case of the year judge Rosemary Barkett, a Clinton appointee, ruled that a fifth grade girl could sue her school in the case of harassment by one of her classmates. She stated that suit could be brought under Title IX of the Education Amendments of 1972 (sex discrimination).

For generations the Satori have tried to implement their conquest of mankind through domination of the voting process. They have attempted to implement this through the process of establishing legislation favoring their cause for decades, as they did in 1913. Progress has been very slow. They have spent millions in an attempt to control the legislative branches of governments. But, they made they greatest progress through Judicial Activism. Judicial Activism (JA), is the process of: 1) Judicially created precedence. This procedure pioneers the individual judiciary's interpretation of statute through the origination of new concepts and law, contrary to original intent. It furthermore is in agreement with Satori aims. 2) Judicial interpretation of precedence. This is the procedure of implementing in law cases brought before the court, not on law, but on precedence created by the court.

The United States is a Constitutional Republic. In this form of governance the federal government has enumerated powers as spelled out in the Constitution. All other rights are reserved to the States, respectively to the people. The Tenth Amendment states: *"The powers not delegated to the United States by the Constitution, nor prohibited by the States, are reserved to the States respectively to the people."* That is very lucid. As a consequence we are all able to clearly understand the amendment.

The federal government, as well as all of the various State governments, are separated into three distinct branches: the Executive (president or governor); the Judicial (all the courts); and the Legislative (composed of a Senate geographically apportioned, and a House apportioned according to population).

This then forms the separation of powers, the checks and balances necessary for our republican form of government to survive. It is this separation of powers which is under severe stress brought on by a change in strategy by the Satori. Having attempted the legislative road and found it wanting, even after changing how Senators are chosen, they are now utilizing the judicial and executive branches to further their plans.

What we are witnessing under the tutelage of the Satori is the total destruction of the checks and balances of the system through judicial activism and executive orders (Article II Section I). The word executive appears one time in Article II, "The Executive Power shall be vested in a President of the United States of America." This then represents the only use of the word *Executive* in the entire document dealing with presidential procedure and operation. There is no place in the entire Constitution which authorizes *"Executive Orders." All such orders are unconstitutional.*

Through these two processes the entire system has been short circuited. The issue of judicial activism (JA) can be easily understood if we ask a question. Should the judiciary, in interpreting the Constitution, do so in accordance with the original intent of the framers, or should they interpret it based on the way they personally feel about it? If we allow judges to decipher, not according to what the words actually say, but what they read into it, then we have no constitution any longer. This opens the specter of continual change in accordance with the whim of the judges.

This is, of course, exactly what the Satori want. It creates a climate of legal instability, in that law simply becomes a bunch of rules which change just like the weather. In consequence, compliance is difficult if not impossible, and provides the state with the opportunity to utilize the legal system for harassment and intimidation. Because the boundries of this alternative are so very vague, it is possible for judges to reach decisions based not on law but on personal opinion. Decisions reached in that manner are with us today. For over five decades the Supreme Court, as well as the lower courts, have been creating precedence law based not on written statute but on their own personal ethical, social and economic opinion. The consequences of this must not be underestimated.

The question this then brings to mind is obvious: Are we better off as an outgrowth of these acts, or are we worse off? The retort again is simple — crime is up, moral and ethical behavior is down. What served us so well for 150 years is under judicial assault, and is in the midst of destruction. Our younger citizens no longer view law as rules for right and wrong, they see everything in varying shades of gray. Many criminals have laid claim to victim status. Murderers routinely invoke a defense that their father beat them, and as an outcome are not responsible for their acts. This is the crap of psychologists, psychoanalysts, social workers and judges. Every year individual rights count for less at the expense of yet another special interest group. We are, as you read this, being re-educated into an insect mentality, which is exactly what the Satori want.

For the first 100 years of the republic our national history and jurisprudence was based on a strict interpretation of our Constitution. The nation flourished and grew in spirit and soul. For the past 50 years we have given up that strict rendition, for one of increasing judicial activism. Presently the Supreme Court is not interpreting the Constitution at all — they are inventing, and amending the document. The consequences to our society have been nothing short of disastrous. Small wonder when our Senate confirms a person like justice Ginsberg to the Supreme Court. Long before her appointment to the bench she wrote a book in which she proposed to: 1) reduce the age of consent for a girl to the age of 12 years old; 2) supported the notion of women in infantry combat units; 3) suggested the elimination of the words "husband" and "homemaker" from statute; and 4) eliminate all statutory rape laws. Not one senator at the confirmation hearings had the guts to ask this extremist a single question about the book she had written. She stands for everything the Satori desire. This then is one of the plans. A populace which is self-indulgent, hedonistic, materialistic, and easily lead. The Satori are ever pushing the limits to destroy our culture, ethics and Christian heritage. Let's face facts — a population with a strong moral, religious, and ethical ideal is not the malleable metal on which the Satori seek to build their New World Order.

The debate between Judicial Activism and strict interpretation of our Constitution is a not some obscure academic exercise. It was concocted in the think-tanks, the hatcheries, of Satori planning. It is a debate centering on the question, do you want to continue to live in a free and open society, or do you want to live under a Satori dictatorship? Make no mistake about it, the planned New World Order of the Satori is every bit a totalitarian dictatorship, no different from any of the others in world history. They are as totalitarian as was Stalin, who murdered 160 million of his own people to remain in power; Mao, who murdered 200 million; or Hitler, or Mussolini. We have been informed, by no other then our VP Al Gore, that the world is grossly overpopulated and severe steps must be taken in an effort to reduce world population. Cambodia was a Satori experiment in population reduction in which the communists under Pol Pot of that nation murdered two million of their own citizens. The Chinese Cultural Revolution had two purposes: first the elimination of a bothersome intelligencia who was opposing Mao's iron will and second, the reduction of China's population. It performed both with admirable efficiency.

At issue is a basic concept: should this nation be governed by elected representatives of the people, or should we be ruled by a elite client class working for the Satori? Because the Constitution is a written document, which was debated at length, we know exactly what it means. Because it was not subject to the vagaries of modern legal scholars, it is clear. The only people who seem to have difficulty in understanding the document are judges. If we mean to have our republic survive then we must return to the doctrine of exact and strict interpretation. If judges refuse to comply with this doctrine we must remove them from the bench. The framers foresaw such possibility and provided us the possibility for impeachment of any member of the judiciary (Article II Section 4).

Daniel Webster, a great New Hampshireite of over 100 years ago said:

> "Miracles do not cluster . . . Hold on to the Constitution of the United States of America and to the republic for which it stands . . ."

For over 200 years the document, envied by millions around the world, has been the light in an often dark world. Other nations have patterned their constitutions after it. It stands next to the Magna Carta (1215 AD) as one of man's great achievements. Its singular effect on world history is unparalleled. The greatest tragedy that could befall this nation is that judicial activism succeed in destroying the spirit, concepts, and intent of the Constitution. This, however, is the Satori plan. For as long as the Constitution is the prime law governing the United States, they will be unsuccessful in their nefarious plans. Through the process of incremental JA, they plan to erode the Constitution into a worthless jumble of confusing rubbish, and they are well on their way to succeeding.

Another matter related to JA is the jury process. It was always, at least until 50 years ago, a foregone assumption that the deliverance and verdict of any jury was final and absolute. A judge sitting on the bench is to rule on points of law as they impact the case, and to officiate between the prosecution and defense. Judges in the United States lack the authority to rule on the law itself or on the guilt or innocence of the accused. Judges do not have the right to produce verdict. Judges do not have the right to tell juries to only rule on act, without consideration of law.

John Jay, the ex-governor of New York and one of the authors of the Federalist Papers, was the first Chief Justice of the Supreme Court. In his first trial in 1794 (Georgia vs. Brailsford) he made the following statement: *". . . You had nevertheless a right to take upon yourselves to judge both, and to determine the law as well as the fact in the controversy."* This statement goes to the heart of the jury system in that jurors are allowed to not only judge the matter before them, but also to judge the law in its application and content to the case. Jefferson in the Federalist Papers stated: *"To consider justices as the ultimate arbiters of all constitutional questions is a very dangerous doctrine indeed and one which would place us under the depotism of a (Judicial) oligarchy."* And once again Jefferson: *"I consider trial by jury as the only anchor yet imagined by man by which a government can be held to the principles of the Constitution."* Any review of recent judicial actions shows clearly that judges across the board are in violation of the spirit as well as the written law, never mind their oath of office.

The value of juries in the last 50 years has been seriously eroded. The consideration of the moral content of the applying law is not any longer inculcated by the judges in their charge to the jury. Instead, judges tell juries to consider the facts of the case alone, and thus make themselves the sole arbitrators of guilt and innocence. This is another change brought by a judiciary who feels that their own opinion is of greater consequence than that of the people they are sworn to serve. This assumption is wrong. In doing this they have further eroded the concepts and spirit of the law, and have made themselves legislators.

A large portion of our law has been removed from the grasp of the people through administrative acts. This process has allowed bureaucratic agencies and administrators to usurp the peoples prerogative through bureaucratic function. Yearly thousands of pages of new regulations are written by these bureaucracies. Agencies write Endangered Species Laws, Wetland Laws, IRS laws, OSHA regulations, which few understand and none have the time nor inclination to read. I have read entire pages of OSHA regulations which I could not understand, my lawyer could not understand, and the OSHA employee could not explain, and for years I worked as a consultant for manufacturers to help them comply with OSHA. This usurpation occurs through a process much like judicial activism. In almost all cases it begins its journey in a special interest "Do Gooder" group.

Environmental law which is enforced by the Environmental Protection Agency (EPA) is a case in point. The original push came out of the environmental movement. Unfortunately that movement has numerous adherents who are neither scientifically nor judicially informed. Many of their suggestions, although well intended, are just plain stupid. A large number of these "stupid" suggestions sadly found their way into law. These laws were not written by the environmentalists, nor by the courts, they were a product of the Mandarins of the various congressional committees. The Satori's Mandarins write the laws, and due to the voluminous output of between 70 and 100 thousand pages per year they are never read by our elected officials, they are just voted in. In the case of the EPA, a huge new bureaucracy of enforcement was instituted, along with semi-automatic-weapons-toting officers, 90% of which never had a high school botany course. Who in our society has not been touched by some bureaucrat in one way or another?

Regulations are always written with ulterior motive, and an objective plan. Most regulations in the last 50 years have been the result of pressure by one or another group of individuals on legislators. They then go to the bureaucracy and request them to produce a law that has a specific planned outcome. The bureaucrats are well aware of what direction is intended by the heads of those agencies, which are always Mandarins. So regulations wind up favoring Satori businesses and goals, as well as plans.

Executive orders have been issued by every president since Washington. The numbers have varied, but the intent has often been an effort to circumvent the legal obligation of Congress. With the advent of the election of FDR, all that changed drastically. On March the 9th, 1933, FDR issued an Executive Order placing the United States into a state of *National Emergency*. This emergency has never been nullified, and it has been reinstated by every president since. The Congress, which has the power and authority to cancel it, has steadfastly refused to do so. This is a very dangerous state of affairs because it allows, according to their illegal interpretation, executive authority far beyond the rights granted under the Constitution. FDR's executive orders (he produced more than all the previous presidents combined) were for the most part designed to increase the power of the executive at the expense of the legislative and judicial. The heart of this issue is the separation of powers, which through executive orders allows the president to seize power, to organize and control all means of production, remove elected officials, seize farms, transport companies, power stations, airports, and even highways. All this ties together with FEMA, the Federal Emergency Management Agency. In fact, under present law, the executive could declare an emergency and replace all elected office holders within a congressional district with FEMA appointed personnel.

Again there is no provision in the Constitution allowing for executive orders. All executive orders are unconstitutional. The most insidious acts have taken place under the Clinton administration, where through executive orders, power has been transferred from our government to an international authority, the United Nations. Examples of this would be the various agreements with the UN on world heritage sites and world biosphere reserves in the United States, which areas are now under UN authority. Executive orders comply with the concepts of the Satori because they allow the unchecked consolidation and centralized power which is the ultimate goal of the New World Order. The process of executive orders since FDR has reached completely new highs in that numerous ones have been issued, particularly by Clinton, which are *secret*, even from members of Congress. This then creates a new episode in our nation's history — secret laws illegally issued and enforced by secret police. All such acts further the Satori aims and goals. Secret laws issued by secret edicts and enforced by secret authorities, the ability to harass, arrest, convict, and imprison citizens at will.

As you can see judicial activism, executive orders, and bureaucratic creation of law go hand in glove to destroy our national identity, and our guiding constitution. It is not unreasonable to say that at the present time our constitutional rights have been so severely abridged, that the document has become irrelevant. You can utilize virtually any major legal issue of the last 30 years, and whether you agree or disagree with it, you will find it impossible to prove that the precept is based in the Constitution. In every instance judges invented the law through a personal interpretation of nonexistent constitutional precepts. One can only wonder what new interpretation they have slated for us in the future.

As you read this, plans to subjugate our American Constitution to an international document based in an international court with judicial power over America, is well on the way. The International Court at the Hague in Holland has in the past expressed several times that it had jurisdiction over American citizens, as well as the nation in general. I do not doubt two actions with take place in the very near future: 1) The attempt at a Constitutional

Convention, so that the entire constitution can be negated; 2) A treaty with the United Nations to subjugate the American Constitution to an international one prior to 2016.

The above information is correct. Those events did occur. We now have US sponsored, enforced, and paid for, thought police. What are the UN standards, or code of ethics to be enforced? We don't know. None have been issued. UN command is writing those rules as they go along. Needless to say any criticism of peace-keeping operations, NATO (which is an arm of the UN), or the UN, will not be tolerated and will be cause for closure. This is exactly the same thing the Nazis did in Yugoslavia 55 years ago. Simon Haselock, spokesman for civilian operations, whose nationality is unreported, on behalf of the UN stated: "What we are trying to do is put in place a regime that offers a legal framework that improves and guarantees press freedom." Mr. Haselock obviously views the first step toward freedom of the press as censorship.

In retrospect, does that not sound exactly like the comments by Hillary Clinton, and other administration pros, when they referred to short wave and AM radio talk shows as "Hate Radio"? Was it not Hillary who suggested that stations who broadcast anti-administration programs should have their licenses reviewed, or canceled?

What Can You Do About Judicial Activism

Unfortunately our options in this instance are limited. However there is one thing that we can do which will, in the long run, have dramatic effects.

ASK THAT ANY CANDIDATE RUNNING FOR SENATE OFFICE EXECUTE THE FOLLOWING PLEDGE:

I _____ promise and pledge that if elected to the US senate I will:

1.) Never pass for vote any member to the federal judiciary by unanimous consent.

2.) I will never allow a voice vote for the election of any federal judge. I will in *all* instances insist on a recorded vote.

3.) I will never allow more then one justice to be voted upon at a time.

4.) I will diligently have my staff investigate the writings and past decisions of any judge proposed by the president.

5.) I will do my utmost toward the removal by impeachment of justices Kennedy and Ginsberg.

Signature_____

Today's procedure for Senate Confirmation of Judges is via unanimous consent and voice vote, which are:

A.) Unanimous consent is a process by which most federal judges have been confirmed. It is a process, in the US Senate, whereby names of proposed judges are simply read and then unanimous consent is given by voice vote to all the judges named. It is contrary to everything the Constitution stands for.

B.) Voice Vote is a process in the US Senate whereby a confirmation is made without recording of how the senators voted.

Cultural Marxism

I call Political Correctness "Cultural Marxism" (CM). There are many facets to this insidiously evil process of diversity and pluralism which is sweeping our Republic. The most active participants are all members of our current administration, the President and members of the cabinet, and of course the majority of all centers of learning. I find it ironic that the very people who condemn the McCarthy era are the very ones who support Cultural Marxism. It is wise to remember that in every instance of the development of any dictatorship, a process similar to CM was used for the purpose of citizen intimidation. There are numerous twists and turns in CM, but you must first understand the reason for it. In a totalitarian state there is little room for independent thinkers. It is a known fact that whenever anyone has, in the past, attempted to develop a dictatorship he first had to take several steps to ensure its success. Among these was a method of intimidation specifically developed to stifle opposition. The think-tanks have developed Cultural Marxism to its present form, which covers numerous differing processes.

Our nation is socially and politically disintegrating before our eyes. Over two million illegal uneducated immigrants of different cultures are piling in every year. Our western culture has been and is being subverted. Music, art, literature, and social interaction are sliding into a sewer. Political corruption is greater than it was when Rome was decaying. The process of destroying our culture is central to the envisioned Satori dictatorship. Only through the destruction of the cohesive elements of our society will the Satori be successful in their plan. For this reason we find our nation torn into varying warring factions, old against young, poor against rich, men against women, black against white. The controlled media and government Mandarins strive to implement this divisive program upon America. These all are the hallmark of the politically correct, Cultural Marxism.

The Baltimore Sun had a CM headline on Dec. 15, 1997: "KIDS WHO WEAR TOBACCO GEAR LIKELIER TO SMOKE." To this statement of obvious rubbish I add: Kids who smoke more likely to wear tobacco gear. Unfortunately my headline would not achieve the desired goal of the Dartmouth Medical-sponsored propaganda. This is one example of how CM works.

Hit Words

George Orwell many years ago made the statement: "Words control thought, and thought controls civilization." The process of utilizing short phrases and hit words as a vehicle to influence discourse outcome is not new. Gemeindschafts Dienst means community service, Geteiltes Opfer means shared sacrifice, contributions instead of taxes, social responsibility, all of these came from 1930 Nazi Germany. It even goes to agencies. Hitlerjugend becomes Americorps, or as I call it, Clintonjugend. In an extensive use of this process entire thought patterns have been developed. Consider Cop Killer Bullet, Beat Generation, Skinhead, Choice, Beatniks, Hippies, Saturday Night Special, Assault Rifle, each one of these creates in the mind a picture or association with an act or process directed to implement a specific goal. The reality that not one of these has any basis in fact whatever is irrelevant. This is the process of word creation.

The second process is the act of changing what words mean. Examples are Gay, Homophobic, and Patriot. All of the aforementioned words mean something completely different in the latter half of the 20th century than they did in the first half. One of them, Homophobic, is so out of any reasonable context that it is impossible to classify. This is what CM is all about, the developmental thought process, the use of words and phrases germinating the '"Environment of Change" spoken of in documents published by the Club of Rome. Another phrase we can glean from think-tank documents is "Crisis Adaptation." This would more closely be associated with a phrase like Assault Rifle. You see, there is no such weapon. The phrase was coined in order to blur the distinction between a machine gun and a semi-automatic rifle. Critics will say that there is no real distinction between these, because a semi-automatic rifle can be converted into an automatic one. True enough, but does that mean that a baseball bat is a bludgeon, just because it could be used that way? This represents an insidious way of influencing society as a whole. Through the use of words, phrases and compositions you are in fact being brainwashed with images created by the user which are contrary to your own basic knowledge, without your actually realizing that a thought pattern completely foreign has been instated onto you. This process is then expanded into the legislative arena where the likes of Sen. Metzenbaum (D, OH), introduces a new law proposal called the "Assault Weapons Control Act." As there is no definition as to what an assault weapon is, we are left to our own devices in concocting any description that suits the moment. It would be interesting if Sen. Metzenbaum would tell us exactly what percentage of gun related crimes were committed with this type of weapon, because according to the Urban Institute of a study for the U. S. Dept. of Justice, the percentage of violent crime committed using semiautomatic rifles and machine guns is so low that it does not show up in any crime statistics. In fact, under $\frac{1}{10}$ of a percent.

As if all that was not enough we are treated to the bastardization and debouchment of existing language through the process of changing the meaning of words, "gay," for example. Also, "lacking in learning skills" for "stupid," "differently able" or "physically challenged," for "crippled," "horizontally challenged" for "fat," and on at infenitum. Then along come people like Professor Stanley Fish of Duke University with the concept that words have no specific meanings — he calls the concept "reconstruction." Perhaps the best thing would be for Duke to deconstruct his tenure.

Then there are words which stem from the communist purges of the USSR, like "reactionary." Whenever you hear that word consider the source with care, it is an indication of a communist background of the user. Yes, words have meanings, meanings create mental pictures, and mental pictures create thought control.

Lebos

The most profound pushers of Cultural Marxism are homosexuals. The reason for this is patently obvious — they want change. Well, not the change you might envision, but change anyway they can obtain it. This desired change is a disaster for our society. The destruction of our ability to defend ourselves as a nation is one of the outcomes of this, by the feminization of the military and the attempt to integrate homosexual men and women into the military services. Our draft dogging Commander-in-Chief and the Democratic National Committee have been the strongest proponent of this, in an effort to garnish female and homosexual votes. The fact that the great majority of women and all the military want nothing to do with any of this seems irrelevant. The noisy obnoxious ones seem to get all the attention. There is a place in military for women, but it is not in the infantry, as pilots, or in the artillery or armor. For every soldier in the field an army requires at least three support personnel, and this is the appropriate place for women. Israel learned this lesson as, in battle, male soldiers died trying to protect female soldiers and as a consequence, females no longer engage in battle. They are limited to support personnel.

Virginia Military Institute and the Citadel were all male military schools for the training of infantry officers. Some of America's greatest generals have come from VMI and the Citadel. No more. Supreme justice Ginsberg put an end to almost 200 years of excellence to achieve gender diversity in what is a male vocation. I don't want to hear this garbage that women can do anything men can because they cannot. In hand to hand combat they would be slaughtered by male adversaries. If integrated with males in infantry units they will become responsible for the deaths of most males in their own units. All this has been tried by the Russians, Israelis and even the Greeks, all failed.

As for homosexuals I give you the regular French army, which accepts homosexuals. Since Napoleon they, with the exception of the Foreign Legion, have not won a war or even a battle. Don't ask, don't tell is stupid. The essential push by the homosexuals is for an expansion of the equal rights provision of the Constitution to include "Sexual Orientation" as one of the provisions of the amendment. On October 13, 1997 the Human Rights Campaign, a major homosexual action crowd, ran a full page ad in the *Washington Times*: "Republicans and Democrats agree no one should lose a job merely for being gay," which touted why we need "The Employment Non-Discrimination Act."

There is so much wrong with that concept it is difficult to find where to begin. Provisions of the amendment address gender and race, states to which we are born. Homosexuality is a learned behavior, it is not genetic, no one is born homosexual. Estrogen and testesterone levels can be corrected. If we inculcate sexual orientation into the equal rights amendment, what is to prevent any other social function from being integrated as well. If one chooses to be homosexual that's their choice, but that does not give them the right to force the rest of us to pay for (insurance) and condone their perversion. All this goes along with the effort to destroy our Christian civilization, and to replace it with the New World Order through the use of Cultural Marxism.

In the process of researching this book I was utterly amazed at the preponderance of information available to homosexual activists. Currently their main effort is centered around the attempt to penetrate secondary education. Homosexuals represent a larger percentage, compared to the general population, in teaching and administrative position in schools. The teachers union likewise can boast of a substantial homosexual membership. NEA pro-homosexual positions are well publicized and known. In New Hampshire, the most conservative state in America, homosexuals represent no more than 4.7% of the population. In New England their network provides: rundown of those school board members by name who oppose their issues, information on all Christian Coalition opponents with names, information on all presidential candidates and their position if opposed, suggested letters to the editor, names and telephone numbers of homosexual supporters, numbers of the Gay/Lesbian teachers support network, among which is listed the Plymouth Congregational Church. A list with address of every single newspaper in the state with fax number and circulation data. That is only the tip of it. Now for getting into a more serious matter: a list of every opposing article appearing in the state with the name of the article and date published, a list of every legislator in the state with full address and telephone number, the names and home addresses of every member of the state education committee, membership and home address of every member of the state board of education, name and address of every Superintendent of schools. That the homosexuals are an unwitting integral part of Satori plans is a foregone conclusion.

Educational Cultural Marxism

Lee Bollinger is the head of the University of Michigan. His policies are nothing if not radical. In fact the University of Michigan is presently defending against several suits similar to those lost by the University of Texas. This deals with admission. By plan American universities and colleges represent a sort of monopoly in that they maintain systems which are unable to meet demand. Through this they are able to continuously escalate prices, and select only those which, in their criteria, meet their outcome goal. Into this mix they have instituted racial as well as other preference systems which are illegal for tax supported institutions. All this is arrayed by the federal government in a complicated system of rebates to higher education which to-date only two universities, Grove City College and Hillsdale, have turned down. A substantial portion of this is through federal loan guarantees to students. This then supports the increased tuition costs, professor salaries, and federal mandates on curriculum. As before, your tax dollars are used to implement discrimination against the citizens.

In 1996, 3.5 million student loans were approved by the Fed, each one of then with strings to the school to which the student went. Hinsdale College in Michigan is one of those who have refused to accept federal funds. Their students' scholastic output is about double the capability of U of M, where in the name of diversity students are not accepted based on scholastic aptitude, but on gender, race — yes — and even sexual preference. In fact the entire educational establishment works on this distorted idea. If we as a society plan to grow intellectually, economically and socially, the only possible route is through personal excellence. All other criteria are absurd. The best and the brightest must be given preference. At the University of Michigan there are factors brought into the equation which have nothing whatever to do with education. Race, gender, alumni status of parents, geographic location of domicile, all are factored into the decision of application.

We can then examine the California syndrome: "Hey Hey Ho Ho Western Civ. has got to go." This was actually a chant at Berkeley U of C Northern campus. Worse yet high school graduates were chanting it. Well, what are Plato, Socrates, Shakespeare, Goethe, Einstein, and Heine to be replaced with? There are limited literary blacks in America. Martin Luther King was a plagiarist, and we named a national holiday after him. Great American blacks are routinely chastised, ignored, and worse — insulted. Allen Keyes, and the eminent economist Thomas Sowell are two names that come immediately to mind, along with Clarence Thomas.

In an effort to garnish more electoral support politicos have developed a strong national movement for bi-lingual education. Rejected by the Hispanic community on a margin of 84% the effort has stalled. Challenged by a voter referendum in California it was voted out by an unprecedented margin. It is but another example of the divide and conquer efforts of the Satori.

The latest effort by New Hampshire edu-crats is a program called "A Good Deed So We Can Read." This is an effort at outcome based behavior modification. Parents are provided a monthly calendar. They are then instructed to mark on the calendar all good deeds, and are admonished to reward the child with money. This money is then to be brought in to school at the end of the month to purchase books for the school library. "Heather has two mommies," will in all probability be the first book purchased.

Bureaucratic Cultural Marxism

When invented, air bags were wonderful and safe. Then government took over and now they are dangerous, and you are not allowed to do anything about it. Air bag government regulations mandated they inflate at a speed of 200 MPH when triggered, even though this speed is dangerous. In their preoccupation with safety government released statistical information telling us the most common cause of severe injury or death in automobile accidents stems from the size of the car. If you drive a Honda Accord rather than a GM Jimmy your probability of death by accident is increased by over 200%. Yet, the law says every new car must have air bags installed. There are several problems with this. First, the federal government has no business legislating safety devices. Second 65 Americans have been killed and 300,000 have been injured by air bags, according to statistics from the federal safety division of the Transportation Department. Harvard University did an extensive study on the use of air bags, and concluded that they had not saved the life of a single child. As usual government statistics were falsified. Had a private firm falsified such information, as the government employees did in the air bag testimony provided, there would be fines and certainly the imprisonment of that firm's officers. Not one federal official has even been charged with anything. The basic question is why? The answer may surprise you. The head of the National Traffic Safety Board, Mr. James Hall, stated: "The fundamental flaw in this whole air bag debate has been a lack of guts on the part of public officials to put in place primary seatbelt enforcement laws." In other words what they want is to increase federal enforcement authority for traffic cops to stop a vehicle in which seat belts are not being used. This then creates, according to the latest Supreme Court rulings, the right for police to go on a search and destroy mission in your car and on your person. The further expansion of police power over the citizen. Fits right in with the Satori plan, does it not?

Hate Crimes/Political Crimes

The government has been very busy in the latter half of 1997 in a campaign to "Stem Hate Crime." In fact Clinton has proposed that there should be Federal legislation to prevent these heinous acts. Naturally we find the homosexual lobby involved. Sticks and stones can hurt your bones but insults are what really matter. Naturally referring to a homosexual as a faggot will be a hate crime. If a white man shoots a black in a robbery it will be a hate crime and thus be federalized. If, on the other hand, a black man kills a white man in similar circumstance it will not be a hate crime. You must understand that hate crimes can only be committed by white heterosexual males, which according to FBI figures is one of the smaller minorities committing crimes. The FBI publishes something called a supplemental report — it breaks down, by state, crime rates by race. Unfortunately some states lump Hispanics and whites together. I have omitted those states.

Crime by Race:

Incidence per thousand:

White	Hispanic	Oriental	Black
1	4 8	1.23	101

This statistic shows that whites have the lowest incidence of crime in America, lower even than orientals. Please don't give me the cliches about poverty — there are millions of poor whites who are law abiding, and I might add millions of blacks as well. As an opponent of all racial preference, gender preference, and any system based on anything but personal excellence, I expect to be labeled an extremist. The fact of the matter is that we live in a very competitive worldwide business environment, and private business cannot afford to hire people based on whom or what they like. If they want to compete and grow they have no choice but to hire the best and most able person for the job. Doing anything else is counterproductive, and has a direct effect on the profit and loss of the business. Quotas and all of these race and gender based programs have more to do with empowering mandarins to ride herd over your private property than they do with any egalitarian outcome.

Recently we have heard the president — in an effort to institute even more racial disharmony — speak of the need to institute some laws in regards to hate crimes. The possibility of federalizing them has been made by him. No doubt he is planning a new department, The Committee on Thought. Perhaps he plans to enact Orwell's *1984.*

Feminization

The rate at which America is being sensitized, and feminized is appalling. Just this morning I was in a store where I came upon a young couple. She was dressed as most young women in blue jeans and a man's shirt, he was the same. They had their child in a baby carriage. She gave him instructions on what to do. She told him what items were needed and proceeded to go read a magazine while he carried out the shopping duties. These are simply outward indications of what is taking place. The Feminization process is without doubt one of the major carriers of Cultural Marxism and a strong Satori platform. I very much love my wife, and I admire women. I also understand that they reason differently from men. Their character is different. They are biologically very different, and even their brain functions in a different way from those of males. It is without doubt these differences which cause most misunderstandings between the sexes. We are continuously bombarded by the media with examples of men crying, confronting grief, nurturing, caring, and on and on. Caring and nurturing are female characteristics, not male. Many young men in America lack the male characteristics of boldness, pride and independence. They display female characteristics of submission. The spiritual man is the builder, poet, soldier, the farmer and the priest. It is he who built our civilization, he, with the help of women, made America great. After that came the whiner, the draft dodger, the thoroughly feminized wimps that now run our government. These men are dangerous because they are the type of individuals who start wars. They are the ones who destroy civilizations. They are the homosexuals, the perverts, the pedophiles who cannot stand up to the competitive nature of men and thus choose an easier, simpler path. They become servants to the Satori.

Disagreement With It All

America has brought forth under our Constitutional Republic the most successful nation in the history of the world. The Satori have become eminently successful in their efforts to subjugate this success and the society for which it stands. The Satori have been successful in separating all of society into groups. These victim groups run contrary to everything our nation stands for. Rugged individualism, the driving force which made this nation what it has become, is passe. Teams, social de-individualization, societal groups are in. When I think of great achievements, I think of Jefferson, Franklin, Washington, Einstein, Tesla, Hemingway, Steinbeck, all individuals, none members of any team. The exploitation of one group differentiating another is the medium of exchange of our new masters. Everyone is able to reach fulfillment by obtaining government benefits at the expense of another member of the society, or even another group. Everyone is kept off balance and removed from understanding the actual objective of the Satori.

Our president, in his last inaugural address, admonished us: "We need a new government for a new century." This was his primary proclamation on January 20, 1997. He further stated that this new document would *give* a number of *benefits* to American people. He was indirectly referring to a new constitution which I am sure is already written.

America is one of a kind. We are the only super power left, but we do not bully anyone who obeys reasonable rules of civil conduct. Our national character is promulgated by the concepts of private property rights, the rule of law, individual rights, freedom of speech and the guarantee through the second amendment to have and bear arms in protection of all the aforementioned rights. All of these are under steady assault through all the Satori-sponsored political spoils programs. The ingredients that make up America are like an automobile — thousands of components make up a car. If you proceed to change all the component parts, you no longer have a car. The attempt to replace individual rights with group rights must be apparent to any onlooker. Group rights allows the ruling elites to play one group against another. Is that not what the president does when he speaks of hate crime, gender discrimination, and all the other vile rhetoric?

Just to prove that point:

- Clinton and the Justice Department actively opposed California proposition 209, only to have the courts support the peoples mandate.
- He defended and expanded the gerrymandering of congressional districts even after the Supreme Court struck the process down.
- He defended a racial preference quota hiring policy for the city of Birmingham, AL after the courts struck same down.
- He defended Texas University Law Schools's use of racial and ethnic preference only to have it struck down by the courts.
- He hired Bill Lan Lee for the justice department, illegally overriding the Senate's refusal to hire an activist whose record clearly indicates that he will not comply with rulings of the laws of the land.

If we are to survive as a nation, we must end this contrived social hatred. We must, as individuals, oppose Cultural Marxism in every form. More than that, when a politician uses this method we must chastise him. America is not composed of a bunch of sanctioned groups. It is and must be one nation under God, of individuals which share a common heritage — we are not Swiss-Americans, Black Americans, Hispanic Americans, Catholic Americans, we are AMERICANS, plain and simple.

What You Can Do About Cultural Marxism

If you refuse to play the game, there can be no game!

1.) Don't be politically correct. Refuse all PC, CM dogma.
2.) Refuse to recognize MC hit words. When someone uses them pretend you don't understand and make him clarify in appropriate language.
3.) Homosexuals per example are not gay. If anything they are emotionally sick.

4.) Be aware that our secondary educational system as well as the NEA have a strong pro-homosexual agenda.

5.) Be skeptical of all bureaucrat government issued edicts touted to protect you. They are to control you.

6.) The much advertised hate crimes are a very rare occurrence. The use of proper English in expressing yourself is not a hate crime.

7.) Resist the feminization of males in our society.

CHAPTER FOUR

LEGISLATIVE ENCROACHMENT

Without doubt centralization of all things, including Government, is the current plan. The first step in any centralization of power is the control of societal functions. To this end our Congress has been busy indeed. The swift move to unconstitutionally centralize power in Washington, later to be transferred to the UN, is without precedence. I call this Legislative Encroachment (LE) for short. The most obvious incidence of this is in law enforcement being instituted by the Executive branch. The Congress is neglecting their oversight duties. In fact, the negligence of our Senate and House of Representatives to limit the executive function to our Constitution has become a predominant factor of the latter half of the 20 century, and is in no small part responsible for the rapid Satori success. It is part and parcel of Legislative Encroachment. So we see that there are two distinct directions to LE. First we have legislation enacted by Congress which usurp the powers of the individual states, in violation of the tenth amendment. Second we have the unwillingness of Congress to challenge the executive's unconstitutional actions, which violate the rights of the states and the people.

Electricity

The latest encroachment into an area where the federal government has no business whatever is the distribution of electricity. The regulation, billed as a deregulation bill, emanated from the US Senate's Energy Committee Chairman Frank Murkowski (R,AK). In reality the bill, if enacted, will drive up the cost of electricity for over 35 million Americans because it restricts the ability of utilities to tighten credit standards, and thereby increases the incidence of uncollectable accounts. The largest unified electric distribution network is in California. If this bill is enacted it will make it impossible for participating publicly owned utilities to join the consortium set up by California unless they make a $2 billion rate increase statewide. Nowhere in the Constitution is the legislature given the authority to regulate distribution systems of any type within the boundaries of any single state. This is a clear violation of the Constitution.

Property

In another lunatic vote pushed by the National Association of Home Builders, the House passed a bill, 248-178, that would give landowners immediate access to the federal judiciary in the event of a local zoning dispute. One can only comment that at least 248 congressmen have never read the Tenth Amendment.

Used Cars

No, I'm not kidding! The House passed a bill, 336-72, pushed by the National Automobile Dealers Association, and strongly supported by the House Commerce Committee, that would require anyone selling a car which had been more than 80% rebuilt to disclose that fact to any potential buyer. In essence the idea is good, but the federal government has no business legislating anything to do with used car sales. Furthermore it is not even the State's business. It is a matter between buyer and seller.

The aforementioned are but a few of the types of legislation proposed in our Houses of Congress. These acts lead to more centralization in the hands of government bureaucrats (Mandarins), who act in behalf of the Satori. Centralization is a major consideration of the Satori. Thus we have "Mega-Mergers" "Consolidations" and "Early Retirement." Let me explain in simple terms: it is easier to control one large business or agency than 100 small ones. It is easier to control people employed by governmental agencies or large businesses than by lots of entrepreneurs.

To verify and show the direction indicated, consider the last presidential election. The voter turnout was the lowest in a presidential election in decades. The president won the election with a scant 26% of the popular vote. We now know that of the people voting for him, 64% were either government employees or on some government support program. Has the nation not reached a low point in our life when government employees combined with welfare recipients and social security beneficiaries account for enough votes to elect the chief executive? This gives us pause to reflect on the policy used by the Democratic National Committee over the last few election cycles. Is it perhaps possible that the Satori think-tanks have come up with another formula to win elections? What are the combined numbers of government employees, welfare recipients, police and military? Do they account for more than 50% of the voting public? The fact that more Americans are presently employed by small business than large does not stop the Satori. The full fledged effort to destroy small and independent businesses has been a fact of life for the last 50 years.

Let me relate my own story of woe. When I was released by the Army (I was drafted) I joined my father's import business. I learned from the ground up. I had already taken an apprenticeship in rebuilding machine tools, power tool repair and machining. I learned every aspect of the import business including shipping and receiving. After a few years I wanted to strike out on my own and began Widder Corporation, my father being the major stockholder. I began importing then manufacturing. I bought out some smaller manufacturers and began to export. Eventually I built a large plant in Naugatuck, Connecticut, and had a branch plant in San Leandro, California, as well as Widder UK Ltd. in England and Widder RSA Pty. Ltd. in South Africa. My father died. The IRS promptly advised me that they wanted $145,000 in estate tax on the business.

Mind you I began this business in 1962 with $10,000.00. I did not have the money that the IRS wanted. Funds were tied up in inventory, production equipment, as well as furniture and fixtures.

I told them I would have to close the business down and place everyone on unemployment. They relented and allowed me to pay the required tax over 10 years at prime plus 2%. Along came Jimmy Carter. Interest rates roared to over 20%. I had by that time paid more than the originally assessed amount of taxes, at previous interest rates. All my profit, as well as some of my principal, was going to the government, the banks, and my employees. We had no capital for expansion, we lacked R&D funding, we were forced to purchase production machinery under expensive lease contracts. The government finally destroyed my business, and in the process eliminated $500,000 in annual exports, unemployed over 70 people, and opened the field for my competitors — all foreign multinationals — to take over the market, who then drastically increased their prices. Everyone lost — employees, consumers, the economy, the government.

The legislative assault on family-held business is incredible. Through laws enacted by congress, and enforced by the IRS, small business in America has become unprofitable. I know of at least 15 business associates who shut down their business because they could make more money clipping coupons. Nowhere is this as obvious as in manufacturing. Self-employed individuals pay tax rates higher than anyone else. The entire legislative direction is to tax and tax and then tax some more. Our government punishes success and rewards indolence. Income taxes are graduated in such a manner as to punish productivity and hard work. This sends a message to business investors to curtail their success. Hundreds of thousands of business owners plan their annual business function with income tax, labor law, and environmental legislation in mind. They make sure not to expand beyond a certain size, not to produce above a specific profit, and not to hire over a explicit number of employees. Thus the system protects larger business from competition, guarantees unemployment, welfare participation, and dependency on government.

We further punish success by taxing funds, which have already been taxed, as in capital gains, and we are the only industrialized nation to do so. In fact they even tax social security, which is wholly derived from taxes, and then add insult to injury by taxing private pension benefits, which were also taxed before. The United States is the only nation of the G10 which taxes interest earned on savings accounts. As a consequence at least once a year we have great bewilderment by the body politic as to why the U.S. has the lowest savings average in the industrialized world. The monitory policy of the U.S., individual as well as governmental, is to shift the payment burden to someone else.

Our federal government, in an incredible act of stupidity, has reduced most treasury notes from 30 years to 5. Short term financing is more risky, more expensive, and reduces stability. On the individual side, credit card debt is soaring to levels never before dreamed of. Some yuppies actually use credit card debt to purchase stocks. Imagine paying up to 18% interest on a credit card to get 6% in stock dividends!

Put Them On a Diet

Our legislative branch of government is out of control. They are the fat cats of Washington. I don't mean to miss our other branches, but due to sheer numbers they are the worst. They have unheard of pensions. They have incredible benefits. They have their own subway, parking spaces, barber shops, gymnasiums, restaurants, post office, free travel, and that's only the beginning. Their salaries are over 5 times the national average. They have taxpayer-funded staffs, lawyers, statisticians, bankers, pollsters — you name it — they have it. Anything at all not found on the list can be provided by any of the agencies whose funding is at the discretion of the legislature. It is a spoils system on a truly grand scale. It creates power and power creates corruption. The longer legislators remain in Disneyworld on the Potomac the more they become corrupted by the system. With corruption comes control. Control by the Satori. They know what illegal acts have been committed by legislators, they know who has accepted bribes, they are fully informed about the personal habits of legislators —

after all, it is the Satori's Mandarins who are congressional staffers. Congressional staffers are the people who do the work, they — not your congressman or senator — write the laws. They read the proposed legislative acts. They develop new legislation. Why do you think so little changes when you elect a new congressman or senator? He comes to Washington and hires a staff, probably the same guys who were employed by the previous politician you thought you dumped. The overload factor must not be underestimated. *Consider that the following pieces of legislation which passed the house and senate were never read by any member because they were not published in written form at the time of the vote:* WTO, NAFTA and GATT. All three issues affect every single American, all three influence every congressional district. All three modify our Federal Constitution and through it every one of the fifty state constitutions. These morons voted on all three treaties, passed all three, and had no idea what was contained in the treaties except for a short synopsis. NAFTA alone is over 900 pages for the main document, plus numerous riders. The other two are longer. How can a man elected to represent you, vote for an international treaty not knowing what is in it, without violating his oath of office? Violation of the oath of office is now so commonplace as to render it non-news. From the president on down to the lowest judge in the system, every one of these elected and appointed officials violates the Constitution on a daily basis.

The True Workings of Corruption

So that you can fully understand the way this corrupt system works, let's take an example. Bill Clinton and the present administration are the perfect examples of a totally corrupt executive. We will use only one example of a politically criminal career which is without parallel in American history (there have been, to date, more incarcerations, deaths, resignations, investigations, and corruption than in any other administration in history). For years the entire Clinton political machine was funded through various kickback schemes. Clinton's greatest weaknesses — his perpetual dalliance with one bimbo after another, and his corrupt political finance funding schemes — have certainly come to the attention of some big time influence seekers.

When Clinton ran for his second term in office, his handlers told him that he would require about $150 million to get re-elected. That is not chicken feed, even for the Democratic National Committee. The Chinese communists (PRC) knew this, and were more than just familiar with Clinton's illegal campaign financing habits, as well as the bimbos. (Blackmail has been used in politics since day one). After all, they had been financing the Clinton machine in Arkansas through contributions they channeled through Charlie Trie in Little Rock.

Along comes what seems an impossible problem to the Chinese. Their long range ICBM and space launch missile, the Long March, had a 20% failure rate, and was so inaccurate that targeting within less than 5 miles was impossible. This rendered their entire missile program useless. Into this picture comes one Bernard Schwartz, the CEO of Loral, the firm that has all the required technology to fix this problem. In short order Mr. Schwartz becomes the single largest contributor to the Clinton Machine, with a contribution of $632,000 to the DNC, as well as over $100,000 in soft money. Then Johnny Chung gave them $366,000. Johnny's funds came from Liu Chaoying, the daughter of PRC Lt. General of the army Liu Huaqing. Subsequently millions were dumped into the Clinton/Gore campaign by the People's Republic of China. The deal had been cut — Loral began an expansive export of top secret technology to China, personally authorized by Clinton. These acts were carried out over the objection of the Joint Chiefs of Staff, the State Department, the National Security Agency, the CIA, and virtually every single governmental agency which deals with national security. The outcome of these acts has been the explosion of 5 nuclear warheads by India, who has considerable fear of China, the explosion of 5 by Pakistan, who has had two wars with India. This entire treasonous act by Clinton has started an arms race on the Indian sub-continent, which may be guaranteed to spread into the Middle East and then worldwide. It has also allowed China to target 80% of their ICBM's on American cities, and enabled those missiles to then hit their targets. Part of the deal was, I am sure, the elimination of the American missile defense system known as Star Wars, which was axed by Clinton last year. These treasonous acts have upset the world power structure and made the USA open to nuclear attack by China.

The Election Process

The single greatest farce in the United States is our election process. There is absolutely no way that you can get the best person elected for the job. The reason for this is the two party system. The two party system has an inherent penchant for corruption. Let us take a recent NH congressional election in which I have considerable personal experience. The Democrats fielded their incumbent, who was less than popular with the voters. It was a foregone conclusion that he would lose. He had done so many silly things that he stood no chance at all. Many of us, including a retired Senator, felt that this was an opportune time to get a conservative elected. An excellent conservative Republican was found in Mike Hammond. He did more than just well in the primary — it was, as they say, in the bag. But, the liberal Republican leadership was less than pleased with a conservative candidate or his overwhelming standing in the polls. They acted swiftly and brought a third completely unknown candidate into the campaign. They funded him with more money than Hammond spent on his entire campaign. Soon he took votes from Hammond and by the time of the election he had siphoned off 30% of his support. The primary wound up in the hands of the liberal Republican.

That's the way elections work in America. Pat Buchannan is living proof of it. He won NH, which was disputed by the media, then they conceded Pat won. Then he won the next primary, Iowa, and the establishment claimed he did not (they never did admit to false reporting in the Iowa primary). He won Arizona and they did it again. Dole was the weakest candidate ever fielded by the Republican party. Buchannan should have been the challenger but he is not a Satori dupe. The difference between Dole and Clinton is the same as between Twiddle Dumb and Twiddle Dee. If we examine Dole's and Clinton's political voting records side by side the difference is miniscule.

It is my contention that through a system of political manipulation voters are never given a choice. That candidates are chosen prior to the primary process. Then things are manipulated in such a manner as to ensure that both the Democrat and Republican candidates are "Satori" candidates. The very few exceptions to this, like Congressman Dr. Ron Paul or Senator Bob Smith, are the exceptions that prove the rule. The big money two party system must be abolished and elections opened up to all challengers.

What You Can Do

1.) Continuously demand enforcement of the tenth amendment.
2.) Demand from all legislators a pledge to get us out of the UN.
3.) Insist on State rights.
4.) Demand a reduction in the size and scope of government.
5.) A complete rewriting of campaign finance law, a major part of which should be as follows:
   a.) All candidates may be funded only by contributions from residents within the legislative district.
   b.) No amount in excess of $300 may be given to any candidate by any individual.
   c.) Outlaw all PAC's, business contributions and union contributions.
   d.) Outlaw all group contributions to political campaigns and candidates.

Socialist Environmentalism

There can be no question that the environmental movement has been completely co-opted by the socialist movement in the last thirty years. Socialist Environmentalism (SE) is one of the primary forces utilized by the Satori in an effort to bring their system to fruition. Where in most of the twentieth century socialist/communist philosophy was the predominant force of opposition to free enterprise, in the latter quarter of the century environmentalism has displaced it. This came about due to the continuous failures of all socialist and communist systems worldwide. It is reasonable to state that there is not one single successful model of a socialist society in existence, and there never was one. Environmentalism has nothing whatever to do with the environment, and everything to do with people control. The academicians who have fostered these socialist concepts on us have been stuck with literally hundreds of failures. They required another tractor with which to pull their wagon. Here we come up against an interesting question, namely, why is academia so fervently pushing socialist doctrine? Some might conclude that the reason for this is the caring appearance of socialism, i.e. the humanitarian aspect of the theory. That, however, is wrong. Professors simply love socialism because universities are socialist in nature. And for most, their entire educational life has been in public schools, which are socialist instutions supported by the taxpayers.

The association between the "Greens" and the socialists is nowhere as open as in Germany. In a press-release dated Dec. 1, 1997 issued by the Green party (environmental party of Germany) I quote:

> *Am Wochenende diskutierte der Fachbereich Außenpolitik Von Bündnis 90 DIE GRUNEN mid dem SPD - Außenpolitiker Günther Verheugen über mögliche Grundlinien einer Rot-Grünen Außenpolitik.*

> Translation: At weeks-end a discussion was held between the SPD and the Greens about the possibility of a Red-Green coalition in foreign policy.

---

*Today a coalition of Greens, Socialists & Communists control the government of Germany.

Socialist Environmentalism (SE) is the ideal vehicle for this mischief. There are a number of important reasons for this. First environmentalism is difficult to oppose. Second there is never any peer review of proposed ideology. "What, you're against clean water?" "It's your planet, are you going to destroy it?" "You have to drink that water, do you want polluted water?" Destroy the ozone layer and you will die from radiation. Greenhouse gasses will bring on global warming or another ice age, depending on which decade you listened to them. So just like socialism it has a human side, which can be exploited. It also has one great advantage over socialism, namely that most of the populace lacks the scientific education to understand the issues, thus is unable to repudiate them. This makes demagogic leadership easy.

Third, is the obvious appeal to the millions of Ludites and mystics in our society, who are ceaselessly seeking a new paradigm upon which to return us to those wonderful days of yesteryear. Well, do you remember . . . carrying water to your house from the well . . . the outhouses . . . smoke-filled rooms in an attempt to heat the abode . . . kerosene or whale lamp light . . . only going out in the evening on full moon nights, for lack of electric lights . . . and all that great stuff.

Fourth, environmental and socialist theories are easily linked. Both appeal to the same type of people. These are individuals who are convinced of their "better than average qualities." They are individuals without a proper education in the sciences. They are people who populate our cities, and would be scared to death in the woods by themselves, but who have sincere regard for all our "Endangered Species." These are for the most part people who do not live from or on the land, they are almost universally city dwellers — the perfect do-gooder environmentalists.

The World Resources Institute is one of the powerhouses of the environmental movement. They publish no less than three magazines, scores of reports and papers, and what's more, they print them in English as well as Spanish. Their Board Membership would impress anyone. Maurice F. Strong (who is also chairman of the Earth Council, senior advisor to the World Bank and number two at the UN) is their chairman. The rest is a veritable Who's Who of the environmental movement: John Adams of NRDC, Bret Bolin of IPCC, Robert Burt CEO of FMC, Alice Emerson of W. Mellon Foundation, Jonathan Lash pres. WRI, Robert McNamara formerly pres. of World Bank — you get my drift. What we see here is the usual overlapping of directorships which so well facilitates all Satori organizations. The real environmental nuts are Earth First. Their own statements: *"We believe in using all the tools in the toolbox, ranging from grassroots organizing and litigation to civil disobedience and monkey-wrenching."* (I assume this is the process of willful destruction of private property.) They have a newspaper which is published eight times a year on "pagan holidays" (their statement). There you have the tie-in with gaia worship. A level of action by these groups has recently been noted by Congress. In congressional hearings before the House Judiciary Committee, the Alliance for America, North American Research, and the Center for the Defense of Free Enterprise, testimony was provided for the widening of "Organized Crime Statutes to include Environmental Terrorism." Named as environmental terrorist groups during the hearings were: Animal Liberation Front, People for the Ethical Treatment of Animals, Earth Liberation Front, and Earth First.

Global Warming

Global warming is bunk. You will find it impossible to find one single atmospheric scientist who will say, "Yes, there is definitely global warming," or that humans can cause global warming. For the last 19 years NASA has been measuring world surface temperature with satellites. This is the best way of doing this because cities, due to the large amounts of concrete in high buildings, tend to increase temperatures in their immediate vicinity. As it turns out NASA satellites demonstrate a slight global cooling (.039 Deg. C.) over the last 19 years. The original USSR global warming theory was postulated utilizing a computer model. There were many problems with this but the main one was that they did not measure or utilize any temperature data from the world's oceans. Needless to say the major portion of the world is covered by water. This then makes the entire computer model worthless. The NASA model measures all temperatures — cities, oceans, deserts and forests — and can therefore presume to be reasonably correct.

It goes without saying that the global warming concept was instituted by the Soviets as a propaganda method to de-industrialize the West. This concept was brought to the USSR by agents of the Satori who were eager to exploit Socialist Environmentalism to their own advantage. We are fully aware that the Soviet system, as well as our own, were and are controlled by the Satori. There are two types of scientists, those whose base their hypothesis on scientifically provable assumptions subject to peer review, and those whose assumptions are based on politically influenced, outcome based, unscientific lies. The second type are stooges of the Satori, funded by Satori foundation grants and supplied with the outcome before they make the study. At the present time there are over 4000 scientists who have signed the Heidelberg Appeal, a document produced prior to the Rio de Janeiro Earth Summit, begging politicians not to bind the world to any treaty based on global warming, which is unverifiable.

On a lighter note: In the latter half of the 19th century trams in New York city were drawn by — you guessed it — horses. The rabid environmentalists of the day had a somewhat different platform. They informed the public through ads in the NY Times that an environmental disaster was in the making. They stated clearly that the entire city would shortly become a disaster because everything would be covered in horse manure. Not much foresight, and less imagination, is the indisputable motto of these people. England of the same period also had environmentalists, and one of their heroes was Robert Malthus. He argued that population was increasing at a geometric rate 1, 2, 4, 8, etc. while food supply was only increasing at an arithmetical rate of 1, 2, 3, 4, etc. As a consequence England's population would starve within 20 years — don't laugh — almost everyone believed him. Obviously peer review and science had no more to do with those prognostications than they do today. In 1972 the Club of Rome published an influential document entitled "Limits to Growth." In it they told us that oil supplies were finite and that we had only 550 billion barrels of oil left in the earth. We would use up all these reserves within the decade, and by 1982 would be out of oil. Well, their consumption figures were not bad — from 1970 to 1990 we used 600 billion barrels — so I want you to know that according to the Club of Rome we are not just on empty, we have overdrawn our world's supply by 50 billion barrels. The actual fact is that present normal oil reserves are well over 2 trillion, 500 billion barrels. The Falklands war was fought between Argentina and Britain because the largest oil field ever found, over one trillion barrels of oil, has been located under the Falklands islands. The Club of Rome is one of the really aggressive pushers of goofy theories. They have in the past made similar predictions about zinc, silver, uranium, aluminum, copper, natural gas, ad infenitum. The string that ties all these predictions together is bad science, no peer review, and an agenda driven not by science — but by a predetermined outcome — the required outcome of the masters, the Satori.

In a British high school science textbook of 1983, it was stated that the earth would run out of zinc within a decade. Wrong again, and instead of explaining the mistake the authors simply removed the reference from the next batch of books. Paul Ehrlich, who is anything but honest, has made one disastrous prediction after another, all of them having been proven false. In 1970 he predicted a world population of 7 billion by 2000, with massive famine and hundreds of millions starving to death by 1990. Lester Brown of Worldwatch Institute began his predictions of massive starvation in 1973. He stated then that within the decade, that is by 1984, world population would outstrip food production. He has made the same prophecy for every decade and has been wrong each and every time.

Global 2000 was a report to the President of the United States written in 1980. It predicted an increase of food prices from 35% to 115% by 2000. Why, and how, is it possible for such foolery to continue? Peer Pressure. Three scientists who in 1970 predicted ample food supplies, plenty of minerals, and no population explosion, were Norman Macrae, Julian Simon, and Aaron Wildavsky. All are vilified by the media, and environmental movement, and referred to as "right wing nuts." Their data was correct. The UN, not wanting to be left out, advised in 1984 that deserts were consuming 51.8 million acres of land per year. The fact borne out by satellites from NASA, indicate that not one desert has grown an inch. Al Gore has asserted that 20% of the Amazon is being deforested per year, and that this is continuing at a rate of 197.7 million acres per year. The actual numbers are 9% and 51.8 million acres but it is also being replanted, a fact not mentioned by Gore. If you fly over the rain forest, you see endless trees and no large tracts of "deforestation," clearings, yes, deforestation, no. The same is true with tree cutting in the U.S. The fact that in North America today, there are 45% more forests than at the turn of the last century is always overlooked.

In order for you to understand the issue more clearly let me demonstrate world climate in a diagram. As you are aware there have been ice ages (mammoths) as well as tropical ages (dinosaurs) in the history of the world. Our climate has fluctuated in a continuous sine wave forever. We do not yet know the reason for this, but may someday learn. The sine wave has two repeating cycles: 1) ice age; 2) tropical age. It spans a determined period of time, but we do not know exactly what the time frame is. Worse than that, we do not know at what point in the sine wave we are at this moment. The reason we do not know these things is that we have been here and able to record weather data too short a period to determine those factors. We are an ignorant lot. Our science has barley scratched the surface of knowledge. Yet there are people who will tell you that we have global warming — this without the slightest scientific factual proof. Go Al Gore! In an interesting column in the *Wall Street Journal* Paul Gigot comments on speeches made by Gore in which he, among other things, said:

"We have reached a fundamentally new stage in the development of human civilization. This new stage is a crisis stage, and its spiritual roots are pridefulness (new goreism term) and failure to understand and respect our connection to God's earth and each other."

Mr. Gigot aptly states that the really scary thing is that Al Gore, and others, believe this rubbish. It is of course an interesting fact that almost all the hype about global warming comes from politicians, and vested interest groups, none of it from people who actually have degrees in atmospheric science. Most atmospheric scientists are a courageous lot, because they have not yet subdued to the peer pressure which is beginning to build for global warming fairy tales. The concept, or proposition that man is responsible for variation in world temperature is like the mouse running down the elephant's leg screaming rape. All the greenhouse gases produced by man worldwide account for under 5% of the total world production. If we turn off every automobile in the United States and find an absolutely non-polluting way of transport it will account for 1/18 of 1000th% of the greenhouse gases produced in our nation.

These people who postulate rubbish about global warming suffer from the most monumental superiority complex in history. Humans are just not that important in the scheme of things. Without doubt the most important of all environmental organizations is the IPCC (Intergovernmental Panel on Climate Change) who have issued all the reports on which all environmental theories are based. Or have they? (Climate Change 1995: the Science of Climate Change), (Climate Change 1995: Impacts, Adaptations and Mitigation of Climate Change), (Climate Change 1995: Economic and Social Dimensions of Climate Change), (Climate Change 1994: Radioactive Forcing of Climate Change), and a later 1997 report. Not one of these reports — I repeat, not one — stated that there was any global warming. The closest to that are words like may, or possibly be. In preparation of this chapter I have reviewed hundreds of documents and in none could I find any statement by any atmospheric scientist confirming any global warming theories. All statements about it came from politicians, and other unqualified individuals. The outcome of this entire global warming concept is not environmental but economic. If the United States Senate binds us to the UN Kyoto treaty, it will cost the average American family $4,000 per year, and the US government over $200 billion. Again we have the Satori strategy in place to lower the American standard of living to level the playing field prior to economic integration. If the treaty were really about global warming, why are only the industrialized nations held to the planned standards of reduction of greenhouse gasses? After all, they account for less then 18% of the total emissions, and their percentage has been decreasing while third world emissions of 82% have been increasing for over a decade. Many still used leaded gasoline and their cities make ours look spotlessly clean. Global warming is an excuse for global government.

CO_2

There is considerable discussion by environmentalists about CO_2 emissions. Please bear in mind that vicious CO_2 is what you exhale and what plants inhale. Two fine ladies have now concluded some startling research on this matter: Cindy Werner and Prof. Susan Brantley spent some time at Yellowstone National Park. This evil place must be closed down at once. The gist of their research indicates that the Yellowstone geothermal system is a substantial producer of CO_2. In their December 23, 1997 report they inform us that the park produces about 44 million tons of CO_2

each and every year. For you novices in power plant pollution, that is the equivalent of the total CO_2 production of 20 fossil fuel burning electric generating plants. Now you should know that the Yellowstone system produces only about 30% of the geothermal produced CO_2 in North America, which is only a small portion of the total CO_2 produced in nature. Indication by researchers place geothermal CO_2 emissions in North America at an equivalent of 150 fossil fuel electric generating plants. The total US production of CO_2 produced by man accounts for just under 2% of the total. According to Dr. Bonner Cohen, Editor of EPA watch: 98% of all greenhouse gases are produced by mother nature! If as a consequence we accept Satori sponsored theory and put it into place the draconian economically-stifling Kyoto treaty, we will reduce our GNP, our income and our standard of living, all for nothing.

Well, we might as well get to the real serious nuts. Greenpeace is an organization that promotes ideas totally based in fiction. It is one thing to be environmentally conscious, but an entirely different thing to spread lies about issues just to obtain cash contributions. Greenpeace is an organization which will make any ridiculous statement in an effort to get you to contribute money. The following statements are all taken from Greenpeace fund-raising literature. All of them are totally untrue:

- Arctic oil exploration is hastening the most severe climate changes since the ice age.
- Nine out of the ten warmest years have all occurred since 1980.
- Northern snow cover and arctic sea ice are retreating rapidly.
- Global sea level is projected to rise between 6 and 38 inches by 2100.
- The balance of evidence suggests that there is a discernible human influence on global climate.
- The average global temperature has already risen one degree Fahrenheit in the past century.
- During the 20th century the arctic temperature has risen by 2.7 degrees F.

- PVC is the single most environmentally damaging of all plastics.

They go on to link the production of PVC (Poly Vinyl Chloride) to: Love canal (the product of military chemical production), Agent Orange (a defoliant used and produced by and for the military), PBC's (which they claim destroys the ozone layer), DDT (a pesticide outlawed since the 1960s but still used in Mexico and other 3rd world countries), and make sweeping statements like: The planet is threatened by climate change, the greatest single threat comes from fossil fuels, genetically engineered food is threatening the environment and organic food supply. There is nothing wrong with opposing anything. But if you do so publicly you had better be able to make a scientifically sound case for doing so, or you will wind up looking like a fool — provided the media will report your errors. As Greenpeace is politically correct, their statements are touted as gospel and never reported to be false, which they are.

Captain Planet
Just How Serious are the Environmentalists?

A few days ago one of my neighbors dropped his kids off for a couple of hours. They promptly went to the TV and turned on a program called Captain Planet. I was amazed. The first and most obvious message to be discerned was multi-culturalism — the hero kids of the program represented every minority group conceivable. White, Black, Indian, Mexican, Hispanic, etc. All the bad guys were white American businessmen. Another message was that animals have rights. The God in the program was none other than Gaia the Earth Goddess. The jungle was the rain forest. Wicked white Anglo Saxon males were cutting down trees to build a shopping mall. There was even a bad white male running a pollution spewing factory in the arctic, his name was Mr. Plunder. All of the employees of Plunder Co. were white males. There were environmentally endangered pigs and kangaroos. When our heroes called Captain Planet they did so using their magic rings under the auspices of Gaia the Earth Goddess invoking the minor gods of earth; water, wind, and fire. Incredible! The cartoon program obviously aimed at children under six years of age is designed to brainwash your children to accept beliefs which run contrary to everything true.

Parents should not allow young developing minds to be exposed to this type of trash. The facts are: the largest polluters worldwide are governments; business rarely pollutes because it is economically bad business; there are no endangered pigs or kangaroos; Gaia worship (pantheism) predates western civilization; there are no manufacturing plants in the arctic; shopping malls are where moms go to buy food and toys; white Anglo Saxon males are one of the smallest minorities on earth; and animals have no rights.

This clearly demonstrates that the Satori plan is a long-term one. They are brainwashing your children before they even enter kindergarten. Children who are successful in our modern educational systems are so because they follow the official line. They do as they are told. If not, they are given Ritalin or other mind altering drugs so as to bring them around to establishment behavior. Most of the secondary teachers, certainly those under 30 years of age, are the product of the same system. Teachers colleges represent the easiest path in higher education. Universities simply continue the same rubbish. The only schools which still represent a reasonable education are engineering schools, and a small number of private schools like Hillsdale College.

Die Gruenen (www.greenparty.com)

Rather then relying directly on American Socialist Environmentalism I prefer to tell you of the international view. The reason being, it is an international movement and it is more developed in Europe. The most active SE political party is the German Greens, who also have considerable influence in neighboring Germanic speaking nations of Switzerland, Austria, Holland, Belgium, as well as northern Italy, and some Eastern European nations. The German Green party was founded in 1980. Average age of the leadership is 46. The party grew out of Gruene & Bunte (Green & Colorful) i.e. Environmentalists and Homosexuals. They came to power in the 70's when they succeeded in having members elected to the Bundestag. When the wall came down they merged with the communist greens of East Germany. They, as a party, have very few positive plans. They are known universally as opponents of nuclear electric generation, which they confuse with nuclear weapons. As aforementioned, they are presently working out a coalition with the socialists and communists.

The basis of these beginning discussions relate to foreign policy in Germany. While the Green command is only about 4% to 10% of the electorate the Social Democratic Party (SPD) is substantially larger and more powerful. The leadership of both parties, however, feel a comfortable commonality of purpose. The Greens are 58% female. The majority of their membership is under 30 years of age. The party speaker, Joschka Fischer, is 49. Kerstin Mueller is 34. At party level, leadership may be related to Buendnis 90 which was the communist E. German green party, and which was an adjunct to the communist leadership of Germany. Juergen Trittin and Gunda Roestel, the leadership, are both from that venue. The Red Green coalition presently (1997) holds 10 ministerial posts in different German states. The Green party platform is:

1.) A total consolidated European policy including Russia (thus the communists).
2.) Strengthening of this coalition.
3.) Further democratization and expansion of the EC (Satori goal).
4.) The further development of finance, trade, ecological, and other politics for the development of an international structural politics (totalitarian control of society).

Hamburg is the latest success story of the Greens. In the Sept. 1997 elections they were able to capture 14% of the electorate in mayoral elections, thus ousting the Social Democrats from office. They began to press their advantage through a coalition with the socialists and communists, the so-called Red/Green alliance. A prominent German think-tank, Allensbach Institute, suggests that the Red/Green alliance may be able to attain a majority in the Bundestag with a 10% margin over the Free Democrats within the next few years. Joschka Fischer, party speaker, stated recently that the Greens were a party of protest in the 60's, but were now, through a coalition with the Reds, developing into a party of leadership. Although veiled, the party remains true to its roots:

1.) Anti-nuclear anything.

2.) Radical feminism/homosexual rights.

3.) Support of Socialist/Communist doctrine.

There are presently two factions within the movement, the "REALO" (realist) and the "FUNDIS" (fundamentalist environmentalists). These two factions are locked in combat for the leadership of the party. Presently the leadership may be considered as representing the realo side of the argument. As Antje Moeller (Hamburg Green Parliamentary Leader) stated, "The golden era of the greens may be over. Now we are in power, we are being forced to walk the knife's edge dividing principle and pragmatism." The change in the party since attaining power is nothing short of astounding. Opposition to open cast mining in North Rhine Westphalia, was dropped because it would create 7,000 new jobs. Realo has even succeeded in stopping opposition to NATO, as well as the elimination of the Bundeswehr, once stalwarts of the Greens. As they gain power the hand of the Satori becomes clearly visible. The fact that the previous Green party of East Germany, Buendnis 90, a communist party, was merged into the Green party is, I believe, relevant. It is also noteworthy that the Greens have links with socialist and Green political parties in 28 different nations, including the United States.

How are they funded? An interesting question. Like so many other political movements funding is somewhat nebulous. However, the largest single contributor is the Heinoch-Boell-Stiftung e.v., a large foundation in Germany whose own funding remains unclear. That the Boell Stiflung has very deep pockets goes without saying. In a conversation with Andrea Meinecke, spokesperson for the Boell Stiftung, she stated that they were a social organization and a major funder of the Greens and have a basic pacifist internationalist attitude. They are located in Leipzig which is most peculiar as there were no foundations in the former DDR. The same building also houses Active Seniors, Buendnis 90, German Russian Center, Greenpeace, as well as numerous organizations with links to the communist past of the German Democratic Republic (DDR).

The truly amazing fact of the environmental movement is that they blatantly report lies, pretending that they are fact. The Headline of the Swiss Green home page reads: *climate-change and greenhouse-effect: actuality academic expertise brought to bear. A* lengthy article then goes on to point out that the UN Rio conference on Climate of 1992 proves without any doubt their theorem. Of course nothing could be further from the truth. All documentation introduced at the Rio and the subsequent Kyoto conferences clearly point to the fact that insufficient evidence exists to make any statements in regards to global warming, or greenhouse gasses, the most pronounced issues to environmentalists. One can add to that recent NASA information which completely contradicts the entire scenario. The major document used to support global warming are various IPCC reports, all of which *refute* the entire global warming theory. The German political party Die Gruenen is the most organized of all the world's political environmentalist movements. Just to review their literature is a mind boggling experience. Below is listed the political platform of the Greens in Germany. Can our own be far behind?

Crime: reduction of time spent in prison for all crimes, no incarceration of minors regardless of the crime, criminals to have free access to their families, paying incarcerated criminals a salary, the elimination of constraints in prison facilities (walls, fences, etc.), free medical and drug services, social security and pension benefits, conjugal visits, criminals apprehension about punishment must be reviewed and democratized. **Children:** a change of current law, children are to be given full power before the courts without parental interference. **Eurofighter:** joint EC fighter war plane development to be eliminated. **Electricity:** EMF fields are dangerous and are to be eliminated (no more high tension lines). **PVC:** the use of PVC reduces labor requirements and must thus be replaced. **Vacations:** the government is to develop a national tourist plan. **Income:** it's just unfair that some people earn more than others, this must be corrected. **Organ transplants:** must be strictly regulated by the government. **Women:** (foreign) who marry Germans must be made citizens upon marriage. Not enough women have drivers licenses, this must be corrected. **Foreign aid:** drastic increases to level the playing field. **EU:** must be comprehensively reformed in accordance with Green issues. **Nuclear Power:** the elimination of all nuclear electric generation. **Foreigners:** to be unconditionally made German citizens. **Land Mines:** to be unconditionally outlawed. We learn exactly what they stand for in the official party brochure . . . "We are a social movement, the ecology, opposition to nuclear power, feminist issues, alternative lifestyles, peace movement, and third world support movements." There you have it in their own words a socialist, environmentalist, ludite, lesbian, gaia worshipping, third-world saving, mutual support group. They are by act and deed socialists with green overtones. They represent a perfect vehicle to move society in the direction of Satori plans.

Gorby

In an interview in *Le Monde* from Moscow a very lonely Russian, Mikhail Gorbachev, the last supreme Soviet, expressed his bitter memories of his past glory. What relevance does this have with the environmental movement and the Satori plan for the New

World Order? Funny you should ask. The interview goes on to say how very disappointed the big man was and how he blamed Boris Yeltsin, his old rival, for having banned the communist party (it was only banned for a few months). He referred to the matter as a witch hunt of the 18 million communist party members (The total membership of the party in a empire of over 300 million. The party represented less than 5% of the population).

That was in 1991. Today, seven years later, Gorby is very prominent and popular in the West, but not in Russia, and a leader of the environmental movement. It is really ironic that a man so sincerely disliked in his own nation that he could not get elected as a dog catcher, is so popular in the West. It is even more confounding when one considers the ecological disasters left behind by the Soviets in all the countries they had occupied. The cleanup in East Germany alone is costing the Germans billions upon billions of marks. Make no mistake, Gorby is a hard-line communist, this is apparent from his speeches, his political arrogance, statements, and writings. Looking at the history of the Communist and Nazi parties' actions in the 20th century, historians must come to the same conclusion about both. They were brutal killers of their own population, they waged war against the world, they were suppressors of thought, action, and deed. Which was more brutal? The Communists by a long shot. They killed more than 360 million of their own citizens in their 70 years in power.

This now brings us to a group of organizations under the umbrella of the Gorbachev Foundation. These are:

The Gorbachev Foundation

The Green Cross Family

Green Cross International, Geneva Switzerland

Green Cross National Organizations

Global Green, USA

International Foundation for Socio-Economic and Political Studies

These have offices in Venice CA, USA; Buenos Aires, Argentina; Cochabamba, Bolivia; Komorany, Czech Republic; Tallinn, Estonia; Paris, France; Budapest, Hungary; Den Haag, Holland; Moscow, Russia; Kungsaengen, Sweden; Bern, Switzerland; Surrey, England; Burkina Fasco, Abidjan; Cote d'lvoire, Yono Shi; Saitama, Japan; and Seoul, Korea. When International Green Cross sponsored an international environmental meeting in the United States they were given the Presidio of San Francisco, a closed Army base. If they paid a leasing fee it is unknown by the author. Every luminary in the environmental circus was in attendance, from Shirley McLain to Al Gore. Not one atmospheric scientist was invited or present. On behalf of Green Cross International, their president, Mikhail Gorbachev, made a speech called the Earth Charter Speech Rio+5. We can glean some interesting information from it. To create urgency, i.e. crisis, which is not the case . . . "We all have confronted the choice of either being swept away by time and nature, or facing the present situation in our world, in nature, to our relationship with our fellow human beings, their situation and needs." Then there are the usual doom and gloom predictions that we have heard for the last 50 years about overpopulation, lagging industrial production and uncontrolled growth. He states . . . "Uncontrolled growth of population, add up to total extermination of the human race."

We then find out about the subject of the speech: The Earth Charter. Although little is told of its content, we do learn that it is about "Eradicating Poverty." This again addresses the construction of an economically level playing field. We are informed that Maurice Strong, the kooky Canadian number two at the UN and long known envirofreak, agrees with it all. We are told that the charter consists of rules, but these are omitted. Then, finally, Gorby lets the cat out of the bag. "We all have recently witnessed the crash of one of the largest experiments of our time — the communist model of bringing happiness to humankind." Wow!! I wonder how the surviving relatives and friends of 360 million murdered by that experiment feel about that? Then we are informed that we will see the "future as a cooperation of peoples . . . cultures, religions, and traditions" . . . and that we are "united in a mutual destiny." In a lengthy interview of Gorby by the *LA Times* on May 8, 1997, we really learn exactly what the Satori plan is and how very little it has to do with the environment. The questions were posed to Gorby as the president of Global Green USA. The questions are all loaded, the answers are, nevertheless, enlightening.

Q. When communism collapsed, there was euphoria in the West. Jacques Cousteau said at the time, "This is a big mistake. The (free) market system is doing more damage to the planet . . ."

A. I absolutely agree with Cousteau. Communism is certainly dead, but capitalism is not the alternative for the 21st century . . . we need a new synthesis, which incorporates democratic Christianity, Buddhist values . . . social responsibility, a oneness with nature, stabilization of population growth, stabilization of poverty"

. . . and on and on ad infenitum. If this is not an establishment Satori straight man I'll eat my hat. On the home page of the Gorby family we find a speech by Dr. Charrier, a member of the World Bank, a prime Satori controlled institution. I have no idea what this guy's doctorate is in but just listen to what he tells us in his speech, *Reaching for Utopia*. 40,000 years ago Neanderthal man was wiped out by us evil Homo Sapiens. On Easter Island the entire population committed suicide 350 years ago — they did this by destroying their ecosystem. Our entire planetary system will collapse within 20 years. We must stabilize population by limiting birth rates per female. We must eradicate world hunger. And finally we come to the conclusion: Activities of mankind threaten the balance of the world ecosystem, but we can all be saved, all we must do is choose *Sustainable Mankind Development*, a true strategy for humankind as formulated by M. Gorbachev, Pres. of Green Cross Int. Hurrah . . . Gorby to the rescue! He will save us, just make him dictator of the world.

Kyoto

How would Al Gore's proposed Kyoto treaty affect you if the Congress enacted it?

1.) The price of electricity would increase by about 50%. This in turn would increase the price of everything you buy on the average about 6%.

2.) Gasoline and diesel fuel costs would increase dramatically, about 85 cents per gallon. This would increase all trucking costs, transport costs, and all farm products by at least 10%.

3.) There would be, at a minimum, one million jobs lost. The treaty would allow prices in third world nations to remain stable as it does not apply to them. This in effect will make it impossible for American business to compete.

4.) American business would, if they wanted to remain in business, have to transplant operations to third world locations. Steel, clothing, and chemical production would all fall by 30% within three years.

There you have it — everything the Satori want in one fell swoop.

The Union of Concerned Scientists (U.S.)

Before anything, UCS accepts membership from anyone willing to send them $25.00 or more. You do not have to be a scientist, doctor, college graduate, high school graduate, grade school graduate or even be able to read. They are proponents of the idea that we can use solar and wind power to replace nuclear and fossil fuel energy in the generation of electricity. This concept is beyond just stupid. Per example: to generate sufficient power using solar energy to meet California's power requirements we would have to cover the entire state of Arizona with solar panels, and at that point we have not even addressed the storage battery requirements. They also push the concept of biomass use, which is basically the concept of using garbage and human waste to produce methane and to convert that into electricity. The methane replaces fossil fuel. Sounds great, but it is not possible on such a grand scale. I am not saying that such efforts are worthless, particularly the biomass conversion process. What I am saying is that the idea of USC to replace all current methods of generation with their ideas will not work.

All this reminds one of the Ludites moronic bumper sticker: BURN WOOD NOT ATOMS. These confused fools want a reduction of greenhouse gasses and then attack the one source, nuclear generation, which does not produce any. Some other ideas they propagate: increasing gasoline prices and paying for insurance of vehicles through the increase, conversion to electrically powered cars, reducing population worldwide.

The UCS was among the strongest opponents of the Strategic Defense Initiative (SDI). I have personally never understood why anyone would be opposed to a defensive system that would prevent a first strike nuclear attack by an opponent. Even with the development of ICBM's on the horizon by, Pakistan, India, Iran, North Korea, Libya, and Iraq, and with Israel, all former USSR republics, and China. France and England have such capability, yet they have not changed their minds. Why? The concepts of UCS have little to do with environmental issues and everything to do with weakening the United States.

Continuation

I could continue indefinitely just listing environmental establishments and their anti-growth, methusian, ludite plans for the United States and the world. Instead I will just provide the names of the ones that I have researched: the Progressive Foundation, which opposes anything nuclear, including life saving medical treatments; Public Citizen – solar and wind power to replace fossil fuel and nuclear energy; Earth Island Institute – to make oceans safe for marine mammals; The Defense Monitor Center for Defense Information, the total elimination of military; Center for Economic Conversion, to convert all military bases to civilian use;

Elsevier Environment News, primarily environmental issues not singly directed, covers environmental issues worldwide without any particular bias; Save Energy Communications Council, anti-pollution topics with heavy ludite direction; Rocky Mountain Institute, claim to promote the best and cheapest methods of energy use in opposition to un-cost-effective supply side solutions; Center for Health, Environment and Justice to protect society from harmful chemicals; Greenpeace; the Sierra Club; etc., etc.

In Summation

As demonstrated so amply in the foregoing text, as well as in all other documents reviewed by the author, the connection between the environmental movement and the old socialist party is a certainty. This then creates another facet of the gemstone I chose to call the Satori conspiracy of Socialist Environmentalism. Most of the Green documentation was in German and came from Switzerland, Austria and Germany. I believe that the environmental movement is international in scope, and offer Rio, Kyoto, and all the other UN based mega conferences on the environment as proof. Behind all the environmental acts is the director of the United Nations. The most powerful proponents of global warming, ozone hole, and other such myths is the UN's IPCC. The entire cabal is orchestrated internationally by the Satori's Mandarins.

In order to see where we are heading on this issue we need only go to the place where they have gained the most success, Germany. In order to explore the makeup of this movement we can review their literature and major supporters. All of these come from the left fringe of society. Financial support comes from the far left, and is socialist as well as communist. People involved in it are scientific neophytes like Al Gore who had his childish book, *Earth in the Balance*, ghost written for him. When I read it I often wondered if the author had even taken a high school physics course. It is a touchy-feeley operation. The plan is the destruction of private property ownership, and the internationalization of government, under Satori control. This is "touchy-feely" kind of movement, which so appeals to the feminine part of society. "I'm so good I want to save the planet," "Don't you care?" "We could all die," "Gaia mother earth save us from ourselves — give us one world government to control us."

What You Can Do About Socialist Environmentalism

SE's success lies in two different directions: the appeal to the feminine side based on emotion, and the second; the lack of scientific education in the general population.

SE can be defeated only through logic and the scientific use of knowledge and fact. This is because almost all environmentally provided information is scientifically weak or totally insupportable by fact. The primary reason for this is the lack of peer review of postulated information by environmental groups. This weakness must at all times be exposed by the questions:

Who reviewed your proposal, when and what were the reviewers qualifications?

The Ozone hole: What hole? How did it get there? Has it not been present through all history? Is it not caused because the earth is tilted on its axis thus producing 6 months of winter at the polar regions? Isn't ozone produced by solar radiation, and when in darkness no radiation occurs? How can CFC's, which weigh more than air, destroy ozone most of which is in the stratosphere?

Global Warming: Is it not a fact that NASA has produced a study over the last 20 years which indicates a global cooling of .05 Deg. F.? Was the global warming study not a product of poor science by the Soviets, in which they did not measure temperature over the oceans? In view of the fact that over 1000 scientists have signed a protocol denying global warming, would you please tell us the names of several matriculated atmospheric scientists who support your contention?

Greenhouse Gases: Primarily CO_2: Are you aware that the entire industrial production of CO_2 in the United States accounts for no more than 3.99% of the total world production? Did you know that Yellowstone National Park produces more CO_2 than all the power plants in the 11 Western states combined? Are you aware of the fact that man-made production of CO_2 represents less than 12% of the total world production and that all the rest, 88% is produced in nature?

The cost of present environmental policy is catastrophic. In the long term it would reduce the standard of living by 50%.

CHAPTER FIVE

MEDIA

As you read this chapter keep in mind that, just as Germanic people have, over the centuries, been know for their engineering ability, the Jewish people have been known as communicators — writers, playwrites, actors, etc., and for their prowess in the field of finance. In addition, it is also well known that many of the leading proponents of socialism and communism, were, and are, of Jewish heritage. And that mainline Christian Churches have been a dominant voice calling for a collectivist, if not socialist, One World Government for almost 100 years. Should you doubt this statement, read my publisher's new book, *The Libertarian Theology of Freedom* by the Reverend Edmund A. Opitz.

In the world of the nineties no single entity has even a comparable power to that of the media — television and radio have seen to that. The media consists of radio, television, newspapers, magazines, as well as the entire entertainment medias of cinema, music, and theater. America's media is managed by a very small select group of individuals. They decide what news is news, what entertainment is suitable for you, and what products are to be made and distributed. They control the subject, the production, and the distribution. This would not represent any problem whatever if America had a balanced and unbiased media. This, as any intelligent person understands, is not the case. It is not necessary to review all the available statistics in this text about the political and social attitude of journalists in our nation. Enough can be surmised out of the fact that 86% voted for Clinton. In addition a full 92% place themselves on the liberal left politically. So much for objectivity.

When we examine the media, and by that I include print, airwaves, as well as entertainment, we come to the astounding realization that no less than a dozen or so individuals control it with the exception of the Internet. Our media is at the forefront of historic revisionism as well as the effort to destroy western culture and civilization. The real problem stems from the fact that the entertainment industries of television, as well as cinema, display just as great a penchant toward left wing propaganda as does the news. It is a wise man who, when involved in anything to do with all media, seriously questions the motive behind the reason and cause, as well as inducement for method of presentation.

In the 21st century media power will increase dramatically. We have already seen in the 20th century how media is not some removed, distant veiled object, but are in our own living rooms, particularly with our children, indoctrinating them continuously with Satori propaganda. Numerous children's programs such as Captain Planet and the film Pochahantas, more than demonstrate my point. All of us, old and young, white and black, poor and wealthy, are influenced by media. This represents a large change from previous centuries in that more people can now be reached with less effort then ever before, and by a very much smaller group of individuals. Each have an agenda. All act in unison to the same goals, without regard of the profit and loss of their businesses. What could be the driving force behind such acts? Why would they display an across-the-board, heavy-handed propaganda effort against everything this republic stands for, as well as a concerted effort to destroy our culture and lower our standards? Is there something in the character of these people which we don't know?

They seem to display an outright dislike of Nationalism. In our last presidential election it made no difference who would be the next Pontifex Maximus to occupy that hallowed white fortress on Pennsylvania Avenue. The losers of the election were the American people, who turned out in the lowest numbers in decades. In previous chapters you learned of the process of Cultural Marxism, Judicial Activism, and Information Overload — these are the people who put these practices to work. They are the greatest

---

Flash-Back

Dateline: October 14, 1997

Source: **UN NATO Command Bosnia** (Peacekeepers)

Issuance: **UN HQ NYC**

The unified NATO command of Bosnia, including US, Canadian, and European forces, are pleased to announce the successful seizure of four Bosnian Radio and Television stations. Also seized were two publishing operations.

NATO and American forces are proud to have succeeded, without loss of life, the closure of these news sources which were broadcasting and printing anti-UN poisonous propaganda. In future, NATO command will be monitoring all remaining media sources to make certain that they will comply with internationally acceptable standards. Any media source deemed unacceptable with our rules of media information will be promptly shut down by force.

---

implementers of all these practices. No chance is missed, no stone left unturned, no newscast uncensored, no script untouched, no idea un-perused.

We are now familiar with the goals of the Satori in regards to population. The general plan is to reduce world population at any cost. We are informed by no less an authority on the subject than The Club of Rome, and Al Gore, that world human population is to be reduced to below one billion. We also understand about news censorship by omission.

This then, brings us to a special election in California's 22nd Congressional District in 1998. The previous Congressman had died in office and so a special election was called. One of the glaring issues was partial birth abortion, more commonly referred to as infanticide. The opponents of partial birth abortion had prepared some totally un-graphic TV advertisements on this issue, on behalf of Tom Bordonaro, a paraplegic running in the Republican primary on an anti-infanticide platform. Gingrich and the entire Republican establishment began supporting, with money as well as advertising, a late-comer opponent, Assemblyman Brooks Firestone, an ultra-left Republican (for gun control, partial birth abortion, etc.) against conservative Tom Bordonaro. Family Research, a pro-Christian group, wanted to run Tom Bordonaro's ads on the local TV affiliates of ABC, CBS, and NBC. All networks turned down the ads, and refused to run them. The reason given was that they were much too graphic. Not one of the ads showed the partial birth procedure. These are the same networks who bombard society with Friday the 13th, The Alien, An American Werewolf in Paris, and so forth. If that is not censorship, please explain to me what censorship is. The good news is that Bordonaro beat the Gringrich crowd and won the primary.

A process developed by the Satori think-tanks referred to as "People Control," is the act of controlling elections in a manner so that both candidates running will support their basic philosophy. The Bordonaro election is an example of the failure of this process, and demonstrates that we do have a chance. Invariably the root cause of the loss or win in an election boils down to money and media. I have been involved in several national office elections, and can inform you that while outright censorship remains rather rare, the process of inventing a second (staking horse) phony conservative candidate, and then funding him in the primary to split the conservative vote is very common. The process of developing phony opinion polls, linking candidates with a false cause, destruction of advertising, and creation of false issues is just as common. In all this the media plays the major card.

A little Russian history will at this point prove helpful to an understanding of the peculiar political and social positions taken by our media. The Russian rulers, before the communists, were anti-semitic. Over a period of time, this caused Russian Jews to align with the communists. The fact that the communist theorists were also Jews helped this process. At the beginning of the Russian revolution the organizers appointed Commissars (a class of political officer in the military and civil service), almost all of these were Jewish, and it was they who governed Russia under Lenin. This created an unimaginable hatred of Commissars (Jews) within the Russian state. When Stalin succeeded Lenin and the purges began, the first to be purged were the Commissars, and an entire anti-semitic hysteria engulfed the country. Worldwide, however, many Jews influenced by their previous success in a communist state became communists, or at the very least communist sympathizers. This is the reason behind the fact that most reformed Jews in the world represent a leftist ideology. This is why one of Israel's most potent voting blocks remains to this day, socialist, and why Israel is a socialist nation who, without our foreign aid, would collapse.

Have you heard of Aryan racists? Have you ever met one? Have you watched television to find yourself viewing a program about a black brain surgeon, with a Hispanic nurse and a white Anglo Saxon male janitor? The intelligent black businessman who has uncovered the plot of an evil white businessman to steal his business? How about the wonderfully gifted homosexual artist, who can't find customers for his sensitive art because of some evil white male gallery owner? This is the type of propaganda to which we are subjected by the media. It's in the news, it's in the cinema, it's in theater, and in the soaps. It has reared its ugly head in a newsletter *"Managing Diversity,"* which is primarily designed to replace white Anglo workers with minorities in the workplace.

A principal dispenser of this concerted hate campaign against the white race is one Dr. Harris Sussman who poses questions like "What are white peoples values?" Well, if he does not know perhaps we could start by telling him of: Plato, Socrates, Beethoven, Mozart, Rafael, Michelangelo, Shakespeare and Goethe. Sussman belongs with the likes of Al Sharpton and Morris Dees. All this fits in with cultural diversity programs pushed in the media and in educational institutions.

In another statement by Sussman we hear many white people are weary about their own history. They are having a profound identity crisis. Small wonder with an educational system which is eliminating western civilization from their curriculum, and a media whose sole purpose seems to be the destruction of western civilization's culture and ethics, demonizing western explorers and inventors. They all, to the point of historic inaccuracies, now represent the main stream of educational teaching. Presumption of historic occurrences, i.e. cause and effect in history, are rarely even superficially reviewed, and then with such political bias and falseness as to render the exercise as useless and misdirecting.

The average American, who is continuously bombarded with all this misinformation, has become unsettled and unsure of what his own culture is about. That, it appears, is the exact purpose of this media blitz. Historical revisionism of this type, one might say pioneered by Stalin, is one of the most common media efforts of the last 30 years. Historical inaccuracies, and the actual rewriting of history, has become a stylish routine of newscasters and scriptwriters across the board. History of fact has been replaced by one of fiction by the media. The films *Amistad* and *Roots* are fine examples. Even the fiction is made to serve the espoused purpose of the Satori.

In the news the most ill-treated subjects come in the form of Bosnia, the Middle East, and China. It would be really nice if at least one of the numerous newscasters in New York or Atlanta at least read one volume on the history of the Balkans. It wouldn't hurt the White House staff, either. Public TV had a program on Bosnia last week in which they managed to get so many historic facts wrong that I lost count after 18.

Reporting on China has been unduly influenced by the enormous amount of political bribery to the committee to re-elect the president and the Democratic National Committee, and the fact that the media is the single greatest reason that this cover-up is working. In reporting about the Middle East, most news media sources are slavishly pro-Israel. The fact that over 95% of the media is in Jewish hands would not have anything to do with that, or would it?

This, then, brings us to an interesting issue. The Jewish question — you know — the one no one has the courage to discuss. The reason for this is twofold. First, if you write anything in opposition to Jews you are immediately labeled an anti-semite, or at least a Nazi, which is more than just ridiculous. Second, no Jewish media outlets will publish or distribute it. These are just plain facts. The American media is Jewish controlled, owned and directed. By inculcating themselves in the mantel of victimhood (Holocaust) many in the media, as well as in politics, utilize that issue to deflect critics. The holocaust was 55 years ago, it was a dark chapter in human history, but the media that has created an assumption that Jews were the only victims of World War Two is completely wrong.

On the subject of Holocaust, and because of the continuous manipulation of history and the fact that this issue is hammered into us continuously by the media, I will now inform you of the greatest single holocaust in human history. I include this information because the people who are so vehemently pounding that victimhood drum are the very ones who were responsible for it. The Russian revolution was brought about by the violent overthrow of its duly elected government. Over 50 million Russian Christians were murdered. 900 Eastern Orthodox churches were destroyed. Close to 15 million Russians, due to their adherence to Christianity, were sent to the gulags in Siberia. The violent overthrow of the democratic state created after the abdication of the royal aristocracy of Russia was brought about by a group of Jewish elites who hated the government because of its open, antisemitic positions — it was their turn to be in charge.

The first ten years of the revolution was a totally Jewish event. The principal organizers were: Lenin, Trotsky (born Bornstein), Zinoviec (born Apt'elbaum), Kamenev (born Rosenfeld), and Sverdlov, all of them of Jewish decent. In carring out their plan they needed a cadre of helpers. They were called Commissars, of which 90% were Jewish. Of the 600 main actors who were Commissars in the Russian revolution, 17 were ethnic Russians, 1 was Hungarian, 3 were Poles, 3 Fins, 15 Germans, 11 Americans, and 457 Jews. The Commissars were the people who destroyed the churches, led the army, controlled the secret police, and carried out the orders of the ruling clique. Who financed the Russian revolution? Rothschild of London, Frankfurt & Paris; Shiff, Kuhn, Loeb, of America and Aschberg of Sweden. I can only assume that the continuous diatribe about the Nazis is to prevent your asking about the Communist Russian revolution.

The clearest evidence we have of the media's distortion of news, in this case by omission, is the Israeli Dimona facility. Israel decided in the late 1950's to develop nuclear weapons. Through stealth spying, courage and a helping French hand, they accomplished their dream in the Dimona nuclear weapons plant. Not until 1970 was anything of this ever reported in the American press. Knowledge of the Dimona project was certainly far from a secret. After all it's not as if you could hide a nuclear reactor, as well as conversion plants, weapons assembly facilities, and delivery vehicle production, from sight. In 1970 the *New York Times* was given the go-ahead and in an article written by their Washington, DC reporter, Hendrick Smith, reported not only on Dimona, but also on the fuel reprocessing facility and the Jericho I intermediate solid state missile system. Not one single American news agency picked up the story — not NBC, not ABC, not CBS, not PBS — not one news magazine, not one newspaper.

Smith had obtained the information for reports probably from Carl Duckett, a CIA researcher. Duckett had attempted to make Israeli nuclear weapons production information available to members of our government since the beginning of the Johnson administration, but had been continuously blocked by Johnson policies (Johnson's largest cash contributor, and the only man in his administration that had carte blanc within the administration, was a Mr. Abraham Feinberg, who coincidentally was also a huge contributor to the Dimona project). The CIA director at that time was Richard Helms, who was totally unqualified in dealing with this issue. He had not even taken a physics course in high school, and he actively prevented the State Department and the Defense Department from being made aware of Dimona. In other words, it had been a Johnson administration policy to withhold from our own Defense Department the fact that Israel was a nuclear power.

This then, brings us full circle. We now had a State Department which not only did not know what was going on in the Middle East, but to make matters worse, the majority of State Department officials on the Middle East desk were and are Jewish. This has nothing to do with anti-semites and everything to do with common sense. This is hardly a situation leading to a level-headed and pro-American foreign policy.

The exact same thing can be said of the media. With the ownership and management of every single network media firm in the hands of people of Jewish descent, how can you expect pro-American unbiased news reporting on Middle East issues? By the way — don't give me any of that journalistic independence sop — these guys are no more independent from their employer than you are. On this, as well as other issues, the entire media represents a monolithic view. Or have you perhaps noted a great difference between the reporting of NBC, CBS, ABC, PBS and CNN? I have not. They cover the same stories, in the same general manner, and all omit the same items.

As America was preparing for yet another Middle East conflict (which did not come off), I had to learn from DW (Deutsche Welle) that the Turks had already sent divisional strength military units into Iraq (DW report on 2/09/98). Getting at the truth is a complicated project for Americans.

Flash-Back

Dateline: January 21, 1999

Source: *Schweizerzeit* (Swiss National Newspaper)

Issuance: Alexander Solzhenitsyzn

Media has become the greatest power; greater than the legislative, the police and the judiciary.

One would think that this would differ in the print media — not so. The print media is, for the most part, a follow-me-operation in which the three giants, *New York Times, Washington Post,* and *Wall St. Journal,* are the leaders. It is impossible to separate electronic media from print, publishing, distribution, or entertainment. The reason for this is that the American media is totally controlled by a very small number of firms. 74% of all media including distribution (excluding print media) is controlled by just five firms: Disney, Warner, Sony, Paramount, and Universal (Seagrams) (1995).

Consider that Disney, the largest firm in the industry, is in: movies, cartoons, TV, entertainment, theme parks, news, sports, the arts, publishing, magazines, periodicals, distribution, sales, cruise ships — they are in everything and anything to do with media. Sony, Warner, and the other giants are no different.

This is unhealthy for the nation, it represents too much control in the hands of too small a group. It would be the only place where a Justice Department antitrust case would make sense, at the present time. The largest segment of media is the electronic media of TV and radio. Of those two, TV is substantially more important. This is because audiovisual impressions are many times stronger then audio alone, and at present, represent a larger market as well as a larger growth potential. In the immediate past our government has been busily deregulating all of the electronic media — the promise was to allow for a more diverse and open media. Well, like usual, that is not the case. Instead of more we got less. Mergers and acquisitions by the giants of the industry, plus a healthy dose of downstream program distribution, has resulted in fewer programs, more centralization and more control by the big boys. All this in accordance with Satori plans. The four giants of this industry in programming are Time Warner Inc., Walt Disney Co., Turner Broadcasting, and Viacom Inc. The smaller firms are Dream Works SKG, MCA/Universal. Listed below you will find a layout of the principal electronic media firms:

Walt Disney Company
Market Capitalization: $53 billion
Sales: $18.7 Billion
CEO: Michael Eisner
Employees: 100,000
Legal Council: Stanford M. Litvac
Subsidiaries:
    ABC/Cap. Cities
    ABC TV
    ABC Radio
    ABC Holding
    American Broadcasting
    Buena Vista Home Video
    Buena Vista Int.
    Buena Vista Pictures Dist.
    Buena Vista Marketing
    Buena Vista TV
    Childcare Education
    Disney Inc.
    Disney Art Editions
    Disney Channel
    Disney Cruise Lines
    Disney Development
    Disney Enterprises

Disney Educational Prod.
Disney Interactive
Disney Interfinance
Disney Online
Disney Regional Entertainment
Disney Software
Disney/Sports Ent.
Disney Stores
Disney Vacation Club
Disney Vacation Development
Disneyland International
Dream Quest Images
Eurodisney (39%)
Hollywood Records
Lake Buena Vista Communities
Mighty Ducks (Hockey franchise)
Miamax Films
Reedy Creek Energy Services
Walt Disney Attractions
Walt Disney Co.
Walt Disney Co. Consumer Products
Walt Disney Imagineering Co.
Walt Disney Pictures and TV
Walt Disney Publications
Walt Disney Records
Walt Disney TV & Telecommunications
Walt Disney Travel
Walt Disney World
Wonderland Music Co.

The Walt Disney Company

A.) Walt Disney Pictures Group, Joe Roth, Pres.
Touchstone Pictures
Hollywood Pictures
Caravan Pictures
Miramax Films

B.) Walt Disney Television, 14 million subscribers
  Walt Disney Cable
  Buena Vista TV
  ESPN
  Lifetime TV
  A&E Network
C.) Theme Parks
  Disney World, Orlando
  Epcot Center, Orlando
  Disney Land, Los Angeles
  Tokyo Disney, Japan
  Euro Disney, France
D.) Capital Cities ABC
  ABC TV, 225 affiliates
  ABC Radio, 3,400 affiliates, 11 AM and 10 FM stations
  7 daily newspapers
  Fairchild Publications
  Chilton Publications
  Diversified Publishing

The big players in electronic media are ABC, CBS, NBC, and CNN. None are independent, all are members of a conglomerate group. ABC is only Primus under Pares, a small cog in the Disney empire.

The print media represents an interesting comparison. Most people are of the opinion that their local paper is an independently owned and published product. Nothing could be further from the truth. About 62 million newspapers are sold every day in the USA. They in turn, are published by 1,500 different publications. This, it is assumed, will guarantee a wide variance of opinion in editorial content. Unfortunately not. The first thing any newspaper owner learns is that most of the revenues of the paper are not derived from subscriptions or sales, but from advertising. Therefore, the first rule of any newspaper is don't upset the advertisers. Surely you have heard of Chrysler Corporation's insistence that magazines and newspapers in which they advertise must submit articles in which their corporation is mentioned prior to publication. This has been a long-standing fact of life which is never mentioned by most newspapers.

Freedom House is a foundation whose espoused purpose is to promote an engaged ITS foreign policy, whatever that may mean. Every year they issue a prize to some paper or other for "engaging foreign policy." We learn a great deal more in details of where their information is published and who is on their board of directors. First, there is *Foreign Affairs* (flagship of the Council on Foreign Relations), *the Economist, the New York Times, Washington Post, Wall Street Journal, AP, UPI, Today, Newsweek, Time, Int'l. News and World Report*, and of course all the TV networks. And every one of these are insider Satori-controlled publications. Eleanor Roosevelt was a founder of Freedom House and on the Board of Trustees, CEO is Bette Bao Lord, then a long list of CFR members. That this organization has a hidden agenda goes without saying. They offer this prize to dupe you and me into believing that the recipient actually is doing something of benefit, when in fact the award is for supporting Satori outcome.

The Heavy Hitters

VIACOM, Murray Rothstein (Summer Redstone) CEO
    12 TV Stations, Paramount studios
    12 Radio stations, Ms. Shelly Lansing Pres.
    Showtime
    MTV
    Nickelodeon
    Prentice Hall
    Simon & Schuster
    Pocket Books
TIME WARNER, Gerald Levin CEO
    HBO east/west
    Warner Music (largest recording firm in the world)

Interscope Records
Warner Bothers
Warner Brothers stores
CBS, 20%
Turner Broadcasting, 100% CNN, FCNN, CNN Europe
Time Warner Publishing, Norman Pearstino Pres.
Time
Life
Sports Illustrated
People
Fortune

Rupert Murdoch News Corp.

Fox TV
20th Century Fox

Universal/Seagrams

Edgar Bronfman, CEO (Pres. World Jewish Congress)
Universal Studios

Bronfman is the man behind the effort to blackmail billions from World War II neutrals for the World Jewish Congress. The entire Bronfman fortune stems from prohibition, as did the Kennedy fortune.

Next, we have those advertisers' personal beliefs. Let's assume that I am a homosexual business owner. I give the XYZ newspaper $40,000 worth of advertising per year. I tell the editor that I am sure he understands my position on issues and that I would be disappointed to the point of withdrawing my advertising if he were to publish an article in opposition to my lifestyle. That is exactly how it works.

Now back to the 1,500 newspapers. An examination of ownership leads us to the fascinating conclusion that only 26% of all these 1,500 are independently owned. That means that 390 newspapers are privately owned while 1,110 belong to one or another chain. It gets worse — the largest circulation papers with over 100,000 circulation all belong to chains, and number less than 90.

When we now add to this that most independents lack any real news-staff except for some local issues, they become completely dependent upon the syndicated columns and various wire services. Their national and international news is captive to the syndicates. Diversity is not a newspaper trait. The number of cities which have more than one newspaper is less then 50. Those papers we assume to be independent are not. Consider that all news agencies are dependent upon news wire services. UPI, AP, Reuters, the New York Times Wire Service, etc., which are syndicated services to which virtually every newspaper and media company subscribe. Independents are hard pressed to cover local news, never mind international and national. They thus obtain all information from these controlled services.

Nor need you think that the diversity they are perpetually pushing on the rest of us is reflected in their payrolls. The media mirrors the least racially diverse employment sector in all industry. This, then, inevitably brings us to the giants of the industry — mega-papers. The Newhouse group (largest) owns 26 daily newspapers, 12 TV stations, 87 Cable TV operators, including the Sunday supplement Parade. They also own the New Yorker, Vogue, Mademoiselle, Glamour, Vanity Fair, Bride's, Gentlemen's Quarterly, Self, House and Garden, as well as the entire Conde Nast group of publications. This power house of media has an approximate value of $8 billion and is jointly owned by Samuel and Donald Newhouse.

I can see very little diversity in publishing, and when we get to the big three it gets a great deal worse. The three most potent newspapers in America are the New York Times, the Washington Post, and the Wall Street Journal. The New York Times publisher is Arthur Ochs Sulzberger. Executive editor is Max Frankel, managing editor is Joseph Lelyveld. The group owns another 33 newspapers, 12 magazines, wire services to over 500 newspapers and magazines by subscription. The Washington post owner is Katherine Meyer Graham, the publisher, her son Donald. They also own one of the nation's largest circulation news magazines Newsweek, and in a joint venture with the NY Times they publish the largest US international paper, the International Herald Tribune. The Wall Street journal is owned by the Dow Jones company which in turn is run by Peter R. Kann. They also publish 24 other daily papers including Barons. Major magazines are no different. Over 90% of the American news magazine market is covered by just three publications:

Magazine	Circulation	Owner
Time	4.1 million	Time Warner Comm.
Newsweek	3.2 million	Katharine Graham
US News and World Report	2.3 million	Mortimer Zuckerman

It sort of gives one a warm and fuzzy feeling to know that we are in such fine hands, and that of course, none of these people display any favoritism whatever. None can accuse me of being anti-semitic, because I simply am not. I would feel the same way about the issue if the majority of the media were Arab, Japanese or German controlled. This only represents a small portion of the "Jewishness" of the media. As an American of Swiss Heritage I can clearly say that Mr. Edgar Bronfman, family fortune made in Canada during prohibition in the liqueur business, CEO of Universal Studios, and president of the World Jewish Congress, has to date extorted over one billion dollars from a gullible Swiss nation whose diplomatic corps is in way over their heads. The Media support for this campaign has been unrelenting and unilateral. Inflammatory lies, the latest of which produced by the Simon Wiesentahl Center of Los Angeles, claiming the Jews were singled out and forced into labor camps during WW II in Switzerland. That is a lie. Jews, as well as all interns (that's what they were called) had to work. Were we supposed to put them all onto some sort of welfare program? My father was in the Army from 1939 to 1946. My mother was in the civil defense corps. At age six I was on a farm along with 14 other city children of various ages, where we went to school and helped out on the farm. If a six year old can work so can a bunch of refugees. Switzerland had accepted over 30,000 Jewish refugees, a larger percentage versus population than any other nation in the world. Instead of thanks we are treated to extortion by a man whose family made their fortune in bootlegging.

With regard to the media — remember — it is not necessary to control everything, only the dialogue and the program, everything else simply follows. The upper management and major newscasters are members of the Mandarin class, they are Bilderbergers, CFR, and TC to a man.

Chapter Six

FINANCE

Finance is the forte of the Satori. They own it. They control it. They manipulate it to their own profit. The following excerpts from an article by Richard Timberlake published in *The Freeman*, December 1999, tell us exactly how it works.

"What the Federal Reserve does have is a powerful money-making machine that operates through the offices of its New York bank. In activating this machine to raise rates, the Fed's decision-making board, the Federal Reserve Open-Market Committee (FOMC), issues a directive to the bank's account manager to sell more or buy fewer government securities in New York's financial market . . . Since the Fed is a major player in the government securities market, when it buys fewer securities it causes the price to fall and their interest rate to increase.

"Unlike anyone else who buys something in markets, a Federal Reserve purchase is not made with old money but with brand-new money. *The Fed creates the means of payment.* If the seller of the securities wants cash, the Fed uses its authority to print new Federal Reserve notes. If the seller wants a check, the Fed account manager has the authority to issue one that becomes new bank reserves when deposited. Since the Fed creates new currency and bank reserves to purchase government securities, the securities are perforce *monetized.* They are no longer outstanding debt, but by the alchemy of central banking have been converted into money. Likewise, when the FOMC sells securities or buys fewer than it had been buying, the quantity of

---

Flash-Back

Dateline: 1916

Source: National Economy and Banking System
Sen. Doc. No. 3, No. 233, 76th Congress
1st session, 1939

Issuance: President Woodrow Wilson

That Wilson had second thoughts about the privately owned monopoly of US credit (money) he had helped create, is evidenced by this written remark, placed on file in the Library of Congress in 1939.

> "Our system of credit is concentrated in the Federal Reserve System. The growth of the nation, therefore, and all of our activities, are in the hands of a few men."

---

money in the economy is reduced or its rate of increase is slowed.

"Federal Reserve policy is responsible for the quantity of money — cash and bank deposits — that all households and business firms have in their possession at any moment. Furthermore, all severe price inflations and contractions (such as the one from 1929 to 1933) result from excesses or deficiencies of central bank money. All of which means that the Fed's current role in "fighting inflation" amounts to nothing more than undoing things it should not have done in the first place.

"By controlling the basic stock of money in the U.S. economy, Fed policy determines the general level of all prices."

— *Richard H. Timberlake*

There you have it. The Fed, a privately-owned corporation, controls the basic stock of money in the United States, and this is just the beginning. Their ultimate plan is to create, as they have done in Japan and Korea, small numbers of multinational conglomerates which become the government. In order for you to clearly understand the modus operandi of this cabal let me give an example.

South Korea — The Korean economy is totally controlled by a group of unrelated but interconnected huge conglomerates. These are called the "Chaebol." The nine largest of them are listed below along with the 1997 debt-to-equity ratio of each of them.

Chaebol	Debt-to-Equity Ratio
Hyundai	439%
Samsung	286%
LG	347%
Daewoo	337%
Sungkyong	385%
Ssangyong	409%
Hanjin	556%
Kia	523%
Hanwah	778%

I was a business executive for thirty years, and in that time I was a CEO for over twenty years. There is no way an American business, regardless of size, can borrow amounts of over 200% the value of the business, never mind 778 times its value. Hello global economy. Good morning free trade. So you think that the Mexican bailout was a big deal. Ha! The International Monitory Fund (IMF), funded 18% by your tax dollars, has already agreed to loan $57 billion to Korea, which experts now state will not do the job. There have also been numerous side deals. The total as of December 1997 is over $100 billion. Meanwhile South Korea's available foreign reserve is under $10 billion. As in the previous Mexican/Panamanian bailout most of these funds will be used to repay outstanding debts to Satori banks, out of your taxes. Such a loan represents a massive transfer of American wealth to Satori interests.

By the way — South Korea is only one of the nations — Malaysia, China and the entire Pacific Rim is in the same or similar financial difficulty. The reason for this is simple. For about 15 years America has been financing its government debt by selling various types of Treasury notes. In an effort to keep the American public in a buying mood our national debt has been, for the most part, financed by Pacific Rim nations' purchase of U.S. Treasury notes. The Clinton administration has, on average, reduced the time of these bonds from 30 years to under 10. What this means, in effect, is that these nations hold billions of dollars in short-term paper, coming due daily, which is not actually liquid. All this is being financed by the American consumer's binge of imported goods purchasing. The Fed has been printing more and more money at an ever increasing rate, but this will increase inflation. They have, as one might say, painted themselves into a corner.

What the various bailouts mean is that an American wage earner struggling at an income of $30,000 will be taxed at a higher rate to bail out the very companies which are depressing his income to start with. The only beneficiaries being the Satori, for they make money on all ends of the transaction. First, the interest on the loan; second, the fees for the sale of Treasury notes; third, a fee when interest on notes is collected by them; fourth, interest on the default papers which are guaranteed by government. By the way, don't suffer the delusion that any form of capital risk is taken, because government, by performance bond, guarantees that the lender will be repaid. How would you like to make high interest loans to risky clients, and have the government not only guarantee repayment but also the interest?

In our capitalist system people place their capital at risk by investing in a business or process, which they hope will thrive and develop into a going concern that will pay back the investment with interest. What we are witnessing is the removal of the risk factor by socialist government edict. The capitalist system creates new markets, opportunity, and employment. The socialist model

(National Socialism, or state controlled capitalism) which we are being forced into destroys every one of those benefits.

Now just take a guess who was behind the entire South Korean fiasco. In an article in *The European*, dated Jan. 8-14, 1999, we find an interesting item entitled *"How to be a Billionaire."* It seems that Mr G. Soros was unsatisfied with his present income, which exceeds one billion dollars per year. He devised a strategy to do better. He attacked South Korea's currency forcing a 50% devaluation, reported earnings in this part of the strategy were just over one billion dollars. Every leader in South Korea is livid about this; he shrugs it off, after all, who cares about peoples' ire when you just made a cool billion. Less than six months later Soros is invited into the country. He tells a cheering crowd, which does not understand that they have just been had, that he intends to invest one billion in their economy on exporting companies. He purchases the stock of those firms at a discounted and depressed price and — bingo — exports soar due to the lower prices caused by the devalued currency, and he makes another billion. Not only has he made two billion dollars, in the process he attained every single Satori goal. He increased third world exports, he got the IMF to bail out Korea with your tax dollars, he lowered your standard of living, he made it more difficult for industrialized G10 nations to compete on the international markets, and now has two billion more to do it to the next nation. Ain't international finance grand!

What has happened in the Korean, as well as other Asian markets, is that government, ever anxious to increase their share of the American market, have loaned these firms ridiculous amounts of money. *These* subsides were nothing but a connected effort to take the business away from American producers and give it to the South Korean Chaebol. That, unfortunately, is not the end of the story, but just the beginning. To further understand what is going on we must look at American banks, controlled by Satori interests, and review their exposure on those markets. Once you do this all you need is a small amount of common sense to see the entire thing fall into place. First, these banks, jointly with other financial concerns, fund the political process to the hilt. Second, they pay themselves ridiculous salaries. Third, they make stupid loans to emerging economies in order to achieve higher interest rates. Last but not least, they turn to the suckers, you and me, to bail them out when the loans go bad. This is what was done in Mexico, it is what is being done here. All this while earning billions.

On December 24, 1997 a meeting took place at the Federal Reserve Bank of New York. Attendees were Robert Rubin, then American Secretary of the Treasury, and representatives of the major banks with outstanding loans to the Pacific Rim — Citybank, Chase Manhattan, Bankers Trust and Bank America. The very next day Clinton announced that $1.7 billion from the Emergency Stabilization Fund would be loaned to South Korea. The interesting matter here is that it just happens to be the amount of the loan interest due to American banks. You paid the banks with your taxes.

The largest private investment bank in the world is Goldman Sachs, their profits in 1997 were $3 billion. Goldman's connections with government are nothing if not extraordinary. Robert Rubin, the US Treasury secretary who supervised the Mexican, as well as the Korean and Pacific Rim, bailout was a high ranking official at Goldman before attaining his new position at the Treasury. Furthermore, Goldman advisor Romano Prodi was previously advisor to the Prime Minister of Italy. At the present time Peter Sutherland, CEO of Goldman, has his eye on becoming president of the EC commission, and chairman of GATT. If Sutherland secures that position all they will need is the finance ministerial position in Tokyo and they would be able to control world finance.

To understand how firms like Goldman Sachs operate you must understand that partners in the firm are not paid a salary. That would be just too mundane. They do not get a bonus, either. Instead, partners are renumerated on an annual return on equity stake. This equity they build up over time in the firm is the largest money making enterprise without manufacturing or producing anything. One way such firms make money is through IPO's (Initial Public Offerings). Investment bankers will take a firm public for a fee, which in most cases is about 30% of the equity stake. For example: if you had a business worth $3 million and wanted to make a public offering for, say, $15 million, they would handle the transaction for only $5 million. They take no risk, they offer no guarantee. In most cases they do not invest their own funds. They simply act as broker sellers of your stock and for this they get 30%. Outrageous you may well say, but the laws have all been designed in such a way that there is no other way to go public successfully. Last year America had 7,000 IPO's, 6,000 of them have since gone bust. But firms like Goldman, who get their money up front, did not lose a cent. Goldman is presently heavily investing in South Korean export firms to reap the enormous profits that will be made due to the 50% lower prices after currency devaluation. All this at the expense of American industry. Life is grand for the Satori.

It is interesting to note that the South Korean companies existing under a socialist inspired government largess were not driven by planned corporate profits and expansion, but rather by a nationalistic endeavor to dominate world markets in their fields. In other words, to displace American and European firms with their own. Lee Byung Chull, the founder of Samsung, said it best, "Money is not the objective of our pursuit, we want to contribute to Korea's growth and industrial development." Moreover this ideology permeates the entire South Korean economy. Of the 170 largest Korean businesses in manufacturing almost all of them have debt-to-equity ratios of over 500%. When I ran Widder Corporation with a good asset base, a value of about $3 million, and making a profit, I had a hard time obtaining a rotating bank credit line. Only by personally signing was I able to extend that credit line to 30% of the asset value of the business. Compare that to a 500% of net book value. South Korea went from a complete zero on the world market scale to number 19 in a few short years. When

Korean business had exhausted the South Korean economy in money supply they simply went to foreign banks. According to *Business Week,* estimated outstanding loans by the Chaebol's to foreign (mostly Japanese and American) banks exceeds $65 billion.

This is all very peculiar, when we review Korean economic growth. The Korean economy grew by 9% in 1995, 6.9% in 1996, 5.8% in 1997 and is anticipated to grow a maximum of 0.8% in 1998. Why would banks loan such extraordinary amounts of money to customers in an economy that is contracting, and has no possible way to repay such funds? Instead of forcing Korea to close down their two most ailing banks, Seoul Bank and Korea First, the IMF let the Korean government nationalize them, refinancing them with funds from the International Monitary Fund (IMF). Congratulations — you just paid 18% of the money to refinance two Korean banks, without any equity stake or interest earning potential. But we know who's making big bucks in the transaction, don't we.

Hurrah for the New World Order. This is all within the perimeters of the Satori plan. Only by leveling the playing field economically can they hope to create the New World Order. It is simply impossible to integrate economies which have vastly different national income and wealth levels. This then, leads to the ultimate question of how low the economic level of the original G7 nations must be brought in order to level the playing field. In regards to the United States, it would require a transfer of at least 80% of our national wealth in order to accomplish the Satori plan to integrate the United States into a new world government.

On the political front, we have recently heard from all our Republo-crat legislators, as well as our president, that we have a balanced budget. That is an out and out lie. The projection for a balanced budget is after the turn of the century. We have been told that government is being down-sized. Another lie. Let us examine some spending in various programs and agencies for the year of 1998:

Programs and Agencies	1997	1998	% of increase
World Bank	742	1.110	50%
Bilingual Education	262	354	35%
OPIC	1,440	1 933	34%
Corp. Pub. Broadcasting	250	300	20%
Plome energy asst.	1,000	1,200	20%
Pell Grants	5,919	6,910	17%
BATF (Waco, Ruby Ridge)	467	528	13%
Training & Employment Service	4,716	5,260	12%
Energy conservation	570	627	10%
IRS (which was supposed to be fixed)	7,043	7,643	9%
Impact Aid	730	794	9%
Head Start	3,981	4,305	8%
Goals 2000 (OBE education)	491	530	8%
EPA	6,799	7,300	7%
AID	6,017	6 499	7%
Power Mkting. Admin.	229	244	7%
Legal Services (Lawyer full employment)	283	300	6%
Americorps (Clinton youth)	402	423	5%
Nat. Endow. Humanities	110	111	1%

There you have it — the balanced budget, and a downsizing of government all in one fell swoop. All this with a minor increase of spending, lots of smoke and mirrors and, on just the above programs, an increase of $4,870 million. If that does not convince you that both parties are in the same pocket, I don't know what will.

Gigantic Mergers

As the timetable progresses in the Satori plans, so do mergers. This is particularly the case in banking. America lost over 800 banks in the last decade. As we know, larger is not necessarily better. Service, however, has little to do with their plans. In an effort to increase profits banks are merging left and right. As an example, the largest bank merger in history is the one between Swiss Bank Corporation and the Union Bank of Switzerland. Between the two of them they had already gobbled up Rowe & Pittman in 1985 and then S.G. Warburg in England, as well as others around the world. The proposed merged firm has branch operations, not just correspondents, in over 100 nations, and will have an asset base of over $600 billion, as well as managing about $1 trillion of investors' funds. In addition the bank acts as stockbrokers, insurance company, financial managers, financial advisors, and is involved in dozens of other businesses. The proposed bank will have greater financial clout than 90 percent of the nations in the world. If you represented the Satori, what would you rather control — one gigantic bank like this or hundreds of smaller ones?

Bigger Banks

The two largest banks are the Bank of International Settlements (BIS) which is located in Basel, Switzerland, which oversees loans to other banks internationally, and the IMF International Monitory fund. The IMF is funded 18% by US taxpayers. In November of 1997, Clinton funded the IMF with an additional $3.5 billion. The IMF has been involved in the Mexican bailout and is now engaged in the Korean, Thailand, Malaysia, Indonesia, Philippine and other Pacific Rim bailouts. It is interesting to note that America's then Secretary of the Treasury Robert Rubin's former employer, Goldman Sachs, is heavily involved in loans to the Pacific Rim nations. It was the largest benefactor of the Wall Street banks in the bailout of Mexico. Four times since 1970 the IMF has bailed out Mexico. In the last bailout of $17 billion in new loans, all funds were used to pay interest due to Wall Street banks. In addition the billions previously given to Mexico to prop up the Peso were, by devaluation of that currency, cut in half.

This is Global economics on a grand scale. While Satori controlled institutions level the playing field we pay. We pay with lower incomes, through lower purchasing power, more and higher taxes, and value reduction of our currency. We pay through a lower standard of living. We pay by having to work more hours. We pay by having both adult family members fully employed in order to maintain our standard of living. We pay and pay and pay. The rich get richer and the rest of us get poorer. Power is centralized and wealth is transferred. Whatever you do, don't suffer under the delusion that wealthy people pay higher taxes. Really rich people pay either no taxes or such a small amount as to be embarrassing. If you earned about $75K, I would bet that your tax bill would be higher than that of Rockefeller. He, like Perot, undoubtedly has money invested in tax-free and deductible endeavors.

The IMF was created by the United Nations at the close of the Second World War. Its reported purpose was to stabilize world currencies, if so required. Ever fearful of large and sometimes unpredictable currency fluctuations, the Satori needed an instrument to bail them out of bad loans. This is exactly what the IMF has done, and at an exponentially increased frequency in the last decade. The largest single supporters of the IMF are Wall Street banks. What the IMF actually does is to comfort governmental bungling and socialist schemes. Hunger and currency devaluations have always been the prerogative of government. Not in one instance in world history can it be shown that hunger, pestilence, disease, and currency devaluation were not the direct result of governmental action. This is why an open market, with only minimal governmental interference, produces abundance, and why socialist/communist centralized systems yield the opposite effect.

There are 181 members in the IMF and America funds 18% of it. I can say with absolute certainly that the other 180 economies account for more than 82% of the total wealth of the 181 nation membership. The total subscription is $90 billion, so we contributed $34.2 billion of the total amount. The usable pool of cash available at any one time, according to Shailendra Anjaria, IMF director of external affairs, is $50 billion. In addition to this, a credit line of an additional $25 billion has been arranged with the G10 nations, Switzerland and Saudi Arabia. Major nations receiving IMF largess in the last 10 years have been Russia, the Philippines, Malaysia, Korea, Thailand, and Mexico. Each of these nations required bailouts due to governmental ineptitude, socialist policies, and outright corruption. In effect the IMF mission is to level the international economic playing field and further the Satori plan for a One World Government they control.

The Kodak Story

What does all this have to do with the Rochester, NY, Kodak company? Glad you asked. Kodak's largest volume product is photographic film. For eons they have attempted to sell their film in Japan, only to be blocked by Fuji at every attempt. Japan is the world's second largest consumer of film. Fuji has a market share of 70 percent while Kodak's is under 10%. In 1997 Kodak brought a complaint to the international tribunal of the World Trade Organization (WTO). As in every other case, the WTO ruled against the American Kodak company.

I have had a personal experience with the International Trade Commission, the agency that deals with international trade issues for the Department of Commerce. I can firmly tell you that their decisions have nothing whatever to do with trade, fairness, equity, reason, or law. They are a wholly political animal, dealing in expediency.

In the late 70's my firm, Widder Corp., brought a dumping complaint to the ITC against Robert Bosch Corp. of West Germany. Bosch had begun selling a Nibbler (a sheet metal working tool) that directly competed with our American made unit at a price 34% below their market, i.e., their American wholesale price was 34% lower than their German wholesale price. American prices were lower in retail, trade, and wholesale than their German prices. Discounting their price 34% is dumping, and it is illegal.

We went to the hearing, which required over 200 hours of paperwork to be filled out, in complete confidence. Our case was air tight. We had German and American price lists, discount structures, and OEM pricing of Bosch in Germany and America The first hearing proved inconclusive. The second hearing, with Bosch represented by no less than 5 DC law firms, caused the panel of judges to rule that Widder was only a small firm and that loss of labor would be minimal. Bosch was a large firm, and that although we were right, they would rule for Bosch.

So much for justice and the American way. Results were predictable. Widder went out of the Nibbler business, leaving it to

German firms, who promptly increased their prices, and took over the American market. I lost, Widder lost, American labor lost, consumers lost, prices increased, and the Satori won again. In Kodak's case, the ITC stated that Kodak did not have the right to free and fair access to the Japanese markets.

American firms must not only fight foreign companies, they also get to fight the Justice department (like Microsoft) for ridiculous antitrust action. Kodak announced that they would lay off 16,600 workers, and terminate 5,000 by the end of 1997. While all this was taking place our government was busy bailing out Korean firms whose debt-to-equity ratio was as high as 778%. Say, could that be the solution, do you suppose? If Kodak found a federal bank stupid enough to loan them 778% of their net worth, would Uncle Sam then come and bail them out? I guess, but only if Robert Rubin's firm was the loan agent.

This is in reality what free trade is all about. The destruction of America's manufacturing base, and the conversion of the only world super power to third world status. In the interim, a trade war between Fuji and Kodak finds us with Fuji cutting prices (only on the American market) by as much as 30%, much below Japanese domestic prices. Did the ITC (International Trade Commission) bring a dumping complaint? Hell no — they informed Kodak that, "No, this is not a predatory act, they did it openly. There was no element of surprise." All this has nothing to do with trade and everything to do with Satori control of society and people.

The Microsoft Story

Lest you think that foreign competition is the only worry of American manufacturers, we have the US Department of Justice and Microsoft. The antitrust division of the Justice department has for years picked on successful American firms in an effort to assert their petty authority. IBM comes to mind. They were forced to spend in the neighborhood of $25 million defending themselves, only to be vindicated. Needless to say the government did not reimburse the stockholders for the unprecedented loss. In the current Microsoft case, the Department of Justice claims that Microsoft licenses their Windows 95 to personal computer manufacturers (right so far), but they then say that they force these manufacturers to accept Microsoft's Internet Browser called Explorer. (They get this additional option for free.) Justice, however, sees this in a different light. They claim this to be a tying agreement in violation of a previously agreed upon arrangement reached between Justice and Microsoft.

I have Windows 95. I don't use their browser. Neither I nor anyone else I know has a problem with this. What this actually is, is a bunch of stupid, misdirected government employees in Washington who lack the courage to go after the DNC for money laundering, illegal campaign contributions, conspiracy and treason, and as a consequence waste taxpayers money on a witch hunt that is destructive of taxpayers interest, Microsoft, and American competitive edge. Just what the Satori ordered!

China, The Wild Card

Into a financially chaotic world steps Mr. Wang Jun, who is, one might say, the CEO of communist China. China has been running a $40 billion trade surplus with the United States for the past few years. It is assumed, due to their reissued most favored nation status, this surplus will continue to rise. China is a totalitarian state. This in effect means that Mr. Jun controls all the basic assets of the PRC. He is chairman of China International Trust and Investment Corporation (CITCI). It is a ministry level organization, with 36 subsidiaries worldwide. It is engaged in trade, export/import, manufacturing, petroleum, transportation and finance. There are additional subsidiaries in North and South America, Europe, and Australia. They even own a gold mine in Colorado. Mr. Jun is also Chairman of Poly Group Corp. (PGC), a wholly-owned subsidiary of the People's Liberation Army (PLA). The PGC imported automatic AK 47's for distribution to gangs in Los Angeles, CA. In May of 1996 fourteen members of Poly Technologies, another subsidiary Jun controls, were charged by the US Justice Department in the attempted sale of the aforementioned AK 47's, modified to full automatic. PGC is also the company which sells military hardware, including missiles and nuclear technology, to many of the rogue states of the world: ship to ship missiles to Iran, nuclear equipment to Pakistan, ground to ground missiles to Libya, etc. In February of 1997 Jun met with Clinton in the White House for tea. We do not want to discuss in this book the huge amounts of cash which subsequently flowed into the coffers of the DNC and the Committee to re-elect the president from that meeting.

China will be the world's largest economy shortly after the turn of the century. The exact date is only determined upon how much longer we give them most favored nation status, and tolerate a $40 billion deficit per year. Attempting to contain China without trade action is a waste of time. With the incorporation of Hong Kong into the PRC, Mr. Jun's financial fortunes have improved dramatically. China, at the present time, holds $67 billion in U S Treasury notes (these are the ones we know about).

Let me now give you a speculative scenario. Just before the congressional deliberations for China's MFN status, Mr. Greenspan gets a telephone call, "Good morning, Mr. Greenspan, this is Wang Jun in China. I would look favorably upon your nation's extension of MFN to us. We do hold $67 billion of your debt and would hate to have to divest ourselves of it." "Yes, Mr. Jun, I can assure you absolutely that MFN status will be confirmed by the US Senate immediately." We were over the proverbial barrel. It could not have taken Greenspan more then 3 seconds to agree to do as Jun suggested. China, you see, has been unwittingly financing Satori plans for the last ten years. But now the chickens, as they say, have come home to roost, and the chickens seem to be calling the shots. The end result meets, or even exceeds, Satori goals: the transfer of American wealth to make possible their New World Order. The question is — will China one day decide to control it?

Global Financial Chaos

Commencing in the summer of 1997 and spreading all over the Pacific Rim nations, financial chaos is now endemic around the world. Thailand was first. It then spread to Communist China, Japan (whose economy has been shaky ever since the overvalued real estate crash in Tokyo), and then all the rest of the Asian Tigers. Russia, for all intent and purposes, is completely in the tank. None can argue that this financial virus has not spread around the entire world. We can also clearly see the hand of the Satori in this, along with the speculative profits they have reaped. It was sparked by a currency collapse in Thailand which then triggered a failure of the Thai stock market. From there it spread to Malaysia and then in order, to the Philippines, Indonesia, Hong Kong, Taiwan, Communist China, South Korea, and finally to Japan. Hong Kong's market dropped 40% while the Japanese market took a 36% hit. Almost immediately all other markets responded — our US market lost one trillion in value in one day (13% of value). This was the single largest drop in market value in world history, greater than the 1920's, or the great German inflation. All this was followed up with the largest bailouts in world history of over $200 billion in public funds to bailout Satori investments. Subsequent payments cannot, at the time of writing, be estimated but the total amount is in excess of one trillion dollars. Understand that no individual investors were bailed out — only Satori banks. This is not only without precedence but it is completely illegal — to use public funds (your tax dollars) to bail out large multinational banking enterprises.

Since the inception of the Clinton administration this has been taking place continuously. Mexico, Malaysia, Indonesia, Thailand, Japan, Hong Kong, every one of them have been bailed out by your taxes. In fact, none of the funds actually go to those nations. What you are not told is that the funds appropriated to those countries actually go to the bankers who made the bad loans to those nations. Your taxes are being diverted to Satori banks. The words normally associated with such a market collapse were completely omitted: *crash, collapse, Black Monday,* were not heard. Instead we were treated to a soft pedal of the situation with: *drop, tremble, tumble,* and *unrest.* The worst was yet to come. Then we were informed that this drop represented a marvelous buying opportunity, in fact, the words used were: *A silver lining. Buying opportunity of the Century. Only a temporary correction. Economic stability of the underlying stock prices is unquestioned.* Pure rubbish. No market since the beginning of time has ever steadily gone up, and to make such a prediction is irresponsible.

At the present time we have the development of a worldwide deflationary cycle. This is when production outstrips demand. This has been brought about by various Satori sponsored initiatives. First of these is population reduction through reduced birthrates. Euthanasia is now commonly practiced in Europe. Birthrates in America, Switzerland, Germany, France, and most of the industrialized nations is now static, if not declining. The populations in those nations are, as percentages, changing to one of a larger number of older people then young. Old people purchase less, spend less, and don't have children.

Our Economy

Reported in the media that we have the strongest, most robust economy in history, is just plain untrue. All statistics emanating from "Disneyland on the Potomac" can be assumed to have been concocted by "Goofy" himself. What is taking place as you read is the incremental devaluation of income levels of wage earners, and the change in America from a manufacturing-based society to a service oriented one. No nation can hope to survive the 21st century grounded in a service economy. Third world nations are based in service economies. The government vastly overstates personal income statistics — they understate unemployment and inflation. Pick any commodity at all — according to the government, inflation is non-existent. Name one line of goods whose price has been static for the last 12 months. There are none.

Added to this are personal bankruptcies. In 1984 the incidence per thousand was about 70. Today we are at 360, the highest level in the history of the Republic. Since 1990 over 7 million households have gone bankrupt. Consumer debt in 1997 topped out at one trillion two hundred and twenty eight billion dollars. This is sick. Americans have been instructed to live beyond their means, and as a consequence we have become the most materialistic society in history. Along with materialism always comes self-indulgence, perversion, self-engrandisment, hedonism, and the destruction of the state. Rome, Greece, Babylon, we surely have ample historic samples to examine. Clinton reported, "The administration is proud to announce that we have the US deficit under control. It will be only $22 billion in 1997" (November 5, 1997). The December figures reported show this to be a lie. Again, the latest figure is officially reported at $5.421 trillion. In December of 1996 the reported number was $5.232 trillion, this indicates an increase of $189 billion. Note that those figures do not contain $81 billion taken from social security that year. Nor do they include all the unfunded mandates of the government.

I do not make predictions. I am unable to see into the future, but surely all the aforementioned Satori concocted financial information gives one cause for reflection.

As there is considerable confusion about political and economic systems I shall now offer some explanations which I hope will help you understand these better. These terms are often thrown about, especially by the media, people who have no factual idea what they really mean.

CAPITALISM: There are three basic forms of capitalism, the first of which we most commonly think of as related to "Free Markets." Capitalism in this sense refers to independent producers who use "capital" equipment to produce a good. For example let's use a machine tool company, manufacturing power and machine tools as I used to do. A "capitalist" is an individual who purchases capital goods and uses them to provide a product to the market.

The second form of capitalist can be, and often is, a government. The US Army, Navy, and Air Force are all capitalists in that they produce much of their own equipment, thus we have government capitalism. This becomes much more pronounced in a "Command Control" economy like existed in the USSR where the government becomes the sole capitalist. The third form of capitalism is "Financial Capitalism." It is the control of the capitalist function by the financial markets through control of investment capital (money). This clearly shows that when we use the word Capitalist we must very carefully explain what it is we actually refer to.

We notice that even in a closed communist system, capitalism, and I may say profit, coexist with communism. It is a fact that modern technological societies cannot function without capitalists. For example, the Soviet central bank, the Gosbank, controlled all Soviet financial transactions. It was the ultimate capitalist system because industry, production, and manufacturing were all dominated by one single banking system which acted as the "Financial Capitalist."

DEMOCRACY: In this system, government is ruled by the will of the people. What his means is that law is malleable and may constantly change with the will of the people. It eliminates moral absolutes, because public opinion sways legal procedure, and law, to come within compliance of current dogma. This is one of the worst forms of governance one can imagine. It opens the possibility of corrupting statute (laws) ad infinitum. Thus it allows government the opportunity of mischief. By changing law continuously citizens lose sight of what the law is and government utilizes this advantage. As Seneca stated, "Government is ill constructed when the mob rules its leaders." Unfortunately this is the type of governance America has degenerated to, thanks to Judicial Activism. Need I add that a controlled media influences and directs the mob to the benefit of the Satori?

REPUBLIC: A republic is a state ruled over by a written law (constitution). Laws are absolute and defined. Through it we have an inculcated principal in laws as written by the framers of those laws. In the United States the founding fathers created a Constitutional Republic. As Franklin said, "If you can keep it." We are doing a poor job at that.

COMMUNISM: This is socialism in a hurry. What I mean is that communists, at least in the current vein, believe in the violent overthrowing of any opposing systems, while socialists believe in the gradual erosion of opposing systems.

SOCIALISM: This is the most evil political economic system developed in man's history. It is directly responsible, in the 20th century, for more mayhem, murder, starvation, pestilence, and death than all the combined wars of the previous 3000 years. It is not unreasonable to state that over one billion people have lost their lives due to socialism. The concept of socialism is that the state (government) should be the sole capitalist and property owner. All property is owned by all the people through their government. Herein lies the rub. The government thus requires a huge, inefficient bureaucracy to administer everything. The bureaucrats (mandarins) become abusive with power, which is absolute. The rulers (Satori) promise the people everything, and when unable to deliver, the system in every known instance immediately deteriorates into an authoritarian dictatorship, and eventually economic collapse.

FEUDALISM: This is the system most recently in use in Japan and many third world countries. Europe was ruled this way through the middle ages, in many regions, until the First World War. The system is based on a relationship of rule of "Lord" and "Serf." The lord owns everything and the serf is his servant. The servant is tied to the land, which the lord owns. Realize here and now that the current attempts to construct a New World Order are in fact the process of creating a worldwide socialist (international socialist) feudalistic autocratic political system. Such a system is based on State and Private Capitalism, very much like the Nazi system, but worldwide. It is envisioned by the Satori to create a linked system between huge multinational corporations and a centrally controlled "UN" government which is staffed by the Satori's Mandarins, and whose power is absolute. When it was said, "Marx is out, Keynes is the new Radicalism," this is exactly what was meant.

IDEAS HAVE CONSEQUENCES

"After WWII, I began to sense the ways in which economics, politics and theology are mutually implicated; I understood for the first time why theology had once been called 'The Queen of Sciences.' I came to realize that many of the modern world's ills are due to the fact that politics (whose symbol is power) and economics (whose symbol is wealth) have usurped a role in our lives which borders on idolatry. This usurpation occurs because the western religious vision has dimmed; the dimension of transcendence is no longer a vibrant part of modern temper. Such are among the consequences of embracing certain unsound ideas."

— THE REVEREND EDMUND A. OPITZ, 5/12/89

CHAPTER SEVEN

CHILDREN AND RELIGION

Hitler was one of the first in this century to recognize the importance of child indoctrination for political and social ends, and the political use of children to sway their parents into social acts supporting his party. The Satori have learned this lesson well and through several surrogate organizations have been on a rigorous campaign to indoctrinate our youth. One of the establishments utilized to these ends is the National Education Association (NEA). This is the largest union in America. They are the furthest to the left of any union in the United States. They utilize laws instituted under the guise of protecting special classes of citizens in order to further Satori gains.

The Disabilities Education Act of 1975 is one of these statutes. This particular law restricts individual public schools from disciplining problem children by saying that they are disabled. According to the *Wall Street Journal* (May 14, 1997), the law is presently under review and is to be rewritten, but the new proposals will not strengthen the ability of schools to deal with the unruly child problem. The process is called *"Inclusion."* Children with disabilities are not handled separately, nor are they segregated into special classes. They are *"Mainstreamed"* into the general student population. Now comes the problem of defining exactly what a disability actually is. Unfortunately it's anything the NEA or the principal or the teacher desires it to be. Let's assume that we have a child who disrupts the class, starts fights, is abusive to other children and swears at the teacher. Such a child will be labeled as being disabled. What absolute crap.

Unfortunately in today's America, spankings are out and drugs are in. The single most popular method of dealing with active, stupid or intelligent children is to drug them. As a past member of a school board I have heard the statement that we do not have undisciplined children in this school. That statement is beyond the pale, it's a stupid statement. We all went to school and we know very well that there are kids, who, if not disciplined, just get worse as they figure out they can get away with it.

Standards have been lowered in all education. The last graduating class at Harvard had 84% of the senior class graduate with honors. What the heck does it mean to be a Harvard graduate with honors when everyone gets them? What does it mean to graduate from Sara Lawrence, the prestigious (formerly girl's) College, when we learn that you are not required to take one single exam on any subject and can still graduate? This then brings us to *"Grading Systems."* No one fails in modern education. In a prominent NH public school the average mark in fifth grade was 89%. Teachers interviewed said that parents complained if their little darlings did not at least get a B. Outcome-based education brought to its zenith. Parents dictating what their child's grade is to be before the child has even entered the classroom. The major effort is not education, learning, or self-improvement, but a concerted effort to make the child feel good about himself.

"Developmental Education" is another vehicle. According to the *Cider Press*, summer 1995, "The essence of developmental education is not just what we do, but how we think about education and about our children." It is the step of relinquishing individual excellence and achievement and replacing it with the team process of *"Cooperative Learning."* Just in case you don't know, that is the process by which children are grouped, usually in fives, always making sure that one of the five is smart, and then working out the problem or assignment as a team. Naturally, the smart kid winds up doing all the work while the rest goof off and learn nothing. The group then gets the grade of the scholar, and — bingo — the school gets a higher rating, as does the teacher. This entire team concept is contrary to everything America stands for. It is an alien con-

cept, it is destructive, it is anti-education, and it is collectivism. It gets worse — the developmental education programs give teachers great latitude to approach the subject in their own way. Thus the teacher is free to instruct your child in whatever social, moral or even political theories they prefer. Through these systems it becomes impossible to review the progress your child is making. It becomes impossible to gauge the competence of the school system. You don't even know what your child is learning.

These systems are workable in most courses, because the teachers make up the examinations, as well as grading them. One would think that in mathematics this would represent an insurmountable problem. 2 x 2 = 4 is correct. 2 x 2 = 5 is wrong. Well, not exactly. According to the new grading systems you grade 50% on effort, 20% on content, and 30% on right or wrong. Soooo, 2 x 2 = 5 gets you a grade of 70%. It actually gets worse — in many secondary, and even high schools, grades are being inflated based on the concept of attendance. In other words, all you have to do to pass is show up.

It is notable that the entire philosophy of modern education leads us directly back to the turn of the last century and Germany. The very concept of public, i.e., tax-funded state-sponsored, education is a German concept. If we now think of the results of that system in Germany, the First as well as the Second World War, we become much more attuned to the actual purpose of this system. State sponsored public education is permanently formatted to benefit the state. In opposition to this we have private education, which is formatted to benefit the student. Everything fostered in present American public education, and I do speak from a point of knowledge, is directed at building a submissive-to-the-state citizen. The political education necessary for any citizen in a republican state, which will enable him to reach correct decisions when voting on issues, is completely omitted from the curriculum. I have actually heard a social science teacher inform her students that America was a democracy. When I corrected her she was unable to differentiate between a Republic and a Democracy. If you don't know that, you should not be teaching in any school system.

It is much the same on economic issues. When I lived in Connecticut, I gave a lecture to teachers at the University of Bridgeport. The topic was the economics of modern business. Not one single teacher out of a class of 40 was able to guess, within a margin of 10, what the average profit margin of a manufacturing concern was. The majority thought it was around 35%. When I informed them that most manufacturers work on after-tax margins of under 5% they would not believe me. Our problem with education is not only the NEA, the curriculum, the textbooks, or the lack of discipline, but more than anything the unqualified teaching staff. In June of 1998, 59% of all new teachers to be hired for Massachusetts schools failed a test given them prior to employment. On a second chance 48% failed. The test, which I have seen, is not difficult — any high school graduate from the 70's could pass it.

The majority of public elementary school teachers are totally unqualified to teach anything. Teachers colleges are the easiest higher education alternative. When I was on the school board in NH, a state whose education level was in the top 10 states, and which expends one of the lowest per pupil outlays in America, we had many problems with payroll. Teachers salaries stand at about $22,000 for full-time. On top of this was a social benefit package amounting on average to $7,500, a total of $29,500 for 40 weeks of work per year. At that time the average college graduate in NH had a starting salary of $21,500, on a statewide basis, for 51 weeks of work per year. This demonstrates that we paid teachers on average a starting salary of $8,500 more than the private sector. We had a 6th grade teacher who made $56,800 including benefits. He had been teaching 6th grade for over 10 years.

Once children become adolescents the game changes. Hitler created a replacement for the Pfadfinder (Boyscouts), and called it the Hitler youth (Hitlerjugend). Clinton created Americorps (Clinton youth). We were told that the purpose of Americorps was to teach adolescents the necessary skills to keep and maintain a job. What the entire program demonstrates is that it has nothing whatever to do with teaching anything, except how to be a good party follower. First, the General Accounting Office (GAO) informed us that the entire program was so mismanaged that an accounting audit was impossible. Then the administration asked for, and received from Congress, an increase in funding. The program was then expanded. In 1998 Clinton again proposed an expansion of the program. Not one of the revisions recommended by the GAO have been implemented. Reasoning for this is very difficult to follow. Why would a Republican majority in both houses authorize an increase of funding for a program whose sole purpose is the creation of "New Democrats?" Clinton youth is by design, operation, management, and function a device to train young people for political activism in the Democrat party. Annual costs of operation per person runs from a low of $8,500 to a high of over $45,000 when administered by the US Navy. Like all government run programs, more money is consumed in management, payroll, and operational costs than anything else. Not one member of the Clinton youth can be shown to have learned a skill, job, nor anything else of personal value. Community service projects may be nice and even serve a purpose, but they should be carried out by unpaid volunteers, not by salaried government Clinton youth. To add insult to injury we are continuously told the Clinton youth members are volunteers. They are not. This is all further indoctrination by government of its citizens toward the brave New World Order.

The education of youth in the past was the process by which our children were brought to civilization, the process by which we instilled in them the meaning of our civilization, our culture and an understanding of ethical behavior. Multi-culturalism, the destruction of western culture, ethics, and the process of civilized behavior is the vehicle utilized by the NEA to destroy those values. The entire concept of a multi-cultured society is ridiculous. It is founded on the totally false concept that different cultures have similar value systems and are compatible. This is a myth. The concepts of group education, i.e. *Team Teaching,* is likewise a fallacy. Just as the false *Equality* notions. Team teaching, multi-culturalism, and equality are the concepts which are used by the NEA to destroy our culture, and along with it our republic. So different are many cultures from one another that the very notion of assembling them is ludicrous. The core belief of multi-culturalism lies in the notion that all other cultures are at war with western culture and civilization. If that is the case, why then is everyone in the world attempting to emulate us? The concept of multi-culturalism is, as the British philosopher Thomas Hobbs (1678) called it, "The war of all against all."

Value systems between cultures vary greatly. For instance, the concept of private property is undefined in the languages of Australian Aborigines and most nomadic cultures. It is the backbone of western civilization, and only since the concept of private property has become commonplace has civilization flourished. The idea that we as individuals are equal is so stupid that one would think it unnecessary to even mention it. Equality before the law, however, is an entirely different concept. To link civil rights to the premise that we as creatures are equal physically, mentally, and spiritually is false. The preposterous notion that women are able to compete with men in a combative action. Example: On Saturday evening February 14, 1997, a young female police officer was overpowered by a 20 year old hoodlum who proceeded to beat her with her own nightstick. In self defense she had to kill him with her gun. Might the outcome have been different if the police officer was a 220 pound male? Another example: I am not equal physically to Mike Tyson. He could beat me to a pulp with both hands tied. I am not equal to my wife. I cannot bear children. I am not intellectually equal to a Thomas Jefferson. This does not make me any less of a man, all of us have abilities in different ways and in different fields. We are, however, not equal.

The contemporary conception of late, the darling of the revisionists, is *Team*. This foolish sentiment is to be found in business, education and government. The idea is that a group of people will come up with a better way than will an individual. OK, let's say that's correct. Now list all the great inventions, developments and ideas which evolved through team effort. Literature is out. Mechanics are out. Optics are out. I cannot come up with one great achievement of man, with the exception of the Constitution of the United States, that were team efforts.

All of the concepts, as taught to our children today, may be seen as wanting. The worst of these is the total failure of today's educational systems to teach our children a fundamental understanding of our government and those of other political systems. They are unable to distinguish right from wrong (this is evidenced in a recent poll showing that 74% of the population think that the president's lying, adultery, bearing false witness, perjury, and the inducement of others to perjure themselves is irrelevant in holding the office of president). They are unable to act on their own and require a team effort for every action.

If you do not understand how the government works, or what the various functions of government are, or indeed what types of other options in governance exist, then you are unable to exercise your right to vote in a intelligent manner. Such a population will eventually come to a despotic leadership. Such is the plan of the Satori.

Our educational system has become nothing more than a program to instill our youth with socialist concepts in which all rights are granted by government. And, the National Teachers Association (NEA) has a death grip on the process.

Of course, Americans probably should have known that a socialist educational system (the government taxes everyone to give free benefits to some) would teach the students that income redistribution and government control (Socialism) is the "American Way."

To correct this situation we must begin by regaining local control of our schools, in which parents have a strong voice. I presented such a plan to the New Hampshire Legislature. You may have other ideas as to how local control can be re-established, and ideas how to gain it through local financing.

The best solution would be to privatize education. Doing so would improve education through competition between schools and reduce costs. The reduced taxes would help parents pay for the education they want their children to have. Churches and other charitable organizations are the non-governmental agencies that should provide education (or education funds) to indigent parents. However, to go from almost 100 years of a socialist education system directly to a private system may be too big a step. Therefore, the plan I presented to the NH Legislature centers on local schools, local financing and local control with tax credits to encourage the development of private sector schools to instill competition into the educational marketplace. Here is the concept I proposed.

A Logical School Tax Proposal
By the Author to the NH Legislature

Now that the ABC plan has finally been rejected, hopefully for the last and final time we can all apply ourselves to a solution to the court-ordered equalization of educational costs. It must at the outset be stated, and clearly so, that the requirement of the court is in violation of the state and federal constitution, and that the justices have, through Judicial Activism (JA), exceeded their authority. It behooves us to also reflect on Arcticle 28, NH Constitution, which prohibits all, except duly elected members of the legislature, to levy taxes. The judicial act may therefore, be moot. Furthermore it is unrealistic to equalize educational expense statewide, because it costs more to live and work in Nashua than in Lancaster. This act also opens the possibility of creating a precedence in civil employment, thereby opening similar action for fire and police departments. That said, it is necessary to address three different and separate issues.

The three issues are:

1.) How to collect the tax on an equitable basis,
2.) How to develop a cost containment model,
3.) How to ensure an improved graduating student.

The Proposed Tax:

All present taxes are collected by local towns for regional schools. In order to maintain local control over education, that should remain the practice. To make collected funds equitable we need only a statewide formula equally applied to each district, and based on an alike cost. Therefore:

1.) The state adopts the total cost of education number for NH, as reported by the USDC Statistical abstract (cost per student abstract NH) of the United States statewide, and multiplies it by the number of school aged children in the state.
2.) Each town has their assessor count the exact number of bedrooms in each dwelling within his jurisdiction.
3.) The total number of bedrooms (2) is divided into the number derived at for the cost of education (1) total cost, (number of student multiplied state-wide).
4.) The arrived at number is applied to each dwelling as the assessed cost of education. Taxes are collected locally same as now.
5.) No property owner or renter over the age of 65 pays the tax.
6.) Renters, not landlords, pay the tax (reduction of rents by the landlord equivalent to savings mandated, but cost assumption by the renter for the tax burden now indirectly applied, empty apartments are not taxed). Renters get tax deduction on federal returns.
7.) Special Education funding is in violation of the NH Constitution Article 28-a. The attorney general of the state is to institute legal action to eliminate this program in its present configuration. Until legal matters are settled it is to be

capped at either 2 times the per child cost #(1), or the total amount contributed by the federal government. Continuing education funds are to be eliminated for individuals judged by two medical doctors as incapable of learning.

8.) Welfare recipients living in either title 8 housing or whose rent is paid by the state or federal government will have those funds directly paid to the school district.

9.) Commercial properties are assessed based on a dollar number per sq. ft. annually. Amount to be arrived at.

This we believe will be acceptable to the courts, and is a fair solution to a difficult problem.

Cost Containment:

That brings us to the very troublesome problem of cost containment, in an educational process that everyone will agree has gone awry. At present American education is rated number 19th in mathematics, 16th in science, and 35th in literacy worldwide, and New Hampshire is now in the bottom of the bottom third nationally. We cannot accept this — it is unsatisfactory. We believe the major cause to be the NEA, the teachers union. To rectify this New Hampshire education must return to a policy of open employment; educational employment must be instituted with "Right to Work" legislation. Furthermore school districts are no longer to pay for: Teachers Union dues, Teachers Association dues, Principals Association dues, NH School Board Association dues, and Superintendents Association dues. Also the processes of "Tenure" as well as the practice of "Paid Sabbaticals" must be terminated. We do not oppose collective bargaining, we strongly oppose forced unionization. In the case of the NEA, we oppose most of their undesirable and failed education programs, as well as political meddling.

Educational Improvement

To improve the outcome product we believe that just as in the private sector the product, in this case the students, be tested in aptitude upon finishing a subject. This should come into play in the teachers financial remuneration, as well as advancement in position. The process of increasing pay, due to time in system, step increases, and lofty degrees must be put to an end. Just because a person has a Ph.D. and has been teaching for many years or has a master's degree does not mean that they are a better teacher. All teachers must pass a competency test upon seeking employment, and be periodically tested in all subjects offered in the school of employment (excluding languages). The only determination of a teacher's competence is the performance of the students upon completion of the class, assuming the students are of average IQ. When IQ of students is below average, these factors must be incorporated in a review of the teacher's competence. Therefore, the state should issue a test to be different each year for every subject offered in every grade (similar to the Regents system in New York). Social promotions, the practice of advancing students who fail, is to be stopped. Test for student competency should be delivered to each school, sealed, 3 days prior to testing of the students. Parents and administrators will know exactly who the good teachers are after the grading of the tests. They will also know who deserves a bonus and advancement, and who should be removed.

Religion

There are two avenues being persued by the Satori in the field of religion. These are Pantheism, based on Gaia the earth goddess; Secular Humanism, which is atheism and socialism. It is intended that Gaia worship will succeed over Secular Humanism in the end. Secular Humanism is simply a vehicle on the way to the pantheism of Gaia worship. Socialism, on the other hand, is the old Fabian political and social spoilage system, elevated to a religion by the Fabians.

Secular Humanism adherents state that they accept a view of philosophy called naturalism. This means that they believe that the physical laws of the universe are natural and that no super-natural being or spiritual structure exists beyond man. They believe man to be the supreme being in the scheme of nature, and that nothing above man exists. All Secular Humanists describe themselves as atheists (without the belief in God, gods, or super-natural beings). On their home page on the Internet they try to imply that Secular Humanism dates back to the Greeks and Epicureans as well as the Stoics. That is simply not so. Secular Humanism is an advent of the late nineteenth century, and a product of the early Satori. Numerous so called intellectuals were adherents of this philosophy. It was an outgrowth of the German philosophies of Hegler, Nizsche, Kant, etc. It wound up giving the world Communism, Socialism, and Nazism. Federal courts have ruled that Secular Humanism is a religion. There are numerous public institutions which subscribe to this religion and among these are the National Educational Association (NEA), The Socialist Party of America, the Communist Party U.S.A. (CPUSA), along with a whole raft of would be intellectuals.

It's very trendy to be a Secular Humanist. They are at the fore-front in efforts to undermine the republic. They are behind the movements to remove from US coinage the phrase "In God We Trust." They were behind the efforts that removed prayer from our schools. They are behind the efforts to remove the Ten Commandments from public buildings, and they are behind the efforts to strike any reference to God in any public document. As we have become informed by the courts that Secular Humanism is a religion, would it be reasonable for monotheists to bring a legal action in the courts to halt the teaching of the Secular Humanist religion in public schools? I for one will not hold my breath for that occurrence. A large percentage of mainline Protestant churches are closer to secular Humanism than to Christianity.

They are the handmaidens of the Satori in all efforts to destabilize organized religion and replace it with the new pantheism of Gaia worship. On Public TV, October 10, 1997, Roberta Nelson, a

Unitarian Universalist minister from Massachusetts, was busily defending a new program introduced by her and her Church. The interviewer, Bryant Gumbel, an icon of political correctness and left wing espousement, was questioning her about their new program using a film for sex education of 12 and 13 year olds. The film is, to say the least, explicit. The film includes graphic descriptions of lesbians and homosexuals, autoerotic techniques, and transvestitism. The program is called "About Your Sexuality" (AYS). So explicit is the material that Concord, MA concerned parents found it very difficult to view. The Unitarian atheist program is now in use in over 300 of their meeting places, and has been used since 1972.

Gaia

Pantheism is nothing new. As a religion it predates Judaism and Christianity, as well as Islam. Gaia is a female goddess which may be linked to the female fertility goddesses of the Celtic culture, as well as numerous Middle Eastern ones. The basic concept is that God, i.e. Gaia, is in everything. American Indians are often depicted as believing in such a female deity. This is untrue. Gaia worship does not stem from the Americas.

Pantheism is the preferred religion of the Satori because it represents an easy way by which one can manipulate people. More than that, it ties in very well with environmental issues, and through them into socialism. The fact that Religion, Environmentalism, Socialism, and Communism are interrelated in Satori plans is indisputable.

Interfaith Center on Corporate Responsibility (ICCR)

Let us first understand that there is lots of money in all this religious and environmental nonsense. Membership for an association in ICCR is a flat $2,000. Individual membership is a mere $600. When you consider that the head of the Ford Foundation draws a salary of $900,000 per year, you have to understand that all the others must be able to at least keep up appearances. Naturally, like all other such organizations, ICCR is tax exempt. What kind of actions does the ICCR boast about? Challenging business on sweat shops, global warming, landmines, affirmative action, equal opportunity employment, etc. I like to think of those issues differently: hard work is how you succeed, there is no global warming, landmines without Iraq, Chinese, Libyan, Iranian, and North Korean participation is unworkable, affirmative action is racial preference, and equal opportunity comes with skill and perseverance — it is inherent in free enterprise.

The ICCR can be considered so thoroughly infiltrated by Satori agents that they are a shill for them. They were behind the extortion of millions of dollars from Texaco in racial litigation. They are behind the diversity movement; they push ridiculous glass ceiling issues, in fact there is not one left wing issue in which they are not at least peripherally involved. These people have been more than just successful in pushing their particular brand of anti-capitalist rhetoric. To date 275 well-meaning religious denominations have been sucked into their convoluted plans. The list of American manufacturers under assault is over 250 firms.

As for the Wall Street Project, Community Lesbian & Gay Rights Institute, etc., how much cash do they raise, and how is it distributed? Their income — $988,836. Salaries — $535,341. Just show me one public or privately held corporation that is under their assault who pays out 54% of their income in salaries. The stockholders would fire the entire board of directors.

In their corporate responsibility crusade the first item mentioned is forced labor. Fine. I agree it is reprehensible for an American firm to sell products produced in slavery. The largest supplier of slave labor produced products into the United States is Communist China (PRC). Not one word is said about China in any of the literature I have seen. It appears to me that at least the entire purpose of ICCR, like other such organizations, is to ensure a fat salary for its directors, and to undermine the free enterprise system.

Tie-In

The threads that tie religion and environment together can be found on the home page of the World Council of Churches. If ever in human history there was a worthless organization this is it. I have personally seen representatives of the World Counsel of Churches involved in the distribution of guns and ammunition in Africa. I have seen them actively push communism. I have seen them attempt to start revolution, inspire to riot, and generally wreak havoc on society. They are now fully committed to all the socialist environmental (SE) garbage put forth.

I quote from their home page, "There is now strong scientific evidence that the atmosphere is warming as a result of human activity." I ask, whose consensus? Certainly not climatologists or atmospheric scientists. The World Council of Churches goes on to say, "Industrialized countries are the main source of these emissions (CO_2 and greenhouse gases — wrong again) while the first victims will be the small island states such as in the Pacific and low-lying countries like Bangladesh."

I have several problems with this statement. First, the last time I looked at a map Bangladesh was located on the Bay of Bengal in the Indian Ocean, not the Pacific. Second, to call Bangladesh a small country stretches credibility. Poor, yes — small, not particularly when it comes to population. Third, who established that there was any climatic change taking place? Fourth, industrial nations produce less than 1/3 of the so-called greenhouse gases worldwide. When and how did they arrive at this conclusion?

The World Counsel of Churches is presently circulating the following petition:

> Climate Change . . . Urgent Action Needed . . . Intergovernmental Petition to Governments of Industrialized Countries.
> Then we have the statement (try to remember that this is supposed to be a Church organization): "By signing this petition, we declare our commitment to accept the consequences of reductions for society, economy and personal

lives. We are prepared to take responsible steps in our lives to reduce our energy consumption and greenhouse gas emissions. We believe that such changes would improve the long-term quality of life for all."

This document is being circulated in English, French, German, and Spanish. The finalized petitions were turned in to the UN in January, 1997. I should say that this constitutes a trail which is effortlessly followed. Church to environmentalists to the UN. However, much more interesting is the background document it lists — among others, Gorby's Green Cross International based in Geneva Switzerland. In the lead-in statement the WCC says that the IPCC has confirmed the second assessment report that climate change is caused by human activity. This is not true. The disclaimer at the beginning of every single IPCC report states that they are not even sure that there is climate change. What is of considerable interest, however, is the indisputable fact that the aforementioned scenario reflects exactly the plans for the de-industrialization of North America and Europe. "... we declare our commitment to accept the consequences of reductions for society (western society only), and our personal lives."

Socialism

What the heck is socialism doing under religion? Well, with the advent of people like Freud it has gradually become exactly that. It has displaced, through government social programs, the previously occupied position of the church. Instead of improving the situation it has considerably worsened it. Leaders like Wilson, FDR and Johnson have utilized it to garnish power and dependency. Socialism is the false concept that government can, at no cost, provide for the needy, the massive punishing of success. Graduated income tax is used solely to punish achievement and redistribute wealth to others. The history of the socialists runs from the British Fabian society to the British labor party to the American Democrat and Republican parties to the South African ANC, and on to many of the left-leaning political parties of the old British Empire. Created by the Fabians, financed by Cecil Rhodes, the entire theory is false. It has never worked in any place that tried it, and it accomplishes exactly the opposite from what the espoused goals are.

The Socialist International lists full party status beginning with Albania and ending with Venezuela, 78 nations in all. What strikes one is the Associated Organizations list. Here we find the International Federation of the Socialist and Democratic Press, (media), the International League of Religious Socialists (Christian religion), the International Union of Socialist Teachers (education), the Jewish Labor Bund (Jewish religion), and the World Labor Zionist Movement (Radical Jewish religion). Interesting that three of these are religiously affiliated and one educationally.

There are several purposes for this system. The first and foremost is the perpetuation of an entire class of civil servants — welfare workers. The majority of all funds, about 70%, which is spent on public welfare is consumed in the cost of administration and payroll for the workers in the system. The previously church-administered volunteers system cost society nothing and required goods were donated by the more fortunate. Even today chuch organizations must keep overhead under 20% or lose donations. To date, since the inception of the system under FDR, America has spent over $4 trillion on welfare. The number of people to whom it administers benefits has remained constant over the entire time frame — even during the LBJ "Great Society" expansion of the system.

By segregating every deviation from Anglo Saxon males found in society into special groups, the system has created dozens of victim classes. Illegitimates, criminals, illegal immigrants, homosexuals, Blacks, Hispanics, Orientals, Indians, lesbians, and yes, even women, which represent 52% of the population, are victims of the evil white males. It is a fact that if we count up all minorities found on government contract forms by percentage we come to the astounding conclusion that 81% of America's population is a minority. All this is what the Satori want — a society that is self indulgent, and materialistic dependent upon government so that they can use you to their self-enrichment.

Cause and Effect

Probably the most important single factor which has allowed religion and religious institutions to be supplanted by the afore-mentioned three factions is a single, simple concept brought forth from the Satori think-tanks. This concept is equality. The egalitarian concept that all people, all races, both genders, are equal in all aspects. This was not the idea of Jefferson, nor any of the Founding Fathers of the republic. This concept was promoted in the early fifties. Any logical, reasonable American wants and demands equal treatment before the law, and equality of opportunity for all citizens. This was always the equality assumed to be found in the Constitution.

What this new equality concept has done is to confuse law with individual potential. It has allowed the state to co-opt religious institutions through legislation and enforcement. It has replaced the spirit of our society, in which we help one another through the facilitation of the church and other voluntary associations, and replaced that function by the state. The church's social function has all but been eliminated, and simultaneously, the watering-down of long held truths has made religion all but irrelevant. Thus the state becomes the arbiter of our needs. We cease to be self-reliant and rely more on the services of the state. We have become wards of the state, which controls more and more of our lives.

This is the reason present-day organized religion has been undermined and decimated. All we have do is look at Europe. In Germany, for example, participation in religious events, Sunday church, church support of the poor, meals to the hungry, all have been co-opted by the state. Thus the state is supreme and the individual its serf. Exactly what the Satori want. Again, it must be clearly emphasized that the state has nothing and that everything the state gives to someone, or some group, it has to first confiscate from another. The only purpose of such a system is political spoils. By the exercise of these acts a politician or the state can say, vote for me, see what I am giving you? The ignorant masses are swayed by this argument. It has been used by every single despot in the development of his power base since time began.

Sadly we can now see that all of the mainline Christian religions have this virus, which has also effected the Reformed Jews. Virtually all religions have been compromised by the Satori. This was accomplished through finance, infiltration, and the founding of organizations like the World Council of Churches, which would be more aptly named the Satori Church Subversion Council. Religion is not, as Marx said, the opiate of the people. Religion is the source of our ethics, morals, and solace. Through the destruction of the organized religions, the arbiter of decency is destroyed. This is very similar to what happened in Rome. Their religious organizations were brought under attack and gradually perverted. When the moral and ethical fiber, which is the cement that holds a society together was desolved, the empire disintegrated and mob rule (Democracy) took over. The existing Roman religions were overtaken by Christianity, and thus we see again the Hegalian Dialectic at work.

What You Can Do About Religion

Religion is a very personal view, and for this reason it is difficult to advise on it. There are certainly several universal things which can be done by any individual that will better the picture for their denomination.

1.) Insist that your church not support the UN or any UN functions.

2.) Ask your minister if your church belongs to either the World Counsel of Churches or the American Counsel of Churches, If membership in either is a fact demand immediate removal, and if that is not possible insist that any contributions to your church be used locally.

3.) If you are Roman Catholic write the Pope about the American Council of Bishops. Tell him how you agree with him and hope that he can help in correcting the Bishops.

4.) If you are Jewish do not support any efforts by the JDL, and other reformed Jewish organization which are secular in nature.

5.) If you are a Unitarian or member of the First Church of Christ, it's to late.

CHAPTER EIGHT

SOCIALISM
ALIVE AND WELL IN AMERICA

Not only is socialism alive but it is growing. Once citizens are drawn into the welfare state scenario they become hopeless pawns of the politicians in power. Lest we forget, the Nazional-sozalistische Arbeiter Partei Deuchland (NSDPA, National Socialist Workers Party of Germany), were the Nazis. Many of our current crop of politicians evidently admire the Nazi accomplishments and appear to be parroting their programs, methods, and systems.

The DSA is the Democratic Socialists of America. They are the largest socialist organization in the United States. They are affiliated with the Socialist International. They refer to themselves as "Progressive Democrats." Understand that there is nothing whatsoever progressive about socialism. In its egalitarian concepts, it teaches that all in society should be financially equal — except — of course, the ruling elite. Regardless of effort, all should have an equal share. Not only does this not work, it results in the type of societal breakdown as we have seen in the last portion of the 20th century. Every socialist state eventually becomes totalitarian with a centrally-planned and -managed economy, which, like a cancer, needs new, healthy tissue to feed itself. In all of history there is not one single case where such a system proved successful. Socialists believe that Democracy is a means to their end of restructuring society to a fairer socialist model, in which the "have not" populace is empowered by wealth re-distribution from those who have. This is the exact reason why our forefathers gave us a republic and not a democracy governed by majority vote. Read what the DSA says about themselves on their web page (www.dsausa.org):

"We are socialists because we reject an international economic order sustained by private profit [free enterprise],

---

Flash-Back

Dateline: June, 1976 (Habitat 1) Section D preamble

Source: United Nations

Issuance: Vancouver Plan of Action

"Land, because of its unique nature and the crucial role it plays in human settlements, cannot be treated as an ordinary asset, controlled by individuals and subject to the pressures and inefficiencies of the market. Private land ownership is also a principal instrument of wealth accumulation and concentration of wealth and therefore contributes to social injustice; if unchecked, it may become a major obstacle in planning and development schemes. Social justice, urban renewal and development, the provision of decent and healthy dwellings — and health conditions for the people can only be achieved if land use is in the interests of society as a whole."

Karl Marx and Adolph Hitler could not have stated their respective communist/socialist positions any better than this UN program which violates every tenant of a free society.

---

alienated labor [people working for other people], *race and gender discrimination, environmental destruction, and brutality and violence in defense of the status quo."*

I assume they speak of the over 66 million people killed by the Soviets, and the 100 million plus killed by Mao, in their socialist workers paradise.

They go on to say that they want to *"regulate markets,"* meaning centrally-planned economies which were all utter failures in the over-40 economies of the USSR, all of which had top-down centrally-planned economies. They want to *"protect the environment,"* like Chernobyl, Love Canal, Hanford, and all the other government-created ecological disasters. They also want to *"ensure a ba-*

sic level of equality and equity for all citizens," meaning to take from those who've earned it and give to those who are socialist members. Then they go on to inform that they *"plan to institute this plan by national and international multilateral regulation,"* i.e. a new world order.

According to the Democratic Socialists of American home page, the following members of Congress are members of the DSA:

House of Representatives (1998)

Earl Hilliard	AL 07
Eni Faleomavaega	American Samoa, non-vote
Ed Pastor	AZ 02
Lynn C. Woolsey	CA 06
George Miller	CA 07
Nancy Pelosi	CA 07
Pete Stark	CA 07
Henry Waxman	CA 29
Xavier Becerra	CA 30
Julain Dixon	CA 32
Esteban Torres	CA 34
Maxine Waters	CA 34
George E. Brown	CA 42
Bob Filner	CA 50
Diane DeGette	CO 01
Eleanor H. Norton	Wash. DC, non-vote
Corrine Brown	FL 03
Carrie Meek	FL 17
Alcee Hastings	FL 17
Cynthia McKinney	GA 04
John Lewis	GA 05
Neil Abercrombie	HI 01
Patsy Mink	HI 02
Jessie Jackson	IL 02
Luis Gutierrez	IL 04
Danny Davis	IL 07
Lane Evans	IL 17

Jullia Carson .... IN 10
John Oliver .... MA 01
Jom McGovern .... MA 03
Barney Frank .... MA 04
John Tieney .... MA 06
David Bonior .... MI 10
Lynn N. Rivers .... MI 13
Johnn Conyers .... MI 14
Bernie Thompson .... MS 02
Melvin Watt .... NC 12
Donald Payne .... NJ 10
Jerrold Nadler .... NY 08
Major Owens .... NY 11
Nyda Velazquez .... NY 12
Charles Rangle .... NY 15
Maurice Hinchey .... NY 26
John LaFalce .... NY 29
Marcy Kaptur .... OH 09
Dennis Kucinich .... OH 10
Louis Stokes .... OH 11
Sherrod Brown .... OH 13
Elizabeth Furse .... OR 01
Peter DeFazio .... OR 04
Chaka Fattah .... PA 02
William Coyne .... PA 14
Carlos A. Romero-Barcelo .... Puerto Rico, non-vote
Robert C. Scott .... VA 03
Bernie Sanders .... VT
James A. McDermott .... WA 07

Here you have 56 elected members of Congress from 22 states and territories, each and every one of them an avowed socialist.

Who is financially supporting these people?

ADA – Americans for Democratic Action

AFL-CIO

Americans for a Sustainable Economy

Flash-Back

Dateline: June, 1976

Source: Conference (Habitat 1)
Chapter 5, Page 37, Earth Summit

Issuance: United Nations

"A human settlement policy must seek harmonious integrations or coordination of a wide variety of components, including, for example, population growth and distribution, employment, shelter, land use, infrastructure, and services. Governments must create mechanisms and institutions to develop and institute such policies . . ."   *(pure Socialism, ed.)*

Amnesty International
Bookings Institute
Catholic Charities
Campaign for America's Future
Campaign for New Priorities
Center for the Advancement of Public Policy
Center of Concern
Center for Defense Information
Center for Law and Social Policy
Center for Responsive Politics
Center on Budget and Policy Priorities
Children's Defense Fund
Child Welfare League
Citizens for Tax Justice
Coalition on Human Needs
Council for a Livable World
Consumer's Union
Defense of Wildlife
Demilitarization for Democracy

Development GAP
Economic Policy Institute
50 Years is Enough Network
Friends of the Earth
Friends Committee on National Legislation
Fund for New Priorities in America
Human Rights Watch
IPS – Institute for Policy Studies
Institute for Woman's Policy Research
International Labor Rights Fund
Latin American Working Group
Leadership Conference on Civil Rights
Long-Term Care Campaign
National Jobs for All Coalition
National Council of LaRaza
National Committee to Preserve Social Security and Medicare
National Council of Negro Women
National Rainbow Coalition
National Associations of Public Hospitals
National Council of Senior Citizens
NEA – National Education Association
NOW – National Organization for Women
National Priorities Project
National Black Child Development Institute
NETWORK – National Catholic Social Justice Lobby
Peace Action
Preamble Center for Public Policy
Public Citizen
Public Campaign
Stakeholders Alliance
The Campaign for Health and Security
United Electrical, Radio and Machine Workers of America
United for Fair Economy
Urban League

USA Network for Habitat II
U.S. Campaign to Ban Landmines
U.S. commission on Civil Rights
UNITE
Unitarian Universalist Service Committee
Veterans for Peace
Witness for Peace
Washington Chapter Alliance for Democracy
Working Assets
Women, Law and Development

These groups are what may be called the "network of the political left." They represent a coalition of environmentalists, communists, socialists, and homosexuals. All are interrelated through the Institute for Global Communications (IGC), the Association of Progressive Communications (APC), and the Democratic Socialists of America (DSA). Almost all of them have web sites hosted by IGC, APC or DSA.

Remember when you hear your favorite network media newscaster backing up a story with a quote from a member of the aforementioned organizations, where on the political spectrum it is coming from.

---❧---

*"A new world order under the United Nations as it is
presently constituted is guaranteed to be a socialist, not
a free-market capitalist, system."*

— PAT ROBERTSON
THE NEW WORLD ORDER (C) 1991, PG. 58

---❧---

*"My vision of a New World Order foresees a U.N. with
a revitalized peacekeeping function. It is the sacred
principles enshrined in the U.N. charter to which
we henceforth pledge our allegiance."*

— PRESIDENT GEORGE BUSH, FEB. 1, 1992

---❧---

CHAPTER NINE

THE UNITED NATIONS AND POLITICS

No summation relating to the Satori plan can be made without a concerted look at the UN. There is, and has been, considerable movement in the US House of Representatives to get us out of the UN. The most recent of these is H.R. 1146 "The American Sovereignty Restoration Act" introduced by Congressman Dr. Ron Paul. The UN Charter is a virtual copy of the former "constitution" of the Union of Soviet Socialist Republics (USSR).

United Nations supporters use two arguments to justify the existence of the organization. First, we must have an international forum to discuss differences so as to prevent wars. We can unequivocally say that in this field they have been a monumental failure. At the present time there are about 100 wars raging in various places around the world. The second argument relates to this touchy-feely rubbish of global harmony, and how we are all living on just one tiny planet. The UN is a one world government whose founding principle is — "Man's rights are given him by government, not God." That principle is in direct opposition to our Declaration of Independence. If that were not bad enough there is considerable movement afoot by the LPN secretariat to develop several worldwide tax schemes in an effort to give the UN an unrestricted access to funds and an international army via the SEATO and NATO treaties. The two major fund raisers are:

1.) An international tax on all international money transfers. This to be a percentage of the total amount in transfer. This scheme is very clever because it will not be immediately obvious to most citizens. It would accelerate the movement toward geopolitical centralization and monitory unification as our federal income tax laws.

Flash-Back

Dateline: January 13, 1918

Source: *New York World* (A former NYC Daily Newspaper)

Issuance: William Boyce Thompson

In a statement made for the *New York World*, Mr. Boyce Thompson stated; "Russia is pointing the way to great and sweeping world changes. It is not in Russia alone that the old order is passing. There is a lot of the old order in America that is going to go too . . . I'm glad it's so. When I sat and watched those democratic conclaves in Russia, I felt that I would welcome a similar scene in the United States."

Why should this statement interest you? His statement was made at the exact time during which the Soviets were, by force, starving to death over 30 million of their citizens. A fact that Mr.Thompson was well aware of.

William Boyce Thompson was founder of the Council on Foreign Relations (CFR). He was later a Director of the CFR and Director of the Federal Reserve.

2.) A tax on all international airline tickets as a percentage of total cost. A very clever idea, as there are so many taxes and fees attached to airline tickets that are all simply presented in the total cost so no one even knows what they are.

The major force behind most international treaties emanate from the UN, either in Geneva or New York. These may be characterized in three differing groups: trade, environment, and social. Through social issues they attack the family. Through environmental issues they attack private ownership of land, and through trade issues they attack business and, more specifically, the manufacturing sector. UN sponsored conferences are held around the world. In every instance, with a very specific purpose

- The Vienna conference focused on children, i.e., your right to bring up your child.
- Cairo on forced sterilization of women for population control.
- China on feminist lesbian issues.
- Copenhagen on worldwide taxes in support of the UN.
- Rio on "internationalizing" borders to protect the environment (one world government).
- Kyoto on implementation of treaties to give the UN authority over national issues.

The most important documents which are in preparation to empower the UN are:

- The Biodiversity Treaty. Awaiting US Senate radification.
- The Climate Change Protocol scheduled to be signed by Clinton.
- Convention on Forests which will destroy the American and Canadian timber industries.
- Agenda 21, outlining how communities may develop. The destruction of personal land ownership, and control over construction, urban planning, and development.

Each of these initiatives go directly to the heart of the Satori plan. Government control of your life. Control of your children. Control of private as well as public property by an international authority. Control of natural resourse development. Control of what and how industry produces. Control of vehicle type production.

How do these international treaties affect us as a nation once they are enacted and ratified by the Senate? Mickey Kantor who was our trade rep at the negotiations for WTO (World Trade Organization) was very candid when asked by a Congressional House Ways and Means Committee: (Q). what are the implications to national sovereignty of the WTO treaty? (A). Mr. Kantor: There is no right of blockage under the WTO. Once an appeal of a WTO ruling has been effected and completed they (the losing

WORLD HERITAGE SITES and BIOSPHERE RESERVES IN THE UNITED STATES

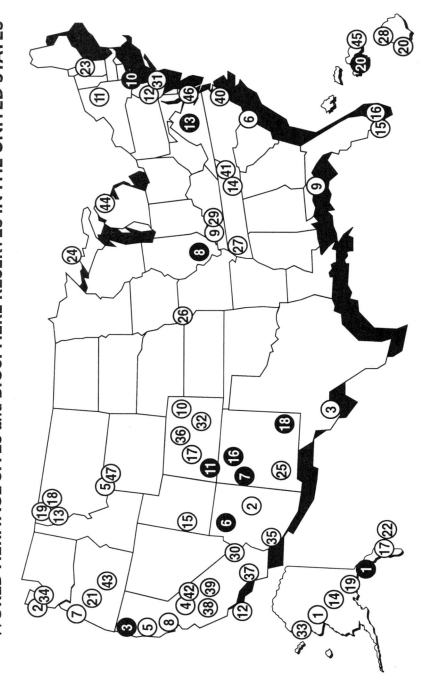

Biosphere Reserves

1. Aleutian Islands
2. Beaver Creek
3. Big Bend
4. Big Thicket
5. California Coast Ranges
6. Carolinian-South Atlantic
7. Cascade Head
8. Central California Coast
9. Central Gulf Coastal Plain
10. Central Plains
11. Champlain-Adirondack
12. Channel Islands
13. Coram
14. Denali
15. Desert
16. Everglades
17. Fraser
18. Glacier
19. Glacier Bay-Admiralty Island
20. Guanica
21. H.J. Andrews Exper. Forest
22. Hawaiian Islands
23. Hubbard Brook
24. Isle Royale
25. Jornada
26. Konza Prairie
27. Land Between the Lakes
28. Luquillo
29. Mammoth Cave Area
30. Mojave and Colorado Deserts
31. New Jersey Pinelands
32. Niwot Ridge
33. Noatak
34. Olympic
35. Organ Pipe Cactus
36. Rocky Mountain
37. San Dimas
38. San Joaquin
39. Sequoia-Kings Canyon
40. South Atlantic Coastal Plain
41. Southern Appalachian
42. Stanislaus-Tuolumne
43. Three Sisters
44. University of Michigan
45. Virgin Islands National Park
46. Virginia Coast
47. Yellowstone

World Heritage Sites

1. Wrangell-St. Elias NP/ Glacier Bay
2. Olympic National Park
3. Redwood National Park
4. Yosemite National Park
5. Yellowstone National Park
6. Grand Canyon National Park
7. Chaco National Park
8. Cahokia Mounds Site
9. Mammoth Cave NP
10. Statue of Liberty
11. Mesa Verde National Park
12. Independence Hall
13. Monticello & Univ. of Virginia
14. Great Smoky Mts. NP
15. Everglades National Park
16. Pueblo de Taos
17. Hawaii Volcanoes NP
18. Carlsbad Caverns NP
19. Glacier National Park
20. La Fortaleza & San Juan

This map indicates the sites and areas that the United States has submitted for special United Nationas designation.

nation) are required to implement the decision of the World Trade Organization (WTO). Furthermore any treaty ratified by the US Senate *becomes a subsection of the US Constitution.*

The United Nations Heritage and Biosphere Programs lists 20 World Heritage Sites and 47 World Biosphere Reserves. Without the recently confiscated lands in Utah by President Clinton, known as the Escalante land grab, the present UN system includes 74,904,245 acres in National Parks, National Preserves, and National Monuments, of which 51,367,716 acres are in the United States. Think of that. Over 51 million acres of American territory has been granted to United Nations control. According to the Constitution the federal government does not have the right to own land (tenth amendment). How can they give away the sovereignty of that land when they do not own it?

In 1997 Bill Clinton, in a Satori-motivated move, confiscated 17 million acres of land in southern Utah (the Escalante land grab). Rep. James Hansen (R.,UT), has been reviewing subpoenaed documents from the administration. The ultimate plan is to have these lands turned over to UN administration. The subpoenaed documents show: (1) The deliberate evasion of National Environmental Policy Act compliance; (2) Finalizing the transaction under the 1906 Antiquities Act, an act never intended for the appropriation of raw land; (3) Violation of the Antiquities Act in that anything procured under that law must be "endangered" or "of cultural historic value," neither is the case; (4) Kathleen McGinty, chairman of the White House Council on Environment (CEQ), stated in an E-mail on March 25,1997 that "These lands are not endangered."

Now some will say, what's the big deal? The amount of land involved is a very big deal! It is bigger than at least one of our states. It contains the largest low sulfur coal deposit in North America. The confiscation placed over 600 people out of work. The confiscation violated the mining rights of the property owners, and the rights of the mining company. The confiscation removed lands from county property tax lists thus making it im-

---

Flash-Back

Dateline: February 9, 1950

Source: U.S. Senate

Issuance: Subcommittee on Foreign Relations

The Senate Foreign Relations Committee introduced today Senate Resolution 66. The resolution reads:

"Whereas, in order to achieve universal peace and justice, the present Charter of the United Nations should be changed to provide a true world government constitution."

Senator Taylor later made the following statement:

"We will have to sacrifice considerable sovereignty to the world organization to enable them to levy taxes in their own right to support themselves."

---

possible to sustain public education, as well as roads and general public services in an entire portion of Utah. Many people have said that our present president has no foreign policy. All policy in his administration is driven by polls and only polls. This is false — there has been an underlying direction in all American policy as directed by this executive. That policy is Globalism and one world government.

While no policy is present on any issue in this administration, be it domestic or foreign, the fact that our national policy is directed toward a New World Order is undeniable. American politics in the Clinton years is said to be driven by pollsters, to give you the idea that this is what people want. Phoney polls are used to justify every violation of our Constitution. "Save the world under one Globalist UN power structure" is undeniably the single decision on which all policy in the United States appears to be centered.

Thirty years ago when Clinton was a student at Oxford, he had time to lead anti-American protests in front of our London Embassy, and to take tours all over Europe, as well as the USSR. He then demonstrated his hatred of everything this nation stood for. Nothing has changed in thirty years. Clinton the draft dodger's programs remain the same — do everything possible to destroy the Republic, and help establish the New World Order. Clinton's mentor, C. Quigley, a Georgetown professor, was a leader in the intellectual development of the entire Satori/Mandarin cabal.

The problem is that as president Clinton can do a great deal more harm than as a radical student agitator. Bill's roommate at Oxford was Strobe Talbott, who is now ensconced as the number two man in the State Department, where he is actively directing foreign policy for the UN, rather than for America. In fact, Talbott has even publicized his vision in a *Time Magazine* article entitled, "The Birth of the Global Nation." In this article we find the unbelievable quote:

". . . nationhood as we know it will be obsolete; all states will recognize a single global authority." Further on in the article, *"All countries are basically social arrangements, accommodations to changing circumstances. No matter how permanent and even sacred they may seem at any one time, in fact they are artificial and temporary. Through the ages, there has been an overall trend toward larger units claiming sovereignty and, paradoxically, a gradual diminution of how much true sovereignty any country actually has."*

Aside from being totally erroneous, the Under Secretary of State's sentiments amount to treason. I point to his oath of office . . . to support the Constitution of the United States. The actual world trend has been in exactly the opposite direction. By 1997 at least one hundred new nation-states made their appearance on the world stage. Talbott is aping the socialist indoctrination that both he and Clinton underwent as Rhodes Scholars at Oxford. How do these elitists plan to institute their scheme on us? We can again go to the writings of Talbott, who informs us, *"The internal affairs of a nation used to be off limits to the world community. Now the principal of humanitarian intervention is gaining acceptance."*

Flash-Back

Dateline: 1992

Source: *UN Internationl Council for Local Environmental Issues*

Issuance: **LA 21 CLEI Toronto, Canada**

The official beginning of internationalizing American Cities and urban centers begins with this program. The purpose of the intitiative is to "develop a partnership" between cities and the United Nations. Twenty three American and Canadian cities have joined the program to date. Included are Toronto, Chattanooga, Portland, and Atlanta, among others.

There you have it. American military under UN command and UN flag — in violation of the president's oath of office, the oath of office of every officer in the military and the oath of every American soldier; Global arms control; GATT, WTO, NAFTA; Global climate control treaties; Global population control, via Planned Parenthood initiatives.

Just a few samples:

- Iraq – For Americans killed in the Gulf War Clinton eulogized them, "Condolences to the families of those who died in the service of the UNITED NATIONS."
- Somalia – On May 5, 1993, Clinton sent our troops to Somalia stating "A humanitarian mission in Nation Building." He placed those 5,000 American troops under the command of Turkish Brig. General Cevik Bir as UN Commander.
- Bosnia – In dispatching American Air Force units over the Balkans, Clinton said, "This redeployment was a clear expression of the will of NATO and the will of the UN." Michael

New, Spec. 4, US Army combat veteran, was court-marshaled by the US Army at the command of Clinton, the Commander in Chief, for refusing to serve under UN command, nor to wear UN uniform, both of which are in violation of a soldier's oath of office.

In the most recent poll taken of Americans in December of 1997, 87% of all citizens polled expressed fear of their government. This represents an increase of almost 20% since the beginning of the Clinton administration. They have good reason for such fear. The abuse of power by the executive branch of this government is unprecedented in American history. Every agency in government has been put to the task of enforcing unwanted, illegal, oppressive government edicts, this specially being the case with anyone daring to oppose any legislative act, or who is in opposition to the presidency.

In the case of the IRS, they have harassed with income tax audits virtually every right-side political force, including: The *National Review, The American Spectator, The Christian Coalition, Citizens for a Sound Economy, The Freedom Alliance, The Heritage Foundation, The National Rifle Association, The Western Journalism Center, The National Center for Public Policy Research, Fortress America*, and *Citizens Against Government Waste*. Last but not least, they even audited with a vengance Paula Jones, a woman with an income under $40,000, and who had a personal lawsuit against Clinton. According to IRS statistics, the likelihood of an audit of someone in her tax bracket is 11,000 to 1. Few of the hundreds of left, and socialist organizations have been audited by the IRS. This is the most powerful message that government can send: mess with us and we go after your income.

The FBI has been used extensively and illegally in numerous nefarious ways. In the case of Billy Dale, the head of the White House Travel Office who was fired so that a political crony of Clinton could profit, they instituted a White House incited FBI investigation. When the matter finally came to a lengthy trial it

---

Flash-Back

Dateline: **May 18, 1998**

Issuance: **Executive branch, Clinton Administration**
(G8 Summit, Global Climate Treaty)

Source: **Small Business Survival Committee**

The Clinton administration has abandoned any remaining appearance of complying with the US Senate. The senate voted 95 to 0 that the administration should neither sign nor send to the Senate for ratification any Global Warming Treaty that excludes third world nations from participation in the reduction of "greenhouse gasses."

This treaty deals with the de-industrialization of the developed world, and particularly with North America. Under the precepts, agreed upon by the administration, will be the lowering of greenhouse gas emissions by North American manufacturers. Only minimal compliance is required in the third world, which is the largest producer of CO_2. Furthermore the 3.99% of CO_2 produced in America is inconsequential. If we reduced CO_2 production to 0, it would have no effect on the world environment.

---

took the jury just 90 minutes to pronounce Mr. Dale innocent of any wrong doing. In the Waco genocide massacre the FBI murdered 80 Americans, including helpless children. Then there was the case of over 900 FBI files found illegally in the White House, for which no one has yet been prosecuted. In a previous Republican administration, one file holder got two years in jail.

Ken Masterson Brown brought a case against Hillary to compel her to give out the names of the health care task-force. He was audited by the IRS. In the case at Ruby Ridge the FBI, US Marshals Office, and the BATF were all used. An FBI agent murdered a mother holding her baby, while another one shot a teenage boy in the back. We are not examining some isolated few incidences of illegal acts. What we have here is concerted, organized, systematic terrorism by the political left.

Where did this type of very un-American action come from? It seems that we can trace all of it to a meeting held in 1989 at the RAND Corporation, an old-time Satori surrogate, who arranged a series of international meetings which, among others, included the US-Soviet Task Force to Prevent Terrorism. I have no idea what strange thoughts permeate the brains of people at Rand, but it does seem to me ridiculous to have a joint Soviet-American Task force on Terrorism. First, the Soviet's have been the primary sponsors of state terrorism, and second terrorism in the west is based on entirely different causes than terrorism in a totalitarian dictatorship. There is absolutely no relationship between the two systems. The reason for those meetings, according to Rand spokesmen, was to *"Turn the fight against terrorism into a joint struggle."* This concept is far past stupidity. Terrorism in Russia was *caused by* internal opposition to totalitarian oppression. Terrorism in America (at that time) was a function of external 4th generation war sponsored by the USSR.

Regardless of these facts the USSR and its co-chairman, Igor Beliaev, had an overwhelming influence on the Americans as well as their co-chairman John Marks. The former Rand consultant, Konrad Kelley stated *"experts have embraced Soviet assumptions, methods, and tactics."* Here comes the KGB. Added to this we have all the various terrorist experts like Kelley, who inform us the tax protesters, the John Birch Society, and other such government opposition groups qualify as "domestic terrorists." Leftists like John Nutter tell us that people who have bumper stickers on their cars like, *I fear government that fears my gun, Don't tread on me,* and *I support the tenth ammendment* are dangerous and should be watched by police. Kathy Marks of the Southern Illinois Criminal Justice Training Program states that "Right-wing terrorism poses insidious and ominous threats to law enforcement." These people should be forced to memorize the US Constitution before being allowed back on their job. The fact of the matter is that it is the political left which is prone to violence, be it state or non-governmental in sponsorship. Not one single identifiable American terrorist organization in the last 100 years can be shown to have been affiliated with the politically conservative right.

The largest unfortunate outcome of disastrous policy was Waco. Another includes Ruby Ridge. America is not a totalitarian state, our delegates to this odious meeting should have read our constitution before, during, and after the meeting, and realized the different political system represented, unless of course they were committed to the communist system. We must bear the UN/Satori plan in mind. The left does not oppose their plan, the right does. The left is being utilized in an effort to implement their plan, the end of the sovreignty of the United States by 2016.

What You Can Do

Help get the United States out of the UN!
Support Congressman Ron Paul and all others in this effort.

Politic

The saying is "Politics makes strange bedfellows." Either nothing much has changed in the last 200 years or history does repeat itself. America is stuffed full of political action groups, all of which appear to be interested in forcing their particular brand of politics on you so as to gain their advantages.

Many political action groups have the same agenda, and are simply persuing the objective in a different manner. The Institute for Policy Studies (IPS) is such an organization. IPS calls itself "Progressive." Progressive is one of the words we must watch out for, it means the political left — no, not liberal — Left. Their annual report informs us of that. IPS unabashedly blames American business for all our social ills.

There are several spin-offs of IPS. These include Economic Policy Institute, Center on Budget and Policy Priorities, and the Center for Policy Alternatives. They are involved in Economics, Environment, Public Policy, and Education. They are strong backers of multi-culturalism, one of the Satori's most destructive policies. It must be said that not all IPS policies are bad. They are the only organization I am aware of who opposes NAFTA and the internationalization of business interests. As I said in the lead-in to this paragraph, politics do make strange bedfellows. IPS, due to its perceived left stance by our left media, gets a great deal more media attention than most organizations on the right. These are true pseudo-intellectuals in the strictest meaning of that phrase. With the exception of their opposition to Satori world trade policy they represent a complete capitulation to Satori plans.

The Royal Institute of International Affairs is located at Chatham House in London, England. They also run an auxiliary outfit called Chatham House Enterprises Ltd. They are connected with The Round Table, The Milner Group, and various other English as well as American and Canadian groups (Canadian Counsel on Foreign Relations) and our Council on Foreign Relations. They appear to be connected to the British government much in the same way as the CFR and Trilateral Commission (TC) are in the United States.

Like all the other groups within this sphere their involvement is in Economics, Politics, and the Environment. The Royal Institute of International Affairs (RIIA), offers a large assortment of services, CHEL is their Climate Change Service. They are very aggressive. Together with their affiliates, Trexler and Associates, Inc. and The World Recourse Institute of Washington, DC, the RIIA offers vast services including: briefings, assessments, analyses, recommendation for action, and even management of environmental projects. RIIA funding is a nebulous operation but, obviously, such a large operation requires substantial funds. They are not at all aggressive about membership, so their funding comes from elsewhere. They are international in scope with branch operations in almost every English speaking nation.

Flash-Back

Dateline: May 29-31, 1954

Source: *H du Berrier Reports*

Issuance: **Hilaire du Berrier**

A secret meeting chaired by Prince Bernard of Holland, the man who will inherit one of the greatest fortunes in the world when his mother, the Queen of Holland dies, was held at the Hotel de Bilderberger in Oosterbeek Holland to institute a new secret organization. Because they do not name themselves, observers gave them the name of the hotel where they held their first meeting. The name, Bilderberger, has stuck ever since.

The Bilderbergers are one of the world's most secretive organizations. Membership is international. The strongest contingents are European. The most pronounced occupation of members is banking. They are enormously influential, membership includes Prince Bernard, the Prime Minister of Britain, and numerous American Executive, Legislative and Judicial branch members, and the CEO's of most central banks.

Let us pause at this point to make clear a matter of great importance. All the organizations mentioned in this chapter are related to the governments of which I write. I do not mean to imply that they have any direct relationship with the governmental institutions. What I am saying is that, through membership by either the politicians or their advisors and staff personnel, these organizations have undue influence upon political decisions. For example: every one of Clinton's cabinet members is also a member of the Council on Foreign Relations, some are also Trilateral Commission, Bilderbergers and/or Bones. No one in his right mind is going to tell you that such membership does not cause the members to be of one mind on most political topics. They are all influenced by the CFR's publication *Foreign Affairs*, they are party to meetings of fellow members, and they belong to sub-groups within the organization which plan strategy. To deny that this constitutes any covenant between members as to the outcome of government policy is nonsensical.

The Tavistock Institute of Human Relations is located in London, England. This organization is difficult to explain because they are not actually active in political matters. They deal with the social sciences and the integration of all social sciences. Their slogan is "social science in action." They tell us that "(we) . . . have the independence of being entirely self-financing, with no subsides from government or other sources." Now that is a fascinating statement. Just exactly how one becomes entirely self-financing, without any contributions from government or other sources is not explained. Perhaps the Satori's numerous papers, documents, books, a monthly magazine entitled *Human Relations* (Plenum Press) and another by the name of *Evaluation*, published in conjunction with Stage Publications, are income sources.

What exactly is Tavistock involved in? According to their documents, academia and consultancy, anthropology, economics, organizational behavior, political science, psychoanalysis, psychology and sociology. Let's see now, could these things include the process of manipulating citizen polling for predetermined outcome? The process of revising history to be favorable to your particular desired outcome? The process of changing actual cultural heritage to one that meets your outcome goals? The process of changing human behavior? Yes they could, and this is what Tavistock is all about. Some of their programs include: Advanced Organizational Consultation (AOC), the process of education through directing the student toward a specific outcome; Center for Decision-Making Studies (CDMS), how to direct the decision making process in a desired and predetermined direction; Group Relations Program (GRP), to modify and change group thought;

Flash-Back

Dateline: 1998 Congressional Session

Source: US Congress

Issuance: Federal Register

Public Law 104-193

This legislation was cleverly concealed from the public through riders on other legislation, and tacked onto the "Deadbeat Dads" legislation. The last portion was FIR 3610, part of the 1996 defense appropriation bill. A staffer for Senator Allen Simpson inserted section 656 onto the bill. The act is now called Public Law 104-193.

This new law establishes the "Machine Readable Document Pilot (fingerprinting) Program." It states that all Motor Vehicle Departments nationwide are to have this program by the year 2000. Members of Congress were unaware of the new legislation because then speaker Newt Gringrich (CFR) scheduled the vote before the new section regarding fingerprinting was published.

---

and last but far from least, the Program for Organizational Change and Technical Innovation (POCTI), to change, influence, and alter group thought, as in police forces, the military, and the judiciary.

To explain exactly what the Tavistock institute is up to, let's pick one example. They are at the forefront of the citizen's identification card called *"Smart Cards."* This is the concept launched by Tavistock in 1977 to report all aspects about citizens to a central authority. They have launched a monumental effort to institute this system worldwide. The effort includes the already installed super computer in Brussels, Belgium, named the Beast, a joint US and EC commission to study the issue, a research project to study using Smart Cards in all compliance and accreditation worldwide.

As it so happens a trial testing project is at this time installed at the University of Michigan where all students are issued Smart Cards. The card includes a magnetic strip, photo ID, university seal, hologram, student ID number, and student name. Exactly what information is contained on the magnetic ID we are not privy to. We can inform you that the card is universal in design, it can be used as a debit bank card, a pass, a library card — it's universal. This is exactly the card which is planned to replace your social security card. It will contain your employment record, medical record, educational record, and be required for employment, medical services, and all government services. It is the heart of the Satori plan for PEOPLE CONTROL.

The Club of Rome was founded in 1968 and is international in scope. Members come from all five continents. It is headquartered in Paris, France. They inform us very modestly "that in a world whose predicaments are far beyond the capacity of individual countries to solve . . ." they will solve them for us. They will do this with "global perspective, deep understanding, and will provide effective solutions with a long-term perspective" in solving these problems for us. How will they do it? "With the contributions of their eleven main global issues about the world and how we should manage it." They further inform that they will teach us "The capacity to govern . . . how to protect the environment, and how to deal with nuclear issues."

One thing is absolutely indisputable — these people do not have a problem with modesty. The philosophy of the Club of Rome is that man is the master of his own destiny, and has badly screwed up. They are the ultimate saviors who will rescue mankind from the perilous course on which we are presently traveling. We are informed that, "The world is undergoing a period of unprecedented upheavals and fluctuations in evolution into a global society, for which we are not mentally prepared." They, on the other hand, are, and will take us by the hand and lead us into their New World Order. They claim a membership of 100 individuals, located on all continents, and from 52 different nations.

They go on to tell us that there is a great conflagration confronting us:

1.) population explosion
2.) technological explosion
3.) social change
4.) cultural and ethical factors

Nothing, they tell us, will escape this tidal wave that will carry everything before it. Talk about apocalyptic. They go on to explain their role in this new Satori invented society. They will correct the shortcomings of the free market economies by leveling the playing field using government controls. They have it all wrong. Any shortcomings in this world are and were created by governments and their policies. In all failing societies the cause was either socialism, communism, or some other command/control society, not a free market. Yet a command/control world government is exactly what they plan for us. Then they inform that they will balance the rate of population growth worldwide. Their plan to bring down the average income in all the industrialized nations to the level of the third world, will eliminate poverty. It will make everyone, except the Satori, miserably poor. We already mentioned in previous text that their initial book, entitled *The Limits of Growth*, is surely one of the most insidious documents produced in this decade. It was published in 37 languages and sold 12 million copies. Talk about a large scale brainwashing exercise. Since that time they have published twenty-one additional reports. The Club of Rome is the principal flagship of the New World Order, and thus of the Satori.

Principal issues list:

- Environment
- Demography
- Development
- Values
- Governance

- Work in Future
- Information Society
- New Technologies
- Education
- The New Global Society
- World Economics and Financial Order

These are, according to the Club of Rome (CR), the major avenues which they are persuing (on behalf of the Satori). The Gorbachev Foundation was started on April 10 ,1991, when the President and General Secretary of the Communist Party the Supreme Soviet (USSR) was finally deposed. So popular was he in Russia that his best course of action was to leave his homeland. "Go west young man," appears even in this day and age to be valid advice. In the United States an eager political left went out of their way to financially support the man who was responsible for over one million dead Afghans. He raised millions of dollars for his Green Cross organization meeting in San Francisco. $250,000 from just one American corporation, Archer Daniels Midland (ADM). Lenin, I believe, said it, "The West will finance their own demise."

Gorbachev was the leader of a nation which rivals only China in the number of its own citizens killed, 100 million. The Gorbachev Foundation is an umbrella organization for a whole string of Gorbi-run environmental cash cows. The touted issue here is environmental, the actual product is the raising of funds for Gorbachev to advance the Satori agenda. One really must wonder how Gorbachev, the man who gave us Cher-nobyl, the greatest single man-made ecological disaster in human history, is going to protect the environment. This is the man who left several of the Russian Republics with regions that look like the surface of the moon. This is Mr. Gorbachev, the Communist. We know this from his own lips. On November 9, 1987, he stated before the Supreme Soviet, "In October of 1917 we parted with the world, rejecting it once and for all. We are moving toward a new world, the world of communism. We shall never turn off that road." Who are some of the Gorbachev Foundation's more substantial supporters, all with over $5,000 in contributions?

Ted Turner	Jane Fonda Turner	James Baker
George Schultz	Carl Sagan	Bill Gates
Shirley McLaine	Colin Powell	Ted Koppel
Al Gore		

At "The State of the World Forum," a meeting held at the posh Fairmont Hotel in San Francisco, people paid $5,000 each to hear Gorbi and Thabo Mbeki of the African National Congress and Communist Party Republic of South Africa proclaim the arrival of the New World Order. The meeting called for, among other things, the expansion of UN authority, international population control, the implementation of the Rio accords at Kyoto, a UN army, and an international court whose edicts could be enforced by the UN army. They discussed the need to redistribute world wealth, to level the playing field. This, they thought, could be done by binding the United States to the Kyoto environmental treaty in 1998, which would lower the American standard of living by at least 35%, while at the same time decimating American manufacturing enterprises.

What is to be the primary weapon in this war against humanity by humanity? Learn what New Age Philosopher, Sam Keen has in store for you . . . *"Reduce the World Population by 90%."* Question is, will you be in the 10% of the survivors? If that's not enough to turn your stomach, listen to Barbara Marx Hubbard in her book, *The Book of Co-Creation*, *"Out of the full spectrum of the human personality, one fourth is elected to transcend and one fourth are destructive, defective seed. In the past they were permitted to die a natural death. Now as we approach . . . the human who is an inheritor of god-like powers, the destructive one fourth must be eliminated . . ."*

Just take a guess at who is going to choose the people to be eliminated. It certainly won't be you! The Russian concept is called "Convergence." It refers to the convergence between political ideologies of the East and the West. Gorbachev was sent to the United States specifically to implement that convergence. The Satori are financing the entire project. The purpose of the Gorbachev Foundation was provided to us by none other than Dr. James A. Garrison. In an article in September of 1995, in the *San Francisco Chronicle*, he states: "The purpose of the foundation is to convene a global brain trust to focus on the principles, values, and actions, that should guide humanity as we enter the next phase of human development." Then Gorbi chimed in with, "the continuation of building a new world order and international relations. This will be a long and difficult process . . ." There you have it in a nutshell: a new world order by a group of self-appointed pseudo-intellectuals to guide us into the Satori-managed New World Order.

The Aspen Institute is an outgrowth of the Markle Foundation. In late 1997 a new president was appointed by the board — her name is Zoe Baird, who you may remember was one of the women not confirmed for a cabinet position in the Clinton administration. As you recall, foundations are one of the avenues by which the Satori fund their nefarious schemes. Markle Foundation (MF) has a capital base of $145 million, and as a foundation pays no state, federal or any other tax. They are required under their rules to give away a scant 5% of their income on charitable activities.

I have three serious problems with that. First, how is a charitable activity defined? It appears that the definition is up to the founder of the charitable activity. We find that when the Satori set up foundations, at the same time they also set up charitable organizations, and through this process are able to pay no taxes while funding their favorite activities. Second, income from investments exceeds 5%, as a consequence tax exempt foundations have, over the last 50 years, shown a remarkable asset growth. Third, the growth of these foundations, with their overlapping directorships, into major corporations skews the entire voting process for corporate officers directing US business enterprises.

We must also remember that these foundations give grants to those who (in their opinion) serve the public interest. When do you think was the last time that the MF sponsored a grant to any conservative cause, author, or activity? Never!

Interactive Communications Technologies is an organization which is devoutly involved in communications, and and advises one world planners as to how you listen and respond to their communications.

I have only covered a minute portion of the thousands of politically active foundations, but I believe it is enough to give the reader a sense of their direction. What you must understand is that there is a motivated political agenda in all of these organizations and it is the uniform direction of that agenda which indicates a hidden hand behind them. Surely there are also conservative and "right-wing" foundations which oppose Satori dictum. The difference between them is one in quantity, financial prowess, and uniformity of political and social direction. One is for human freedom under God, the other serfdom under an elite. I do not believe that this assertion is disputable.

---◈---

"Mr. Jefferson remarked that 'it is the manners and spirit of a people which preserve a republic in vigor. A degeneracy in these is a canker which soon eats to the heart of its laws and constitution.'"

— *A STUDY IN MANNERS*
ALBERT JAY NOCK

---◈---

*"When the State has granted one privilege, its character as a purveyor of privilege is permanently established, and natural law does not permit it to stop with the creation of one privilege, but forces it to go on creating others . . . which in turn culminates in the decay and disappearance of the society . . . Such is the grim testimony borne by the history of six civilizations, now vanished, to the validity of the law that **man tends always to satisfy his needs and desires with the least possible exertion.**"*

— *THE GODS' LOOKOUT*
ALBERT JAY NOCK

---◈---

Quotes are from essays by Albert Jay Nock, *The Disadvantages of Being Educated And Other Essays,* 1996 Hallberg Publishing.

CONCLUSIONS

As normal average people we tend to hold many people, and especially intellectuals, in high esteem. I am sorry to say that we must, with diligence, reject the elitism of the intellectual class. First, I am sure that you will agree that just because a person is intelligent does not necessarily mean that they have what we call "common sense." I believe we can agree that in numerous instances very intelligent people act in a stupid manner. We are instructed by a fable made up in the middle ages about Aristotle and his lover, the beautiful Phyllis, and how he let her ride on his back and whip him when he was too slow crawling about his garden. It demonstrates my point amply. The inteligencia, ever hopeful of approval from their fellow travelers, are more susceptible to peer approval than any other societal group.

Consider some statements made by a past American National Security Advisor to President Carter. I quote from Zbigniew Brzezinski's book, "Marxism represents a further vital and creative stage in the maturing of man's vision," and "Marxism is simultaneously a victory of the external, active man over the inner, passive man and a victory of reason over belief," and "Marxism has served as a mechanism for human progress." The man is a communist, plain and simple. Worse yet Carter hired him to be his advisor, as did Rockefeller. Brzezinski founded the Trilateral Commission and then sold the idea to Rockefeller, who promptly financed it. How much more conclusive proof does one need to tie Satori influence to both capitalist as well as communist camps?

Many intelligent people are not cognizant of the Satori plan. Others are, but both support the plan. Why, is a very important question. There are numerous reasons for this support, but I believe they can be boiled down to personal greed.

Let us first consider the people who are unaware of the Satori or their plan for world conquest in the guise of the New World Order. The mandarin organizations, as listed in my previous book *The Satori and the New Mandarins*, I would categorize into two groups — knows and naivete's. In both cases these individuals are driven by the factor of peer pressure and greed to succeed and be recognized by their peers for achievement. All are in the spider's web. All are happy to be there, and all enjoy the benefits of the web. None of these people are either anti-social or in any manner opposed to present society, they simply go along to get along.

In the beginning of this book one of our first considerations was Information Overload, and the consequences this has on modern society. We can, now that you have progressed to this point, demonstrate how Information Overload, Judicial Activism, Cultural Marxism, Legislative Environmentalism, and Special Education all come together in a master plan of conquest. This is not a military conquest, it is a new type of subjugation — the bondage of society through scientific means, with only limited force. This is the beginning of the New Dark Age. Unlike the medieval dark age this one is different in nature. Our new coming dark age is a period in which we lose our freedoms to an ever increasing in power, international state controlled by the Satori. The major portion of this plan is taking place at the present time, and may be seen in the incrementalism of legislative, environmental, and other changes at the direction of the Satori. A considerable factor in societal change is the growing nature of urban areas. It is reasonable to assume that by the beginning of the 21st century well over two-thirds of the world's population will be domiciled in cities. This in itself creates a serious problem, as Julian Huxley stated, "overcrowding in animals leads to disorientated, neurotic and downright pathological behavior." The same thing is of course true for humans. In his document *Why Is Man So Aggressive*, G.N. Carstars clearly points out that cities and overcrowding, the anoniminity of which plus the lack of moral guidance, is the cause for a large percentage of our urban problems.

The radical change in the way we receive information compared to a previous time is also taking on a life of its own. In our present time the function of reading to learn is rapidly disappearing. Replacement for it is audio visual information, as supplied by television, movies, and computers. The sheer volume of information available to the individual is mind-boggling. Satellite TV has expanded the availability of even more options and digitalization will in the near future expand available signals to an infinite number of options. An examination of man's mass-media consumption habits serve to reinforce the above demonstrated facts. By examining literate 25 year olds in various epochs we see the rapid change taking place at present:

Per 1000 of Pop.	1965	1985	1995
Books read	15	11	6
Newspapers	326	280	220
TV hours	310	950	1332
Radio hours	1334	960	840
News magazines	40	15	11
International News	5	3	0

The very apparent reduction in the reading of non-fiction books is remarkable. It is my personal belief that this may well be founded in the current job requirements of most employers. Where 30 years ago a Liberal Arts degree was worth a great deal, today it is useless. There are several reasons for this. First, the educational standards have been so lowered that the only degrees thought of as serious by employers are in the engineering, mathematical, or hard science fields. Second, employment requirements have, over the years, become much more single-source directed. Without a good background in computer sciences you are worthless on the job market. Added to this is the more technical nature of current employment. Even an auto mechanic is required to operate computers for diagnostics of modern autos. All this causes great social upheaval, in education and the direction one might take.

When I went to college one of my professor's favorite sayings was, "Of 100% of the population, 1% knows what's going on and does something about it, 3% knows what's going on and does nothing, and 96% are ignorant fools." This may be an overstatement, but in the 21st century it will get much worse. The reason is specialization, demanded by the complexity of technology. This pushes people more and more into separated specialized fields, it eliminates generalists who make the best managers, and might be referred to as renaissance men. A verification of this may be found in the exponentially expanding technical publications field. At the present time we have, worldwide, about 160,000 such periodicals in over 60 languages. Knowledge, more than ever before, becomes the tool and focus of power. This is particularly true of political power, where manipulation of information and how, why and when to manipulate it becomes very important. Today's politicians and parties have rafts of specialists, pollsters, demographticians, mathematicians, advisors, computer experts, cartographers, and who knows what else, just to tell them what their position should be on each issue based on location and demographics. Most of these specialists are in the employ of foundations and think-tanks and are paid for by the Satori through your taxes. In the most able words of Seneca, "Proof of a bad cause is the applause of the mob."

In the field of communications, the TV and computer technology has shrunk the world into a small community where virtually everyone has access to the world net. This, however, has not lead to a sense of community, but just the opposite. The young who are particularly addicted to this media have totally lost their sense of community. They have become the first victims of Information Overload. Instead of involving themselves in community activities like the Boy Scouts, the Brownies, or the YMCA, they become self-centered in a communal visual and auditory electronic scheme. This then distracts human interaction and serves to further isolate them from their fellow humans. This is only the beginning.

To convince yourself of what is taking place, just visit any of the various Video Arcades in your neighborhood and watch all of the young men who should be at work, school or home with their families, pile quarters into various loud, violent "games." All this impedes human understanding, social interaction, and creates a climate in which conflict becomes more violent and prevalent. This artificial extension of interaction through computers may be characterized as the new era. Or according to Z. Brzezinski, the "Technetronic Era." In the below illustration we see the parallels with the 20th century, as well as the espoused outcome.

The Industrial Revolution (20th Cent.)	The New Age (21st Cent.)
Navigation Compass	Space Travel Computers
Gunpowder	Nuclear Physics
Printing	TV / Radio / Electronic communication
Result	**Result**
Agriculture to industry to machine operation	Automation to computer controlled (CAD/CAM) production to Robotics to replacement of humans in manufacturing.

The ultimate outcome of this is more leisure time filled with more frenzied actions and more unemployment, the rapid displacement of entire segments of the labor market, societal turmoil, the increase of crime, and the tremendous specialization of individuals in thousands of new fields, at the cost of societal intercourse. This will require new and different forms of education centered not on individual lectures and classes as today, but in interactive audio visual electronic presentations. Continuing education becomes a necessity because existing technology will quickly be passe' in very short time frames due to the speed of technological advances. At this point Information Overload will become so prevalent in all segments of society that manipulation will reach entirely new levels.

The beginning of this effect has become apparent in the last decade. The majority of people think of themselves as politically isolated. The most common sentiment heard when asked about voting is, "I don't vote anymore, my vote does not count anyhow." This in all probability is an exactly correct assumption made for the wrong reasons. Another good example of this is the separation of society into groups. This is being effected at greatest speed by the Satori through their political surrogates.

In my previous book *The Satori and The New Mandarins,* we explored in some detail the method of financing utilized by the Satori. We basically covered two methods, the funding through tax exempt foundations, and through your taxes. It is important to add drugs. The drug industry, in my opinion, is controlled worldwide. Most federally elected officials are not only aware of that fact but know the lower level management personnel in that industry. To prove this indisputably let us examine the method utilized in the manufacture of heroin. To refine raw opium into heroin, you need a rather specialized chemical which has very limited sources, aceticanahydride. Since the source of this chemical is limited to a specific number of producers, anyone who wanted to find out who was making heroin simply has to demand the shipping manifests of the chemical plants producing it, and follow the trail.

The opium trade has a long history, primarily in England. India was the largest producer and the British made an industry of exporting it to China. From the 1790's to the 1890's opium exports from India to China, completely controlled by the British East India Company, exploded in volume. A large number of the great fortunes in England can be traced to this business, as can the Boxer Rebellion. In 1790 there were around 80 opium dens in Shanghai. A hundred years later over 700. That the same firms are still involved in the same nasty business goes without saying. That they are connected to the Satori is a fact.

The money in the drug business is of such magnitude that no nation has succeeded in seriously disrupting it. The Shaw of Iran outlawed the growing of opium and the use of it in Iran. It got him deposed. Nixon attempted to seriously impede the drug industry and he was deposed. Clinton has basically dismantled interdiction, admitted to using drugs ("I didn't inhale"), and drug use has drastically increased under his presidency. Interestingly no matter what he does, no matter how many members of his administration are convicted, forced to resign, or have an untimely death, he can do no wrong. I believe there is a connection. This inevitably leads us to the pharmaceutical drug culture and its connection with the Satori plans. Quotes Dr. D. Krech, April 3, 1968, "I foresee the time when we shall have the means and therefore, inevitably the temptation to manipulate the behavior and intellectual function of all people." Has this not begun with the drugging of school children, i.e., ritalin?

In order to explore the last avenue of Satori income we must go back to the Boer war and England's Sir Cecil Rhodes. The nicest possible thing you can say about Rhodes is so bad we would not want it to appear in this book. The British coveted the treasures of the Transvaal and the Orange Free State in the Republic of South Africa. These two locales represent the single largest mineral wealth deposits in the known world, even today. I do not know how much in gold and diamonds has been mined, and neither does anyone else, outside of Satori control. However, the amount, in all probability, exceeds trillions of dollars. Rhodes subsequently came to partnership with several others including Sir Harry Oppenheimer. These men plundered South Africa, but not before they defeated the Boers and stole their birthright in a brutal war.

To accomplish this subjugation, Queen Victoria, in 1898, assembled the largest army that has ever been fielded in Africa (including the Second World War) 400,000 men. Not only was the Crown heavily involved, but the usual MI6 and the Round Table (Milner Group), one of the nefarious forerunners of the modern Satori, which is still in operation. The entire venture was financed by the opium trade. When the commanding General, Lord Kitchner, saw that he could not beat the indigenous Boers, he invented concentration camps. In these camps he interned the women and children of the Boers. Forty-six camps were constructed, and about 26,000 of the 117,000 interned Boer women and children died in them.

Rhodes later returned to England and became, through a series of secret and complicated bequest wills, the benefactor to the Fabian society, Rhodes scholarships, and an entire plethora of left-wing socialist causes specifically designed to develop and advance socialist minds. President Clinton, George Stephanopoulos, Robert Reich, and half of the present Clinton administration have been Rhode scholars, subject to that special socialist brainwashing exercise.

From this we can reach the conclusion that financing of Satori efforts is and has been carried out through four differing avenues. To this point we have covered financing and changes brought about through societal and engineering alteration of our world. It now remains to tie together the various remaining threads of the conspiracy, and then to examine exactly what their plans for the future are.

We must not lose sight of illegal drugs, for they are of paramount importance in the overall plan. Money from drugs provide much of the needed financing, and the result of their use meets the need to increase the power of the "police state" under the excuse of fighting the war against drugs. Furthermore, because drug sales are transacted in cash, they represent a large available flow of funds for nefarious purposes. People on drugs cease to be opponents, they become merely dependents of the product they seek.

In the wake of financial market collapses in many of the Asian Tigers, we can examine the full impact of the Satori Club of Rome's plans for America's de-industrialization. In the late 1960's, the Club of Rome produced several documents and white papers dealing with their policy of *"Zero Growth."*

The basic proposal was that the industrialized nations were to be impeded from further growth, socially, economically and in population. There were several methods by which this was to be accomplished:

1.) Unregulated, expanded, out-of-control immigration into the industrialized nations.
2.) Transfer, through economic advantage, manufacturing from the G7 to the third World.

3.) Drastic increase in environmental regulations applicable only to the G7 nations.

4.) Unwarranted expansion of consumer credit in the G7 nations to stimulate purchases of third world products.

Since 1940 America has lost more than 50% of its manufacturing capability (Crisis Adaption). At this point it is important to remember that a service economy nation is a third world nation. Only with active and developed manufacturing is it possible to be a power on the world stage. A very substantial portion of our manufacturing has either moved abroad or shut down. The stable long-term manufacturing jobs based on specialized skills are rapidly being displaced by the service sector. Employment has become short-term, with little or no job security, and even less of a future. While this is taking place in America the exact reverse is occurring in the Pacific Rim. The manufacturing job base is literally exploding. To keep this momentum going, along with the transfer of industries and markets, a correction was required. Prices of products were climbing to the point that in some fields it was again possible for American industry to compete. To reverse that position the Satori took steps to reduce the value of currencies in Mexico, South Korea, Thailand, Japan, the Philippines, and Indonesia. With those currencies safely devalued exports to America and Western Europe could again be drastically increased.

Country	Currency	Drop in Value by% in 1997
Mexico	Peso	50%
Indonesia	Rupiah	70.70%
Thailand	Baht	56.13%
Malaysia	Ringgit	45.86%
Philippines	Peso	39.29%
Taiwan	Dollar	19.52%
Singapore	Dollar	20.60%

These odious acts have been occurring for years but news sources avoid any mention. Government, being one of the Satori vehicles for implementation of these plans, is not going to tell you what is taking place. In examining the value of the dollar we can clearly see the trend. Since 1950 the dollar has lost 90 cents (90%) of its worth. In 1950 one dollar was close to five Swiss francs. Today one dollar is worth less than 1.60 Swiss francs, the franc being the world's most stable currency. The actual buying power of the dollar on domestic markets is about 10 cents verses 100 cents in 1950 dollar value. We are not discussing some abstract theory here, we are talking about your income, which is being destroyed with the direct assistance of both political parties.

A pronounced goal of the Satori is the destruction of national entities, and the elimination of nation states. In an effort to accomplish this, the media has unleashed an unrelenting attack on any patriotic group. I cannot recall a single instance in any news report on any media where patriotism was shown to be a virtue. Instead, when we examine our society we find, for instance, there is a strong move to eliminate the pledge of allegiance from school curricula. When I was on the school board this was brought up by various NEA active teachers. Reasons given were that it was out of date, that you could not hear it over the PA system, that it was irrelevant, that it violated the Church/State separation clause and that it did not comply with our global outlook. In every area of Satori plans, we can visit the classrooms of our public schools if we wish to become more acquainted with their strategy.

Please think about how you viewed the society that surrounded you 50 years ago. For you youngsters, let me explain. Fifty years ago your parents and grandparents had a different way of looking at society than the one you have today. We thought of our immediate family first, our relatives, then about the town in which we lived as our community. The state of residence was already somewhat removed. You were however, a New Yorker (or whatever). But last and foremost after family and town, you were an American. Not an African American, not an Italian American, just a plain American.

In the last 20 years the concepts of community, patriotism, and pride in America have gradually been replaced by Global concepts. The very word *"Global"* was not part of anyone's vocabulary. It was "the world." Global is a special word specifically designed to make you visualize the world as a small place. This is part of Cultural Marxism. Rather than people today thinking of themselves as being of German or Italian heritage they think of themselves as being European, Asian or African. This again is in order for you to be divested of your cultural heritage, and to get you into the New World Order thinking mode.

The new concept is *"Regionalization,"* which is the process of destroying your individuality, community and nationality. EC and NAFTA are the examples that will be recognized by most. To again quote Brzezinski, from his *Between Two Ages*, "Regionalization has become the US Foreign policy since 1960." And then in 1970, "The non-Russian states in the Soviet Union are perhaps the only exception to nationalism's successful dissolution of Colonial Empires." He could not possibly have been more iniquitous.

The UN, ever at the forefront of all efforts to centralize everything, has created an empire of agencies all toward the ends of global government. The Center for Development Planning Projections and Policies is the UN organization which overlooks this effort. Under its auspices we find the following: UNICEF, WHO, World Food and Agriculture Organization, World Education and Culture Organization, World Bank, International Monitory Fund, Global Meteorological Organization, International Atomic-Energy Agency, International Civil Aeronautics Organization, World Labor Association, The International Association for the Peaceful use of Space, International Agency of etc. etc. etc. and so on.

The Democrats, once the party of Thomas Jefferson, staunch anti-federalist and pro-private property, are today a socialist party, as are the Republicans. They have created a classic political spoilage system. In this system so many citizens are dependent upon government largess that the party can exist just on the support of those people to whom they have given entitlements. If we count government employees, the military, police agencies, state employees, those on welfare, food assistance, Medicare, Medicaid, Social Security, and all the other programs which make people dependent upon the state, we come up with over 50% of the population. That this is a disaster for the country and a benefit to the Satori goes without saying.

This is why I refer to the two political parties as the Republocrats. They are directed to implement all the varying collectivist programs of which we have been speaking in this book. Each of these systems, when implemented in concert, create a symphony of organized change in our world. It is a movement for subjugation of all society to the will of the Satori. Evidence of the conspiracy is amply presented in all the overlapping directorships of foundations. The amount of interlocking corporate, foundation, and think-tank board memberships, is nothing if not astounding. The same names just keep reappearing continuously.

If we now examine our previous text we see a number of differing acts, some of which, under superficial observation, appear unrelated. The actual fact is that they are all related in that they all contribute to the same goal, namely One World Government. They simply work in varying ways. Each of these acts and processes leads our nation closer to the totalitarian goal of the Satori. The only reason for the Satori plan in the first place is political power. This desire for power is nothing new, it is part of man's history from Alexander to Caesar to Napoleon to Stalin and Mao. All have thought of political power. The only difference with the Satori is that they are not lead by a demagogue, but are a group comprised of some of the richest people on earth. We must examine what the ultimate outcome of a Satori victory will be, and what it would mean to your children. The prognosis is not a pleasant one.

We now find in *The American Future* that the call for a national constitutional convention for 1979 was planned in 1970 but did not develop. A subsequent attempt in 1997 also failed. We can anticipate another effort in 2000. This is nothing more than a veiled attempt at getting rid of the United States Constitution, the single greatest roadblock to World Government. The words used are "redefining the meaning of modern democracy." The author of *The American Future* is none other than Z. Brzezinski, a Polish communist who now goes on to lecture about the inequities of our voting process, etc., with the blessings of the Satori.

In his study we are informed that "Deliberate management of the American future will become widespread, with the planners eventually displacing the lawyers as key social legislative manipulators." Could that be any clearer? Mandarins will replace elected officials as administrators of society. We are then informed that the "process of social planning and legislative action (personal freedom) must be merged." What this means is the creation of top down social and political management by a cadre of Mandarins. Then, "The strengthening of local, metropolitan government already recognized as an urgent necessity." Here comes the dictatorship! We also learn in *American Future* that, "Cultural reform and Social change will be brought about by 'programmatic engineering'." Just so we clearly understand *"Programmatic"* (of or pertaining to, or the nature of a program, planing of a system), *"Engineering"* (industrial organization, maneuvering and controlling). Does that perhaps strike a discordant chord? What we have learned is that the Satori system is to be implemented through a planned, programmed, contrivance. The study goes on to inform us that the implementers of the *"Programmatic Engineering"* will be the National Commission on Techintergrative Needs. This commission, we are informed, will take over all education for all citizens. We are also informed that citizen programming will be a lifelong process, which will be repeated every few years (lest they start to question the system). The document goes on endlessly in an ever expanding diatribe about the need for social and political centralization, and the evils of our fathers in allowing private property ownership, which is referred to as a social evil. I said he was a communist, and so did he. These themes may be found in all the various Satori strategies and are endlessly repeated in every one of their long range penetration documents.

Long Range Penetration

As with all large bureaucracies, a world government would be incredibly clumsy and as a result would become a dictatorship. All you have to do is look at the bureaucratic nightmare that is the United Nations, or the EC at Brussels, or what was the case in the USSR in Moscow. The inflexibility and inefficiency of our Federal Government serves as a small model. In the end scheme, there would be one world currency with a "cashless" society to control the citizens. The continents, according to UN documents, will be separated into regions, with regional administrators. Forget about voting, citizen assemblies, or any of that. Present day China gives us a model, as did the Soviet Union. The difference being that in the Soviet system about 5% of the population (18 million) were party members, who had at least some voice in the state's actions.

Under the Satori system that number will be sharply reduced. There will be the regional administrators, and the Mandarins. At present the number of Mandarins worldwide is under 5,000. The world will be sharply separated into those who have everything, and us, the serfs. The standard of living will be the same for all serfs, except those who are able to garnish the favor of the Mandarin ruling class. World population will be sharply reduced, according to reviewed documents, to under one billion. Birth control will be mandatory. To keep birth rates down homosexuality will be encouraged. All power will come from the state. All acts will have to be approved by the state. Education, employment, movement, and income, will be mandated by state authority. Justice will depend on the whims of the regional administrator. Law will be enforced by a police/military class whose benefits and living standards will be just enough higher than that of the serfs to keep them loyal to the ruling Mandarins. The police/military class will always come from a different region to prevent any emotional ties to the serfs. In other words, a classic top down totalitarian state, run by perhaps two or three hundred individual families (the Satori), and administered by Mandarins, whose mandates will be enforced by a police/military class. Unlike communism in the former USSR, some private property and privately owned business will be allowed. The Communist's learned that is was just too difficult to manage every detail of life. Therefore, you will be allowed to work all you like to buy a home, or to work 70-80 hours a week trying to make a living operating a small business — but — government will tell you how to operate that business. Yes, you may own it, but the Satori will control it, and tax it.

Their timetable for ending the Sovereignty of the United States as an independent nation is the year 2016. A few years ago they had hoped to achieve this by the year 2000, but they have not been able to confiscate the citizens' guns, or push through additional agreements like NAFTA, which are prerequisites. Can we defeat the Satori plan? Yes, provided American's learn about it in time. But without media support, we had better get busy. As the following special report from England indicates, time is short.

December 1999
Portman Papers
North Curry
Taunton, England

GLOBAL DEMOCRACY [SOCIALISM]

A recent internet World Net Daily.com report stated that in less than a year the UN will convene a special Millennium Assembly as a global summit on the future of the world. A Charter for Global Democracy, already signed by influential leaders in 56 nations, will be presented next September.

The Charter for Global Democracy is in reality a Charter for the abolition of individual freedom. The first of 12 principles calls for the consolidation of all international agencies under the direct authority of the UN. Principle three demands world UN taxes on aircraft, shipping fuels and on using the "global commons" — outer space, the atmosphere, non-territorial seas and "related environment."

Principle four eliminates the veto power on the Security Council. Principle five authorizes a standing UN Army. Principle six requires UN registration of all arms and the reduction of all national armies under the authority of the UN. Principle seven requires individual and national compliance with all UN "human rights" treaties. Principle eight activates the International Criminal Court and makes the International Court of Justice compulsory for all nations.

Behind the global government movement is the money supplied by the well-to-do elites headed by David Rockefeller and other money power "untouchables" (i.e. the Bilderbergers, etc.) who operate *ultra vires* legitimate governments.

Yes, the Capitalists did defeat communist USSR but we now know it was not free market, laissez faire, free enterprise capitalism that won, but a very elite group that controls the world's central banks and major industries, i.e. *The Capitalists* (the "Satori"), and they do not like unregulated free market competition. They want a global government which they control to their advantage, that they may attain their utopian goals.

In order to thwart the plans of the globalists, it is important that every American know the principles upon which the United States was founded, and, therefore, I ask you to read and re-read the following "Founding Documents."

Founding Documents of
The United States of America

The Constitution of the United States is probably the most cited and the least understood of all our nation's founding documents. The Constitution was crafted by a group who believed in forming a Federal government and, therefore, are referred to as "the Federalists."

In designing our Constitution the Federalists incorporated everything they could think of to make it impossible for any group to take over the government and take away the rights granted the citizens in the Declaration of Independence. Namely: the right to life, liberty and the pursuit of happiness, given each citizen by God, not by government. These words were "the shot heard 'round the world." There had never been such a government on earth.

Those who know the history of Europe know that Europe had a caste system every bit as strong as that which we today associate principally with India, and it was enforced by their governments. People were born into their "place" in life and they dare not attempt to change it. In Europe of the 17th and 18th centuries, Henry Ford and Thomas Edison probably would have been farm hands and not allowed to leave the farm. And, had they managed to leave the farm, they would never have been given permission by the government to build cars or develop electric light. Government controlled every aspect of one's life. Private property was granted only to nobles, by government.

Men like Thomas Jefferson knew that despite man's best intentions, a government of limited power would find ways to expand its power and once again control the citizen's lives. Therefore, they opposed the Constitution and became known as the anti-Federalists.

As you read the Federalist Papers, you will note that even the Federalists were afraid of what they termed "mob-rule" and what we, today, term "the democratic process." They did not believe that might-made-right, whether it be from armies, guns or popularity contests. They wanted to guarantee the principles in which they believed, such as: the right of private property; the right to a jury of one's peers rather than government officials; the right of free speech and press; the right to bear arms to protect oneself, etc. They did not want their new-found freedoms to be lost, not even to popular vote, so they made only one Federal office subject to popular vote — that of each area's Representative to Congress. Senators were chosen by each State's legislature and represented the interests of their State in Congress. The President and Vice President were elected by a select group of electors chosen by each State. The person who came in 2nd in the voting for President was made Vice President. And, to be sure the "wants" of Congress were within the laws as written in the Constitution, a Supreme Court was established.

Now, after the Federalists had devised this system of checks and balances to forever limit the scope and power of the Federal government, thus assuring citizens that the rights granted them in the Declaration of Independence could never be taken away by the Federal government, the anti-Federalists still said, in effect, "No, we will not join, because we do not think your constitution can or will prevent the Federal government from growing and taking away the citizens' God-given rights."

Madison, Hamilton and others did their best to argue for their constitution, but to no avail. Finally, the anti-Federalists proposed twelve amendments to the proposed constitution. Amendments which were stated in very clear language. Language they felt made abundantly clear the limits of the Federal government. These were prohibitions against anyone, ever, increasing the scope and power of the Federal government over the States or the citizens of those states no matter how popular the idea or how powerful the forces that wanted to take away the freedom of the citizens and return them to "their place" in life. These amendments, stated in short, clear sentences, that such laws were unconstitutional. And, because these amendments were written as prohibitions against the Federal government to forever guarantee our rights, they were called THE BILL OF RIGHTS.

When the Federalists agreed to schedule a vote on these amendments as one of the first acts of Congress, the Constitution was ratified and the United States of America created. As such, we became the first people on earth whose rights are given us by God and not by government, and, we remain the only people on earth whose rights come from God, not government. No other people have such a constitution. Not England, Canada, Germany, Japan . . . no one! In fact, the United Nations Charter is a virtual copy of that of the former Union of Soviet Socialist Republics. Read the Declaration of Independence giving special attention to the words in the second paragraph (bold type added) and the Bill of Rights, before you vote to live under the old system promoted by the globalists and United Nations advocates.

---

*On September 25th, 1789, the First Congress of the United States proposed to the state legislatures 12 amendments to the Constitution that would assure individual citizens' rights and prevent autocracy by the central government. Ten of the 12 amendments were ratified by three-fourths of the state legislatures and were formally adopted on December 15th, 1791. These amendments have since been known as the Bill of Rights.

Declaration of Independence

In Congress, July 4, 1776
The unanimous Declaration of the thirteen united States of America

When in the Course of human events, it becomes necessary for one people to dissolve the political bands which have connected them with another, and to assume among the powers of the earth, the separate and equal station to which the Laws of Nature and of Nature's God entitle them, a decent respect to the opinions of mankind requires that they should declare the causes which impel them to the separation.

We hold these truths to be self-evident, that all men are created equal, that they are endowed by their Creator with certain unalienable Rights, that among these are Life, Liberty and the pursuit of Happiness. That to secure these rights, Governments are instituted among Men, deriving their just Powers from the consent of the governed, — That whenever any Form of Government becomes destructive of these ends, it is the Right of the People to alter or to abolish it, and to institute new Government, laying its foundation on such principles and organizing its powers in such form, as to them shall seem most likely to effect their Safety and Happiness. Prudence, indeed, will dictate that Governments long established should not be changed for light and transient causes; and accordingly all experience hath shewn, that mankind are more disposed to suffer, while evils are sufferable, than to right themselves by abolishing the forms to which they are accustomed. But when a long train of abuses and usurpations, pursuing invariably the same Object evinces a design to reduce them under absolute Despotism, it is their right, it is their duty, to throw off such Government, and to provide new guards for their future security — Such has been the patient sufferance of these Colonies; and such is now the necessity which constrains them to alter their former Systems of Government. — The history of the present King of Great Britain is a history of repeated injuries and usurpations, all having in direct object the establishment of an absolute Tyranny over these States. To prove this, let facts be submitted to a candid world.

He has refused his Assent to Laws, the most wholesome and necessary for the public good.

He has forbidden his Governors to pass Laws of immediate and pressing importance, unless suspended in their operation till his Assent should be obtained; and when so suspended, he has utterly neglected to attend to them.

He has refused to pass other Laws for the accommodation of large districts of people, unless those people would relinquish the right of Representation in the Legislature, a right inestimable to them and formidable to tyrants only.

He has called together legislative bodies at places unusual, uncomfortable, and distant from the depository of their Public Records, for the sole purpose of fatiguing them into compliance with his measures.

He has dissolved Representative Houses repeatedly, for opposing with manly firmness his invasions on the rights of the people.

He has refused for a long time, after such dissolutions, to cause others to be elected; whereby the Legislative Powers, incapable of Annihilation, have returned to the People at large for their exercise; the State remaining in the mean time exposed to all the dangers of invasion from without, and convulsions within.

He has endeavoured to prevent the population of these States; for that purpose obstructing the Laws for Naturalization of Foreigners; refusing to pass others to encourage their migrations hither, and raising the conditions of new Appropriations of Lands.

He has obstructed the Administration of Justice, by refusing his Assent to Laws for establishing Judiciary Powers.

He has made Judges dependent on his Will alone, for the tenure of their offices, and the amount and payment of their salaries.

He has erected a multitude of New Offices, and sent hither swarms of Officers to harrass our People, and eat out their substance.

He has kept among us, in times of peace, Standing Armies without the Consent of our legislatures.

He has affected to render the Military independent of and superior to the Civil Power.

He has combined with others to subject us to a jurisdiction foreign to our constitution, and unacknowledged by our laws; giving his Assent to their Acts of pretended Legislation:

For Quartering large bodies of armed troops among us:

For protecting them, by a mock Trial, from Punishment for any Murders which they should commit on the Inhabitants of these States:

For cutting off our Trade with all parts of the world:

For imposing Taxes on us without our Consent:

For depriving us in many cases, of the benefits of Trial by Jury:

For transporting us beyond seas to be tried for pretended offences:

For abolishing the free system of English Laws in a neighbouring Province, establishing therein an Arbitrary government, and enlarging its Boundaries so as to render it at once an example and fit instrument for introducing the same absolute rule into these Colonies:

For taking away our Charters, abolishing our most valuable Laws, and altering fundamentally the forms of our Governments:

For suspending our own Legislature, and declaring themselves invested with power to legislate for us in all cases whatsoever.

He has abdicated Government here, by declaring us out of his Protection and waging War against us.

He has plundered our seas, ravaged our Coasts, burnt our towns, and destroyed the lives of our people.

He is at this time transporting large Armies of foreign Mercenaries to compleat the works of death, desolation and tyranny, already begun with circumstances of Cruelty and perfidy scarcely paralleled in the most barbarous ages, and totally unworthy the Head of a civilized nation.

He has constrained our fellow Citizens taken Captive on the high Seas to bear Arms against their Country, to become the executioners of their friends and Brethren, or to fall themselves by their Hands.

He has excited domestic insurrections amongst us, and has endeavoured to bring on the inhabitants of our frontiers, the merciless Indian Savages, whose known rule of warfare, is an undistinguished destruction of all ages, sexes and conditions.

In every stage of these Oppressions we have Petitioned for Redress in the most humble terms: Our repeated Petitions have been answered only by repeated injury. A Prince, whose character is thus marked by every act which may define a Tyrant, is unfit to be the ruler of a free people.

Nor have we been wanting in attention to our Brittish brethren. We have warned them from time to time of attempts by their legislature to extend an unwarrantable jurisdiction over us. We have reminded them of the circumstances of our emigration and settlement here. We have appealed to their native justice and magnanimity, and we have conjured them by the ties of our common kindred to disavow these usurpations, which, would inevitably interrupt our connections and correspondence. They too have been deaf to the voice of justice and of consanguinity. We must, therefore, acquiesce in the necessity, which denounces our Separation, and hold them, as we hold the rest of mankind, Enemies in War, in Peace Friends.

We, therefore, the Representatives of the united States of America, in General Congress, Assembled, appealing to the Supreme Judge of the world for the rectitude of our intentions, do, in the Name, and by Authority of the good People of these Colonies, solemnly publish and declare, That these United Colonies are, and of Right ought to be Free and Independent States; that they are absolved from all Allegiance to the British Crown, and that all political connection between them and the State of Great Britain, is and ought to be totally dissolved; and that as Free and Independent States, they have full Power to levy War, conclude Peace, contract Alliances, establish Commerce, and to do all other Acts and Things which Independent States may of right do.

And for the support of this Declaration, with a firm reliance on the protection of Divine Providence, we mutually pledge to each other our Lives, our Fortunes and our sacred Honor.

The Bill of Rights

Amendment I – Freedom of Religion, Press, Expression
Ratified 12/15/1791

Congress shall make no law respecting an establishment of religion, or prohibiting the free exercise thereof; or abridging the freedom of speech, or of the press; or the right of the people peaceably to assemble, and to petition the Government for a redress of grievances.

Amendment II – Right to Bear Arms
Ratified 12/15/1791

A well regulated Militia, being necessary to the security of a free State, the right of the people to keep and bear Arms, shall not be infringed.

Amendment III – Quartering of Soldiers
Ratified 12/15/1791

No Soldier shall, in time of peace be quartered in any house, without the consent of the Owner, nor in time of war, but in a manner to be prescribed by law.

Amendment IV – Search and Seizure
Ratified 12/15/1791

The right of the people to be secure in their persons, houses, papers, and effects, against unreasonable searches and seizures, shall not be violated, and no Warrants shall issue, but upon probable cause, supported by Oath or affirmation, and particularly describing the place to be searched, and the persons or things to be seized.

Amendment V – Trial and Punishment, Compensation for Takings
Ratified 12/15/1791

No person shall be held to answer for a capital, or otherwise infamous crime, unless on a presentment or indictment of a Grand Jury, except in cases arising in the land or naval forces, or in the Militia, when in actual service in time of War or public danger; nor shall any person be subject for the same offense to be twice put in jeopardy of life or limb; nor shall be compelled in any criminal case to be a witness against himself, nor be deprived of life, liberty, or property, without due process of law; nor shall private property be taken for public use, without just compensation.

Amendment VI – Right to Speedy Trial, Confrontation of Witnesses
Ratified 12/15/1791

In all criminal prosecutions, the accused shall enjoy the right to a speedy and public trial, by an impartial jury of the State and district wherein the crime shall have been committed, which district shall have been previously ascertained by law, and to be informed of the nature and cause of the accusation; to be confronted with the witnesses against him; to have compulsory process for obtaining witnesses in his favor, and to have the Assistance of Counsel for his defence.

Amendment VII – Trial by Jury in Civil Cases
Ratified 12/15/1791

In suits at common law, where the value in controversy shall exceed twenty dollars, the right of trial by jury shall be preserved, and no fact tried by a jury, shall be otherwise re-examined in any Court of the United States, than according to the rules of the common law.

Amendment VIII — Cruel and Unusual Punishment
Ratified 12/15/1791

Excessive bail shall not be required, nor excessive fines imposed, nor cruel and unusual punishments inflicted.

Amendment IX – Construction of Constitution
Ratified 12/15/1791

The enumeration in the Constitution, of certain rights, shall not be construed to deny or disparage others retained by the people.

Amendment X – States' Rights
Ratified 12/15/1791

The powers not delegated to the United States by the Constitution, nor prohibited by it to the States, are reserved to the States respectively, or to the people.

These are the revolutionary principles upon which the United States was founded. It is because of these principles that citizens of the United States have the most individual freedom and the highest standard of living ever known to man. These are the principles which we, the benefactors, must proclaim to all the nations of the earth as the global model for the future of mankind — not those of the "Old World Order" touted by advocates of a United Nations global government!

APPENDICES

APPENDIX I
About the Author

Dr. Adrian H. Krieg CfMgE
Curriculum Vita
Updated July 1997

Personal particulars:
Born St. Gallen Switzerland 1938
Dual National, Fluent in English and German

Education:
HS Pembroke Academy, NH, class Valedictorian
Elmhurst College/University of Mex./
    San Miguel De Allende Campus
CCU California Coast University
SME Society of Manufacturing Engineers/Certified
    Manufacturing. Engineer.
Rectified 1996.
World University/Cultural Doctorate Manufacturing Science.

Memberships:

American Nuclear Society	(ANS) Ret. 1997
American Welding Society	(AWS)
American Society for Metals	(ASM)
Society of Manufacturing Engineers	(SME) Certified
Society of Pipe Engineers & Designers	(SPED)
Nuclear Suppliers Assoc.	(NSA) Ret. 1997
American Arbitration Society	(AAS) Ret. 1987
World Affairs Council	Ret. 1990
CT World Trade Assoc. Advisory board	Ret. 1993

U.S. Dep. of Commerce:

CT & RI District Export Council	1980-1992
Co-Chair CT Strike force for Fair Trade	1990
Legislative Committee	1989-1992
Finance Committee	1989-1991

Special:

ASW American Welding Society Speakers Bureau since 1985

Vice Chair AWS Committee Fume & Ventilation 1985-until disbanded

Recipient NATTCO Award 1983 - Best New Welding Product of 1983-AWS

z 48- 1 Committee (standards for welding safety ANSI & AWS)

AWS & ASM & SME consultants directories.

Thomas Award for advertising 1983

AWS Silver Certificate

Académie Européenne des Sciences, des Arts et des lettres 1989

Eli Whitney Entrepreneur of the year (certif. of recognition)

CT District Export Council 1982-1992 (appointed by Sec. Commerce)

Rolex award 1987

Published:

Plate Bending Machines, (FMA)

The Problems with Welding Fumes and what to do about them, (Widder)

Marketing your Product through Distribution Channels (Krieg)

Distributor Marketing, (Widder)

The Satori and the New Mandarins, (Hallberg)

Over 100 technical articles in the world press 1962-1997

Business Experience

CEO of: Widder Corp./Rovic Manufacturing Co./Nugget Realty Corp./Mamaroneck Depot Plaza Corp./A. Krieg Consulting Inc./ Consumable Trading Inc.

Secretary: Vicktor J. Krieg Inc.

Past and present board of Directors: Widder Corp./Rovic Manufacturing Co./Nugget Realty Corp./ Mam. Depot Plaza Corp./ Panox Trading Inc./Widder UK ltd./Colonial Bankcorp./CT World Trade Asoc./Widder RSA Pty.Ltd./ FM Reg. School Board CT District Trade Council./AWS Fume Committee.

APPENDIX II

BIBLIOGRAPHY
and
RECOMMENDED READING
(In addition to books mentioned in the text.)

Allen, G., *Conspiracy*

Allen, G. & Abraham, L., *None Dare Call It Conspiracy*

Atkinson, James, *The Edge of War*

Atkinson, R., *Treason at Maastrict*

Baret, R. J. & Muller, R. E., *Global Research*

Barnes, Harry E., *Perpetual War for Perpetual Peace*

Barnes, Harry E., *Genesis of the World War*

Bastiat, Frederick, *Economic Harmonies*

Bastiat, Frederick, *The Law*

Beard, Charles, *President Roosevelt and the Coming of the War, 1941*

Bennett, J. & DiLorenzo, T., *Official Lies*

Bohm-Bawerk, Eugene, *Capital and Interest*

Burnham, James, *Suicide of the West*

Burnham, James, *Congress and the American Tradition*

Carson, Clarence, *The American Tradition*

Castle, Eugene, *The Great Giveaway*

Chamberlain, William, *America's Second Crusade*

Chamberlain, William, *Appeasement – Road to War*

Chambers, Whitaker, *Witness*

Chesterton, A. K., *The New Unhappy Lords*

Connolly, B., *The Rotten Heart of Europe*

Council On Foreign Relations, The, *1995 Annual Report*

Crocker, George, *Roosevelt's Road to Russia*

D'Sousa, D., *My Dear Alex*

DeLove, Sidney, *Quiet Betrayal*

Douglas, Gregory, *Gestapo Chief,* 2 volumes

Dowd, Kevin, *Laissez-Faire Banking*

Ebeling, Richard, *Austrian Economics: A Reader*

Ekon, Amos, *Founder*

Epperson, A. R., *The Unseen Hand*

Evans, Christopher, *The Micro Millennium*

Finder, Joseph, *Red Carpet*

Friedman, David D., *Hidden Order*

Friedman, Milton, *Capitalism & Freedom*

Friedman, Milton & Rose, *Free To Choose*

Funderburk, D., *Betrayal of America*

Funderburk, D., *Pinstripes and Reds*

Garrett, G., *The American Story*

Gilder, George, *Wealth and Poverty*

Glasstone, S. & N. A.Jordan, *Nuclear Power and Its Environmental Effects*

Golitsyn, A., *New Lies for Old*

Golitsyn, A., *The Perestroika Deception*

Greaves, Bettina Bien, *Austrian Economics*

Griffin, G. E., *The Creature from Jekyll Island*

Grigg, W. N., *Freedom On The Altar*

Gross, Martin, *The End of Sanity*

Hayek, F. A., *Road To Serfdom*

Hazlitt, Henry, *The Critics of Keynesian Economics*

Hazlitt, Henry, *Economics In One Lesson*

Hersh, Seymour M., *The Sampson Option*

Horowitz, David, *Radical Son*

Huck, Dr. Susan, *Why Do We Americans Submit To This?*

Hutt, W.H., *Keynesianism: Retrospect and Prospect*

Hyneman/Lutz, *American Political Writing During the Founding Era*

Ikeda, Sanford, *Dynamics of the Mixed Economy*

Ingrams, Richard, *Muggridge: The Biography*

Jasper, W., *Global Tyranny Step by Step*

Jipping, Tom, *Does the First Amendment Contradict Itself?*

Jones, M., *John Cardinal Krol*

Kellems, Vivian, *Toil, Taxes & Trouble*

Kelly, B., *Adventures in Porkland*

Kelly, C., *Conspiracy Against God and Man*

Kelly, Tom, *Adventures In Porkland*

Kessler, R., *Inside the CIA*

Kilpatrick, James J., *The Sovereign States*

Kimmel, H. E., *Admiral Kimmel's Story*

Kincaid, C., *Global Bondage*

Krieg, A. H., *The Satori and the New Mandarins*

Lambro, Donald, *Fat City*

Lane, Rose, *The Discovery of Freedom*

LaPierre, W., *Guns, Crime, and Freedom*

Lax, Albert, *Consumers' Capitalism*

LeFevre, Robert, *The Philosophy of Ownership*

Locke, John, *Of Civil Government*

Madison, Hamilton & Jay, *The Federalist Papers*

Marx, Karl, *The Communist Manifesto*

McAlvany, D., *Toward a New World Order*

McManus, John, *Changing Guard*

McManus, John, *The Insiders*

McManus, John, *Financial Terrorism*

Mises, Ludwig von, *Human Action*

Mises, Ludwig von, *Socialism*

Mises, Ludwig von, *Bureaucracy*

Mises, Ludwig von, *The Theory of Money and Credit*

Morgenstern, George, *Pearl Harbor*

Morley, Felix, *Freedom & Federalism*

Mullins, E., *The World Order*

Mullins, E., *Secrets of the Federal Reserve*

Nock, Albert J., *Our Enemy The State*

Nock, Albert J., *Mr. Jefferson*

O'Rourke, P. J., *Parliament of Whores*
Opitz, Edmund, *Your Church, Their Target*
Opitz, Edmund, *Religion: Foundation of the Free Society*
Opitz, Edmund, *The Libertarian Theology of Freedom*
Palmer, William, *The Court vs. The People*
Palyi, Melchior, *Compulsory Medical Care and the Welfare State*
Phillips, *The Quest for Excellence*
Pike, James A., *If This Be Heresy*
Pombo & Farrah, *This Land Is Our Land*
Quigley, Carroll, *The Anglo-American Establishment*
Ray, Dixie Lee, *Environmental Overkill*
Ray, Dixie Lee, *Trashing the Planet*
Read, Leonard, *The Free Market and Its Enemy*
Regnery, Henry, *A Few Reasonable Words*
Ressler, Ronald, *Inside the CIA*
Roberts, A., *Victory Denied*
Robertson, Pat, *The New World Order*
Robison, John, *Proofs of a Conspiracy*
Rothbard, Murray, *America's Great Depression*
Rothbard, Murray, *Left & Right*
Rothbard, Murray, *Making Economic Sense*
Rothbard, Murray, *The Case Against The FED*
Sadat, Jehan, *A Woman of Egypt*
Sanera & Shaw, *Facts Not Fear*
Sauborn, F. R., *Design For War*
Sinkin, J. & A. Zelman, *Gun Control: Gateway to Tyranny*
Sklar, H., *Trilateralism*
Slomich, Sidney J., *The American Nightmare*
Soros, George, *The Crisis of Global Capitalism*
Sowell, Thomas, *The Vision of the Anointed*
Stelzer, G., *The Nightmare of Camelot*
Stick, P., *Defrauding America*
Sutton, A. E., *America's Secret Establishment*

Syke, Charles, *A Nation of Victims*

Tansill, Charles, *Back Door to War*

Taylor, Jared, *Paved With Good Intentions*

Theobald, R. A., *The Final Secret of Pearl Harbor*

Trilateral Commission, The, *1995 Catalogue*

Tuchman, Barbara, *The Proud Tower*

Tuchman, Barbara, *First Salute*

United Nations, *Charter*

U.S. *Bill of Rights*

U.S. *Constitution*

U.S. Labor Party, *Dope Inc.*

Vennard, Sr., Wickliff, *The Federal Reserve Hoax*

Walbert, M. W., *The Coming Battle*

Weaver, Richard, *Ideas Have Consequences*

Welch, Jr., Robert, *May God Forgive Us*

White, Andrew, *Fiat Money Inflation in France*

Wolf, Tom, *The Painted World*

Woodward, B., *The Agenda*

Wormser, R. A., *Foundations and Their Power and Influence*

Zahner, D., *The Secret Side of History*

Text Newsletter Sources

Global Energy Outlook

Insiders Report

Earth Island Institute

EPA Environmental News

Nuclear Waste News

Nukewatch

Elsevier Environment

Alliance for America Foundation

Center for Health, Environment
and Justice

SECC

The Defense Monitor

Center for Economic Conversion

ICCR

Worldwatch Institute

The McAlvany Intelligence
Advisor

Earth Island Institute

Earth Share

Ocean Alert

The Spotlight Union of
Concerned Scientists

The Corporate Examiner

Nucleus

Nukewatch Pathfinder

The Defense Monitor

Center for Economic Conversion

Public Citizen (Critical Mass
Energy Project)

Council on Economic Priorities

Personal Finance

Triple R

Analysis & Outlook

Environmental News (EPA)

The Fleet Street Letter

Global Insights

Argus Update

Traders Edge

Oxford Club

Wall Street Underground

Taipan

Text Internet Sources

gruene. de/aktuell/presse/pm97 1 2/pm97- 178. htm
.hbdl.de/infomieter/hbs.htm
admin. ch/bbs/news/pm/kimal-d. htm
hrz.uni-oldenburg. de/~oliver/bg/e.bgindex. html
hummro. org/home. htm
freedomhouse. org/
idsonline. com/sdusa
libertymatters. org
gci.ch/
gci. chgreencrossfamily
gci.chdigital.forum/
worldwide. org/
hrz.uni-olbenburg.de/
wri. org/wril
imaja. com/imaja/chanse
3 cddb. com/xw/cd/rock
gn. apc org/gn/aboutindex. htm
admin. ch/bfs/news/pm/klima
usgcrp. gov/ipcc
wcc. coe. org/climate
usgcp. gov/ipcc/html/getpts/himc
secularhumanism.org/intro/what. html
members. aol. com/skepticweb/atheistorgs. html
gci.ch/
gci. ch/greencrossfamily/gorby/newspeech/newactivities. html
/gorby/gorby. html
/digitalforum/speeches/bc-wb. html
libertymatters. org 4 79 7%201mms. html
wcc-coe. org/climate/
wcc-coe. org/climate/bkgnd-en. html
idsonline. com/sdusa/whatwe. html
gn.apc org/socint/who html
yn.apc.org/gn/about/index html
worldwildlife org
usgcrp. gov/ipcc
hummrro. org/home. htm

idsonline.com sdusa
wn. org/wri]
imaja. com/imaja/cange/environment/ef/whatis. html
brynet. net/~gerryr/index. htmL/
tavinstute.org [etc
clubobrome.org

Globalist Organizations

The Club of Rome

Americans for Democratic Action

America in the Technetronic Age

Socialist International

World Resources Institute

Tavistock Institute of Human Relations

Bildebergers

Trialteral Commission

Counsel on Foreign Relations

The Milner Group

The Round Table

World Council of Churches

Brookings Institute

Institute for Policy Studies

The Royal Institute for International Affairs

Conservative/Patriotic Print Media

Taking Aim
P.O. Box 1486
Noxon, MT 59853

Patriot Report
P.O. Box 1148
Sallisaw, OK 74955

PA Patriot Press
P.O. Box 211
Evlerson, PA

National Review
215 Lexington Ave.
NY, NY 10016

Liberty
P.O. Box 1181
Port Townsend, WA 98368

The Spotlight
300 Independence Ave. SE
Washington, DC 20003

Southern Partisan
P.O. Box 11708
Columbia, SC 29211

The Washington Times
3600 NY Ave. NE
Washington, DC 20002

Culture Wars
206 Marquette Ave.
South Bend, IN 46617

American Survival Guide
206 Cinnamon Deal
Elis Viejo, CA 92656

American Promise Ministries
3000 Great Northern Rd.
Sand Point, ID 83864

Carl Klang Ministries
P.O. Box 217
Colton, OR 97017

The Grass Roots Journal
P.O. Box 7353
St. Petersburg, FL 33734

The Resister
P.O. Box 35046
Fayetteville, NC 28303

Wake Up Call America
P.O. Box 280488
Lakewood, CO 80228-0488

The Jubilee
P.O. Box 310
Midpines, CA 95345

Wolverine Productions
P.O. Box 281
Augusta, MI 49368

The Oregon Observer
PMB 387, 233 Rogue River Hwy.
Grants Pass, OR 97527

The Nationalist Times
P.O. Box 426
Allison Park, PA 15101

Human Events
One Massachusetts Ave. NW
Washington, DC 20001

The Wanderer
201 Ohio St.
St. Paul, MN 55107

Washington Dateline
P.O. Box 5687
Baltimore, MD 21210

The Edgefield Journal
P.O. Box628
Edgefield, SC 29824

The Idaho Observer
P.O. Box 1806
Post Falls, ID 83854

The American Spectator
2020 N. 14th Street
Arlington, VA 22201

The Free American
UH Hwy. 380 Box 2943
Bingham, NM 87832

American Bulletin
P.O. Box 3096
Central Point, OR 97502

New Oxford Review
1069 Kains Avenue
Berkley, CA 94706

GANPAC Brief
P.O. Box 11124
Pensacola, FL32524

The Barnes Review
130 Third Street
Washington, DC 20003

Midnight Messenger
P.O. Box 96
Colton, OR 97017

American Renaissance
P.O. Box 527
Oakton, VA 22124

GSG Associates
P.O. Box 6448
San Pedro, CA 90734

Free Enterprise Soc. News
738 W. Shaw Ave., Suite 205
Clovis, CA 93612

The Trumpet Messenger
P.O. Box 565
Sandy Hook, CT 06482

Mannarain
6248 Lost Creek Rd.
Eagle Point, OR 97524

Media Bypass
P.O. Box 5326
Evansville, IN 47716

Christian Crusade for Truth
HC 66 Box 39
Deming, NM 88030

Sentinel of Freedom
2790 Wrondel Way #41
Reno, NV 89510

The National Investor
410 River Street
Spooner, WI 54801

Analysis & Outlook
P.O. Box 1167
Port Townsend, WA 98368

Insight
3600 NY Ave. NE
Washington, DC 20002

The Register
P.O. Box 47095
Kansas City, MO 64188

New American
P.O. Box 8040
Appleton, WI 54913

Mennonite Weekly Review
129 W. 6th Street
Newton, KS 67114

David Patterson
2816 Darby Falls Drive
Las Vegas, NV 89134-7476

The National Educator
1216 N. Tustin Avenue
Orange, CA 92867

Christian Patriot Association
P.O. Box 596
Boring, OR 97009

Speak Out
P.O. Box 1187
Hillsboro, NH 03244

FFF David Hornberger
11350 Random Hills Rd., #800
Fairfax, VA 22030

World University Roundtable
P.O. Box 2470
Benson, AZ 85602
Dr. Howard Zitko, Pres.

The Monodnock Shoppers News
445 West Street
Keene, NH 03431

Portman Papers
20 Portman, North Curry,
Taunton, EA3 6NL England

Schweizerzeit
Postfach 23, CH 8416
Flaach, Switzerland

Editors Note: *The foregoing lists those publications known to and used by the author. It is not meant to be a complete listing of all "Conservative/ Patriotic Print Media."*

INDEX

BOOKS OF INTEREST
ON
SIMILAR SUBJECTS

Available through all bookstores
or directly from the publisher,

HALLBERG PUBLISHING CORPORATION
P.O. Box 23985 • Tampa, Florida 33623
Phone 1-800-633-7627 • Fax 1-800-253-7323

Ayn Rand's Fiction . . . Today's Reality!

THE Satori AND THE NEW Mandarins

by

A. H. KRIEG

The Satori And The New Mandarins by A. H. Krieg, demonstrates the details of a conspiracy in our government, and does this out of the mouths of the conspirators. The Satori is what the author calls the elite who lead the conspiracy, while the Mandarins are the active participants. Listed are 3,400 Mandarins by name in present world government, as well as the most important international participants.

ISBN #0-87319-044-0
342 pages – $14.95

Praise for

A Cure Worse Than The Disease . . .

"Rigorously argued, and guaranteed to be contro-versial. Mr. O'Shea has made a highly original contribution to the great debate over affirmative action that is sweeping the country."

— WILLIAM A. RUSHER, FORMER PUBLISHER, *NATIONAL REVIEW*

"An extremely valuable book. O'Shea tackles with courage, honesty, and fairness one of the most serious social problems of our time, the damage caused by the proliferation of anti-discrimination law (race, sex, age, disability, etc.). He shows with clarity and wit that the cure (for a problem that often does not exist) is far worse than the disease. Hugely informative and a pleasure to read."

— LINO A. GRAGLIA, A. DALTON CROSS PROFESSOR IN LAW,
UNIVERSITY OF TEXAS

"The best counter to the 'racism, sexism and homophobia' cant of the Politically Correct – the cultural Marxists – is reality, and *A Cure Worse Than the Disease* offers a cold dose of it. It should be required reading on every campus in America, as well as in corporate boardrooms and legislative chambers. Finally, someone has stood up for the truth about race and sex."

— WILLIAM S. LIND, FREE CONGRESS FOUNDATION

M. LESTER O'SHEA

A CURE
WORSE THAN
THE DISEASE

Fighting Discrimination Through Government Control

Foreword by
WALTER E. WILLIAMS

A Cure Worse Than The Disease makes it clear that the long-held American belief that this is a land of opportunity in which "cream rises to the top" and "you can't keep a good man down," is fundamentally valid, and that, as Adam Smith pointed out long ago, free markets and free choice best produce the fairest results.

ISBN #0-87319-048-3
280 pages, hardcover, $24.95

memoirs of a superfluous man

Albert Jay Nock

"This is the kind of book that gets under a person's skin, performing catalytically to persuade the reader into becoming what he has it in him to be."
— Edmund A. Opitz

ISBN 0-87319-038-6
352 pages, Trade Paper, $16.95

"Albert Jay Nock's *Mr. Jefferson, is a superb biographical essay, beautifully written and penetrating in analysis; Mr. Nock understands Jefferson so well that one despairs of going at all beyond him."*
Richard Hofstadter
Columbia University

ISBN 0-87319-024-6
224 pages, Trade Paper, $14.95

"The most captivating single volume in the Jefferson literature."
Merrill D. Peterson
University of Virginia

Mr. JEFFERSON

Jefferson at the time of the French Revolution

by Albert Jay Nock

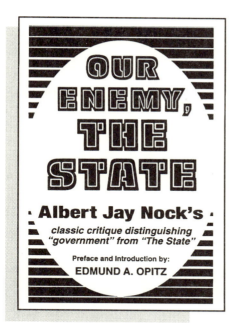

An essential history of Colonial America. Must reading for students of government and advocates of man's right to Life, Liberty and Property.

ISBN 0-87319-023-8
112 pages, Trade Paper, $9.95

Albert J. Nock (1870-1945) was a radical, in the venerable sense of the word: one whose ideas cut to the root and make you think again about things previously taken for granted.

— Edmund A. Opitz

ISBN 0-87319-041-6
224 pages, Trade Paper, $14.95

"A must read to better comprehend the important linkage between religious principals and individual liberty."

— RON PAUL

THE
LIBERTARIAN
THEOLOGY
OF
FREEDOM

by

The Reverend

Edmund
A. Opitz

"This book by Rev. Opitz will go a long way to help those in mainline churches appreciate the critical importance of liberty in the construction of a just society. It will disabuse all readers of the notion that to be a libertarian, one must be a libertine."

— FR. ROBERT A. SIRICO
  ACTON INSTITUTE FOR THE STUDY OF RELIGION AND LIBERTY

ISBN 0-87319-046-7
160 pages, hardcover, $18.95